MASTERS of
SCALE

MASTERS of SCALE

Surprising Truths from the World's Most Successful Entrepreneurs

REID HOFFMAN

with **JUNE COHEN** and **DERON TRIFF**

NEW YORK

Published in the United States by Currency, an imprint of Random House, a division of Penguin Random House LLC, New York.

CURRENCY and its colophon are trademarks of Penguin Random House LLC.

LIBRARY OF CONGRESS CATALOGING-IN-PUBLICATION DATA
Names: Hoffman, Reid, author. | Cohen, June, author. | Triff, Deron, author.
Title: Masters of scale / by Reid Hoffman, June Cohen, and Deron Triff.
Description: First edition. | New York : Currency, [2021] | Includes index.
Identifiers: LCCN 2021012808 (print) | LCCN 2021012809 (ebook) |
ISBN 9780593239087 (hardcover) | ISBN 9780593240700 (international) |
ISBN 9780593239094 (ebook)
Subjects: LCSH: Entrepreneurship. | New products. | New business enterprises. |
Success in business.
Classification: LCC HB615 .H6248 2021 (print) | LCC HB615 (ebook) |
DDC 658.1/1—dc23
LC record available at lccn.loc.gov/2021012808
LC ebook record available at lccn.loc.gov/2021012809

Printed in the United States of America on acid-free paper

crownpublishing.com

2 4 6 8 9 7 5 3 1

First Edition

Book design by Susan Turner

For every entrepreneur who's ever jumped off a cliff and built an airplane on the way down.

CONTENTS

INTRODUCTION

Each of us, in our own way, aspires to make an impact, especially on the people closest to us—our families, friends, and colleagues. Some of us set our sights higher, hoping our ideas will spread beyond our immediate networks, touching our communities, affecting even those people we may never meet personally.

And a few of us dream even bigger. We dream of changing the world; of doing something never done before—or at least not in *this* particular way; of disrupting old models and building new ones; of having our visions for business and social change achieve the kind of rapid growth that becomes self-perpetuating.

We dream of reaching *scale*.

Here at **Masters of Scale**, we believe scaling is not just a science but also a mindset—a journey that requires equal measures of faith and a willingness to fail.

As founders ourselves, we recognize what's at stake when launching a new business initiative—especially in times of uncertainty, when conventional thinking can no longer be relied on. We understand that the arduous path to entrepreneurial success is often a risky adventure rife with contradictions and unexpected turns. And we believe that within each of us is the capacity to cultivate an entrepreneurial mindset that will lead to success—and to scale.

When you talk to people who have scaled a business—and we have talked to many, at length and in depth—you begin to uncover some counterintuitive truths about scaling:

- The best, most scalable ideas are often the ones that seem the most implausible.
- An encounter with resistance at the start of your journey is a *good* thing.
- Early, honest feedback from the right people will have an outsized impact on helping you refine your idea.
- Doing things that *don't* scale—especially at the earliest stages—can set you up for dramatic scale later on.
- Even if everything you thought you knew turns out to be wrong, you can still achieve your goals—as long as you accept the truth and adjust your plan.

Lessons like these were learned the hard way by the seventy extraordinary people featured in this book. They are among the most iconic entrepreneurs behind the disruptive companies that have shaped our cultural landscape.

Among the pantheon of modern scale leaders sharing their stories with us: Bill Gates, Mark Cuban, Starbucks' Howard Schultz, Netflix's Reed Hastings, Apple's Angela Ahrendts, Google's Eric Schmidt, Yahoo's Marissa Mayer, Airbnb's Brian Chesky, YouTube's Susan Wojcicki, Spotify's Daniel Ek, Canva's Melanie Perkins, Xapo's Wences Casares, Spanx's Sara Blakely, the Black List's Franklin Leonard, ClassPass's Payal Kadakia, Duolingo's Luis von Ahn, Minted's Mariam Naficy, Shake Shack founder Danny Meyer, Walker & Company's Tristan Walker, designer Tory Burch, investor and philanthropist Robert F. Smith, and media maven Arianna Huffington.

These leaders represent a wide range of industries as well as the nonprofit world. They hail from all over the world—from rural towns to urban housing projects (and everywhere in between). In the pages ahead, you'll learn not just about their winning strategies but also their embarrassing mistakes and their dark moments of defeat. At times, it may feel a bit like you're eavesdropping on a private conversation between them and the book's expert navigator, Reid Hoffman, who conducted all the interviews.

Reid knows firsthand what it takes to scale a company, both as a founder and as an investor. He helped launch some of the most successful startups of our time, including PayPal and LinkedIn. As an angel investor and later an investor with Greylock Partners, he was among the first to spot the potential in paradigm-shifting companies like Airbnb, Facebook, Zynga, Aurora, and Dropbox, among many others. Reid has even created new and original language on the subject, such as the term "blitzscaling," which refers to the pursuit of aggressive growth by prioritizing speed over efficiency, or risk-intelligent scaling.

So as the host of the *Masters of Scale* podcast, it makes sense that he would help to scale the podcast series itself, turning it into one of the most popular and influential of its kind—a dependable place to find hard-fought wisdom, a resource entrepreneurs and business leaders turn to in times of opportunity and in times of crisis.

Fans of the series know that *Masters of Scale* is a business podcast that doesn't sound like any other business podcast—with immersive storytelling, original music, and a quirky sense of humor. Today it has millions of passionate fans in more than two hundred countries, and its listen-through rate of 75 percent confirms that it has one of the most engaged podcast audiences in the world.

Since 2017 we've produced more than eighty podcast episodes based on hundreds of hours of conversation with the most admired founders in the world. In each episode, we set out to prove a theory about how companies scale, using one founder's story and career as a starting point. The show then unfolds like a detective story, with Reid as the listener's guide, as he tests our theory, pulling insights—and counterpoints—from our guests.

Part of the podcast series' appeal is that Reid uses his own inside knowledge of scaling to probe deep in his interviews. As someone who's been in the trenches himself, he is able to draw out insights and ideas from his guests that the typical interviewer would never think to ask. But Reid also recognizes that these legends of modern business are people, too. Some of the richest, most fascinating material comes from their thoughts on human relationships, problem solving, purpose, and meaning.

But this book is much more than a collection of those incisive interviews. It is radically different from the podcast in format and approach. Each chapter identifies one of ten key themes that carry you through the entrepreneurial journey. The journey begins with surprising ways to surface and recognize your big idea, then proceeds to some of the early-stage challenges of building and funding a new venture, a period when you must do things that don't scale now in order to scale later.

The middle section of the book deals with practical issues like raising money and managing the challenges of rapid growth—including the unexpected twists and turns that require continuous learning, a constant readiness to pivot, and a willingness, at times, to let fires burn.

And the final chapters focus on what happens *after* you have achieved a level of scale, a time when you have the opportunity to be a true leader and a force for good in the world around you.

In the inspiring stories of the founders featured in this book, you will see your own individual stories as entrepreneurs—your ups and downs, your struggles and triumphs; and you will find commonality, community, and courage as well.

Weaving these stories together, we see how the insights from one leader connect to the ideas of another—with Reid's guidance and analysis interspersed throughout. And joining in, along the way, are fascinating creators and thinkers operating *outside* the business world, whose cameo stories and insights provide unusual perspectives.

We believe this book is more important now than ever before. We are living in a time of dynamic change—a period of great upheaval. Our world urgently needs people who possess the tenacity and the will to tackle ambitious challenges, adapt to difficult and volatile circumstances, and offer us fresh solutions.

If you want to bring something new into this world and scale it, you don't necessarily have to be a young guy in a hoodie. You don't need to be an engineer or programmer, or live in Silicon Valley. And you don't need big bucks—in fact, many of the successful startups in this book began with less than $5,000. But you do need knowledge, insight, and inspiration.

That's where these leaders come in. Enjoy their stories and heed their advice. Then get out there and start—then scale.

MASTERS of SCALE

1

Getting to No

When she first pitched her idea for a new kind of career development website to investors, **Kathryn Minshew** was turned down 148 times . . . not that she was counting.

"There were literally days where I had a 'No' over breakfast, a 'No' over a 10:30 A.M. coffee, a 'No' over lunch," Kathryn says. And the "Nos" kept coming: "Disinterest at 2 P.M. Someone who left the meeting early at 4. And then I would go to drinks and feel like I was being laughed out of the room.

"And when we finally raised our seed round, I went back and counted. It was both painful and gratifying at the same time—looking at all those names, and thinking, *I remember that no. I remember that no. I remember that no.* And they sting; every one stings."

Kathryn is co-founder and CEO of **The Muse**, and her idea sprang—as so many great entrepreneurial ideas do—from her own experience. Kathryn had spent her youth dreaming of a career in international relations. Secret Agent Minshew! But after a stint with the U.S. embassy in Cyprus she realized her foreign service fantasy didn't match the reality of the work. So she took a job as a consultant with McKinsey & Company and spent three years in their New York office. When it was time to move on again with her career, she found the experience disappointing—and dehumanizing.

"It wasn't uncommon to type in a keyword on a job-listing site like Monster.com and get 5,724 results—and they all looked functionally identical to each other. I just felt, for someone starting out in their career, that there has to be a better experience," Kathryn says.

So she started brainstorming with Alex Cavoulacos, a former colleague from McKinsey—and her future co-founder. They asked themselves: "What if you built a career site that put the individual at the center of that experience? And what if you allowed them to see inside offices before they applied to a company? What if you connected them with experts who could help them understand—How do you negotiate a salary? How do you manage someone for the first time?—all of those career questions that if you're lucky a mentor or a boss teaches you."

The more they shared their own experiences and envisioned what they might create, the clearer the opportunity became. "After a couple of long nights at the whiteboard batting this idea around, we became convinced that there was an opportunity to create a trusted, beloved, personalized career destination really focusing on the advice that early-stage professionals need," Kathryn says.

Kathryn and Alex had a clear vision for the role The Muse could play in users' lives. But not everyone could see what they were seeing.

"When I started pitching to investors, I ran into a couple of big problems," Kathryn says. "The first is that most investors don't match the user archetype that our product was built for. When you think about the classic venture capitalist, they often have been traditionally successful in their career, went to a top school, worked in banking or private equity. They usually get jobs through a very comfortable, well-developed network. And that's great. But that's not necessarily the case for everyone. So we were pitching this site and this concept to a demographic that looked at me with confusion."

The second problem she encountered: complacency with the status quo. "We ran into a lot of people who were unable to see past the current paradigm and the way things had always been done," Kathryn says. "One venture capitalist—who probably hasn't looked for a job in twenty years—pulled up Monster.com in the office after I finished my initial pitch. He said, 'I don't understand, this looks great to me.' And I was thinking, 'You haven't used that product in two decades. How do you know whether it serves the needs of a thirty-one-year-old woman in the early to mid-stages of her career?'"

The "Nos" just kept on coming. Among the ones Kathryn recalls:

"It's a bit too early for us, but keep in touch." ("No.")

"This is a fool's errand." ("No.")

"It's too expensive." ("No.")

"That's not very tech—it's not a scalable platform." ("No.")

"Aren't you worried that you're going to lose all your users once they turn thirty and have babies?" ("No.")

"I get that women in New York and San Francisco love this product, but I think you're going to really have a hard time finding women who care about their careers once you go outside of the coasts." ("No.")

When you're still early and unproven in your career—and you're getting "Nos" from some of the smartest and most successful investors in Silicon Valley and New York City—it can be difficult not to ask yourself, "What if the naysayers are right?" But at the end of the day, you have to listen to your gut instinct. And Kathryn trusted hers. She remembers looking at these guys doling out the "Nos" and thinking, *Do you know a lot of women?*

Kathryn was right to ask this question. She certainly knew a whole lot more about millennial women than the mostly white, mostly male, mostly middle-aged investors she was talking to. And she also knew more about her business. She held on to what she knew through the arduous pitch process—and it paid off. The reaction to the site when it first launched confirmed all her instincts: "We were getting this incredibly positive feedback from our users, who tended to be twenty-two- to thirty-five-year-old women and men who were saying 'I love this. This solves my problem, this is exactly what I need.'"

As The Muse gained traction among job seekers and employers,

Kathryn started getting a lot of calls. "All of a sudden, the same people that had laughed me out of the room two years before were saying 'Well, of course career-related content can be a great way to engage professionals.'"

Today, The Muse serves nearly one hundred million users. Kathryn has raised more than $28 million and has a staff of two hundred. It's tempting to assume she achieved this *despite* the "Nos." But in truth, each of those 148 "Nos" was a clue that ultimately made her business even stronger. Some sharpened her view on who her user was—and who her user wasn't. Some helped her grasp how her competition might think. And some gave her an early warning about the ways her company might fail. At the end of the fundraising process alone, Kathryn had a roadmap marked with every potential pitfall she'd need to navigate around—and the unexplored territory she could explore ahead of any competitors.

Kathryn's tale in many ways echoes the origin story of most great startups, and indeed, most great ideas. We're taught to get to "Yes" as quickly as we can—but there's so much more to gain by seeking out and celebrating the "Nos."

This chapter is all about "No"—and why that dreaded word doesn't always mean what you fear it does.

In fact, the most overlooked opportunity among early-stage entrepreneurs is the information to be gathered from different kinds of "Nos." A "No" can turn a good idea into a game-changing one. A "No" can clue you in to the size of your idea. A "No" can help you refine your strategy and your goals. In short, the gold is buried in the "Nos."

What follows are some examples of the various forms of "No" that founders encounter when challenging the world with an idea. Notice their willingness to ask for more feedback and hear what the world has to say as they embrace the naysayers in order to refine their product and move closer to scale.

"The lazy no": Or just completely missing the point

In 1904, a man named King Gillette had an idea. For hundreds of years, barbers had used straight razors to cut facial hair. It worked like a charm—the single sharp blade cut whiskers level with the skin, no pulling or tugging. The only problem: Using a straight-edged razor yourself at home is difficult. You had to go to the barbershop to get it done properly and avoid the risk of cutting your own throat. But King saw another possibility: What if you take a single blade, house it within a safe head, attach a handle to it, take it home with you, and shave? That started the mass-market shaving industry as we know it.

Within a couple of decades, King Gillette had many competitors, partly because he lost the patent on safety razors. Those new competitors, to stand out (and secure patents of their own), started adding more and more blades. Safety razors went from having one disposable blade to two, three, even five and six. This ever-growing stack of blades did actually improve the shaving experience for a lot of men. But for people with curly whiskers, like the kind of facial hair many Black men have, the multiple blades often caused painful ingrown hairs, razor bumps, and razor burn. Their shaving experience actually got worse. Such was the state of the razor market for more than one hundred years.

Enter **Tristan Walker**, founder and CEO of **Walker & Company**, whose flagship product is the Bevel, a single-blade razor designed for coarse or curly hair, and whose company is dedicated to designing health and beauty products for people of color.

When Tristan set out to launch Walker & Company in Silicon Valley, he went against the grain in at least three ways: It was a consumer goods company in a market that favors tech; it targeted consumers of color when most investors are white guys; and he wasn't an engineer—in an ecosystem that heavily favors tech CEOs. Now, to be clear, you don't need to be a white, twenty-two-year-old computer programmer in a food-stained hoodie to succeed in Silicon Valley. You do, however, need an overdeveloped sense of curiosity—and Tristan Walker is exceptionally curious.

"I like to say I had the whole 'rose that grew from concrete' story," Tristan says. A self-described "kid from the projects" of Queens, New York, Tristan's family was on welfare for a time. "I had one goal in life, and that was to get as wealthy as possible, as quickly as possible."

Tristan saw three ways to do that. "The first was to be an actor or an athlete, and that didn't work out for me," he says. The second way would be to work on Wall Street, but Tristan tried that briefly and hated it. "So I said to myself, 'I've already exhausted two of the three.' The last one is entrepreneurship—and the day I came to that realization, I applied to Stanford for business school."

Tristan arrived at Stanford in 2008, and quickly took in the thriving ecosystem of Silicon Valley that surrounded him. "I was twenty-four and I saw other twenty-four-year-olds not only making millions of dollars but fundamentally changing the world. And I thought, *Wow. Why didn't I know about this place?*"

Tristan quickly became not just a student of business but a student of every technological shift taking place around him. He wasn't what you'd call a geek, but he did geek out over new ideas. And he started seriously geeking out over Twitter, back when the social media platform had a relatively cozy community of five hundred thousand monthly users. Tristan was one of its more active members, but his classmates? "They just didn't get it," Tristan said. That is, until a fateful incident with the rapper MC Hammer.

"I was in accounting class, and I remember MC Hammer was supposed to speak on campus," Tristan explains. "And there was this commotion going on—people wondering if he was actually going to do it. I opened up Twitter, and I just asked MC Hammer, 'Are you coming?'"

"Thirty seconds later he replied back, and I turned around to my fellow classmates, and said, 'Yes, he's coming. See?'" Getting a personal reply from a multi-platinum artist? It built Tristan's confidence in his ability to spot a trend. "At that point, I realized how important Twitter's part in the innovations within communication were. And it was my first understanding of the way seemingly bad ideas can actually be a good idea. Because everyone else around the table was like, 'Why are you on Twitter? What's the point of this thing? I don't care about what you're eating for breakfast.' And that showed me that there was something there that I had to dive into," Tristan says.

Tristan wasn't just predicting the power of social media. He was learning a crucial early lesson in trusting his instinct. He has a knack for seeing the open space. Where other people saw "No," Tristan saw "YES." And **the earlier you can predict a "Yes" in a field of "Nos," the bigger your opportunity.**

For Tristan, he wasn't just an early Twitter user—he wanted to help build the company. So he started cold calling, searching for the closest connection to the company he could find. "I emailed twenty different folks who I knew were either one or two degrees separated from the company. The last person I emailed was David Hornik, because he was a professor at Stanford, and also a partner at August Capital."

It turns out that David was an old friend of Twitter's first CEO, Ev Williams. And two days after meeting David in his office, Tristan received an email from Ev, offering him an internship. Remember, this is 2008, and the size of Twitter's workforce at the time? Twenty employees, total. Tristan spotted the company's potential not just ahead of his classmates but ahead of the market.

Shortly after his Twitter internship ended, Tristan started his next email campaign, bombarding the founders of a fledgling startup called Foursquare. And again, the CEO, Dennis Crowley, responded.

"I emailed them eight times. The eighth time, Dennis sent me an email—I'll never forget, this is verbatim—he said, 'Tristan, you know what? I just may take you up on some of this. Are you ever in New York? Dennis.' That's it. I was in LA at the time, and I was sitting on the couch with my wife, and I said, 'How should I reply to this guy?' Ten minutes later, I sent him an email and I said, 'Actually, I was planning on being in New York tomorrow.' I booked my flight that night, flew out the following morning, hung out with them for a week, and a month later I was running business development for the company."

The lesson here is not just Tristan's persistence but his prescience. Some people get lucky, and board a rocket ship by chance. But two rocket ships? That's no coincidence. That's a sign you can spot an undervalued idea ahead of your peers. It's like this spidey sense that just keeps tingling. Tristan has a knack for seeing white space. He says "Yes" when the world is still saying a resounding "No."

Tristan moved on from Foursquare in 2012, after building their business development team from the ground up. "When I started at the company we had zero merchants, zero brands on that platform. By the time I ended up leaving Foursquare—even a couple of years later—we had over a million merchants. When I started, we were three people. By the time I left, we were 150. And quite frankly, I wanted to go out and build ambitious things myself."

He landed in the perfect place to plan his next move. Ben Horowitz, a founding partner at the iconic venture capital firm Andreessen Horowitz, invited Tristan to just hang around the office and think big, as their Entrepreneur in Residence, or EIR. He spent several months casting around for his big idea: "I wanted to build a bank. I wanted to fix freight and trucking. I want to fix obesity in the country, in the world. . . ."

Then inspiration struck: "I just got frustrated by the shaving experience."

A better shaving experience may not sound like an idea on the scale of freight trucking, obesity, or banking. But scalable ideas don't have to tackle dramatic problems—they have to tackle neglected problems. And the more that Tristan looked into the history of shaving, the more he realized that there was a hugely overlooked demographic—men with coarse or curly facial hair—who had been living with the curse of razor burns and razor bumps for so long, they no longer even recognized it was a problem.

Tristan envisioned not just a product to solve razor burn for men with curly hair, but a health and beauty company on par with global brands like Procter & Gamble—one devoted to men and women of color. It was blindingly obvious to *him* that this company should exist, but when you're pitching a room full of mostly white, mostly male investors—with mostly straight hair—it can be hard to convey the urgency of an idea serving a very different type of market. It was similar to the hurdle Kathryn Minshew faced in pitching The Muse: Investors consistently miss opportunities that serve an unfamiliar demographic. Smart VCs will educate themselves on the opportunity in front of them. But many others just respond with an ignorant "No."

For example:

"It's niche." ("No.")
"I don't think anyone knows they need this." ("No.")
"The industry's dominated by the multi-blade use case with billions and billions of dollars to attack you with patent protection." ("No.")
"To do it in Silicon Valley—that's crazy." ("No.")

As is often the case when pitching a bold idea, there was one lone early champion. In this case it was the VC Ben Horowitz from Andreessen Horowitz, the one who had invited Tristan to hang around the office for a few months and think big.

"I knew if I came up with ideas that were awful, Ben would tell me the truth. And he did," says Tristan. "Finally, I brought my idea to Ben and he's like, 'That's the idea.'" (It's worth noting that Ben has family members who are Black.) "And at that point I knew I had something."

This may sound like a strangely optimistic reaction. Why should a single endorsement outweigh the chorus of "Nos" from a crowd of investors?

Short answer: Because some "Nos" count more than others. "Substantial nos" can revise your idea. "Skeptical nos" can force you to rethink the size of the opportunity. These are "Nos" worth listening to and learning from. But then, there are "lazy nos," and these you need to dismiss and move on from—quickly.

Tristan has a keen ear for these distinctions. He can pinpoint, down to the PowerPoint slide number, the moment his audience stops paying attention to his pitch.

"I had a slide in there—I think it was like slide 14—where I talked about Proactiv, the acne system, as a good analogy to what we're trying to do. It's the difference between Gillette and Bevel, as Neutrogena and Proactiv; it's a system that solves a very important issue. And this VC looked at me—and I'll never forget this—he said, 'Tristan, I'm not sure issues related to razor bumps, shaving, or irritation are as profound an issue for people as acne.'

"At which point, I said, 'I understand what you're saying, but all you have to do is get on the phone with ten Black men, and eight of them would say, 'This is a permanent thing I have to deal with.' All you have to do is get on the phone with ten white men, four of them would have said the same thing. Could have done it for women too, and you would get the same ratios." Tristan knew at that moment that the VC's comment had nothing to do with the quality of his idea—he was simply unwilling to acquire the context necessary to understand it. "That's just laziness—and at that point, I can't fix that," he says. "So I just move on until I find somebody who understands it."

Notice how quickly Tristan's mind moves on to the next investor as soon as he's detected a "lazy no" in their half-hearted questions. When the quality of the questions drops, he knows, mid-pitch, that the real conversation is over—the rest is noise. "Silicon Valley investors will tell you all the time, 'We want to invest in people who can execute with some semblance of pedigree, chasing a significant white space and a big opportunity.' For us, it was like 'Check, check, check, check'—and we heard 99 percent 'No,'" Tristan says. The VCs were missing the larger picture.

One of the things first-time investors don't often realize is in the end it doesn't matter how many "Nos" you get. The right "Yes" is the only thing you need.

For Tristan, that "Yes" came from the rap star and investor Nas.

"I met with Nas via Andreessen Horowitz, sitting on the other side of the table," says Tristan. "We're both from Queens, and Nas is a person I always looked up to. He is one of the guys most well known for his haircuts, and Bevel was really perfect for him. So I started from a place of pure authenticity. After five minutes, he said, 'I'm in, so what do we do next?'"

After the Bevel trimmer was designed and ready to roll out, Tristan sent Nas a text message with a photo of his face on the box. He replied, "Tristan, for my entire life, I've always wanted to be on a trimmer package. Thank you." "It was a surreal moment for me," Tristan recalls.

Nas went on to name-check the Bevel in the chorus of a hit summer 2016 song, tripling the sell-through rate for that trimmer.

Of all those "Nos" that Tristan received from the investment community, perhaps the most embarrassing for investors were from those who mistook Tristan's idea as "small." As Tristan said in 2017, "A lot of people say that we're trying to build the Procter & Gamble for people of color. Folks talk about it as if it's a niche thing. But people of color are the majority of the world. So if we're the Procter & Gamble for people of color, what the hell is Procter & Gamble?"

In 2018, Walker & Company was acquired, with Tristan staying on as CEO. The buyer? None other than Procter & Gamble.

Fifty shades of "No"

If the stories of Tristan and Kathryn lead you to conclude that being an experienced white guy will guarantee you the easy "Yes" from VCs, **John Foley**, founder of **Peloton**, the at-home exercise and media company, is here to tell you: "No."

In fact, what John thought would be his biggest asset in the eyes

of investors—fifteen years of relevant tech leadership experience—
turned out to be a liability. "By age forty, I'd spent twenty years slogging
it out as a corporate guy," John says, "but then I had enough life experience that I felt confident enough to push away and start my own
company. It turned out, though, that at that point I was 'old.'"

This was a surprise to John. After all, John had the kind of background that ought to appeal to investors: engineering degree from
Georgia Tech, MBA from Harvard Business School, CEO of two
well-known and successful online businesses: Evite and Barnes &
Noble Online. He'd been sure that venture capitalists were going to
throw money at him. He had what he saw as a "10 out of 10" business idea, served up on a silver platter. "The data and the sales and
the retention and the cohorts and everything was there," he says.
"And I thought I was a pretty good salesman, but clearly I wasn't,
because my success rate on these meetings was one out of a hundred."

Not only was he "old" at age forty (in Silicon Valley terms, anyway), but John soon learned his big idea was in the unsexy consumer-
sales category that made it easy for VCs just to say, "Nah. *Next.*"

After three years of pitching Peloton to hundreds of venture capitalists and thousands of angels, John says, "I hadn't raised a dime of
money from a venture or an institution. It was a lot of headwind and
everyone had a different reason. It was so frustrating. . . ."

John became a connoisseur of "Nos." He sorted them into buckets:

"You're too old." ("No.")
"Hardware is hard and capital-intensive." ("No.")
"Fitness is a dopey category with no capital and no software, no
media, and no innovation." (To which John would respond, "Ex-
actly! We are going to be the tech disruptor in fitness.") But still,
"No."

Some of the "lazy nos" were a function of geography.

"Oh, you're a New York City company. I've made a commitment to
my family that I'm only going to sit on boards in California." ("No.")

A lot of people in Silicon Valley didn't understand boutique fitness cycling classes because it was largely an East Coast phenomenon.

"There's two types of biking out here: mountain biking and road biking." ("No.")

One of the biggest "lazy no" buckets was some version of "great idea, but not right for *us*." There were times when the whole investment team John was pitching would love him and the Peloton idea—but in the end they'd decline, because they only invest in consumer internet or healthcare and couldn't tell their LPs that they invested in this weird thing that didn't fit their investment thesis. ("Sorry, no.")

It's true: Conventional VCs like the ones John was pitching can be leery of direct-to-consumer businesses, especially in new categories. Because these categories are unknown, they're highly unpredictable. And while they'll never say it this way to your face, if your product doesn't look like one of the things these investors have made big money on, they're just not interested.

In the end, John overcame all the "Nos" from VCs and institutions by finding other means of financing—"a hundred checks from a hundred angels," as he put it. And he eventually found his way to a contrarian investor, Lee Fixel, former partner at New York–based Tiger Global Management, who appreciated the disruptive premise and promise of Peloton and said a quick "Yes."

In the course of navigating this epic labyrinth of "Nos," John eventually learned he could have saved himself a lot of time—and a good deal of rejection—by focusing his pitch effort on more eccentric, contrarian VCs. Instead of wasting his time on the usual suspects, he could have intentionally sought out investors like Lee who actively seek out unconventional ideas that create new categories.

How did John manage to persist so long in the face of such unrelenting rejection? "It goes back to my parents giving me the confidence, and plus I really believed that there was something there," he says. "But there wasn't much to sink our teeth into other than just our belief in ourselves for years and years and years."

One piece of good news, perhaps, for those who go through the multiyear gauntlet of VC "Nos": If the VCs don't get your idea, they're probably not funding anyone else with a similar one, either. When you make it through, you'll have a lengthy head start on potential competitors.

REID'S ANALYSIS | Big ideas are contrarian

The first truth of entrepreneurship and investing: The biggest new ideas are contrarian. They go so deeply against commonly held assumptions that they seem not only risky but flat-out ridiculous. They're the kind of ideas that draw a lot of "Nos."

And this makes sense: The fact that an idea goes against conventional wisdom is probably why other large companies and competitors haven't already tried it—and why other entrepreneurs haven't already succeeded at it. When you have a contrarian idea, the kind that almost everyone says "No" to, it leaves you the space to create something. And to create something big, you *need* a lot of space. This is why "The Contrarian Principle" is one of the four underlying principles in my book *Blitzscaling*. Being contrarian and right gives you a critical head start on achieving scale.

We see this all the time with truly big ideas. In the early stages of Google, search was seen as a terrible way of making money in advertising. Valuable ad inventory was measured by page views and time-on-site. And what does search do? It shuffles you off the site as fast as you can go. That didn't strike anyone as a good business model. But Google of course stuck with it—and rewrote the rules of online advertising.

Or think of TED Talks. When my *Masters of Scale* colleague June Cohen first pitched the idea of putting TED Talks online, it was widely seen as a very small, very bad idea. Putting taped lectures online? Who would possibly watch them? And wouldn't it capsize the business model of an expensive conference to give the content away for free? Of course, the opposite happened: The talks were an immediate viral hit, and so massively increased demand for the conference that the ticket price rose 5x—to $10,000—in the years that followed.

> Or take Airbnb: At the beginning, the concept seemed absurd: Someone's going to rent their spare room to a complete stranger—for a night? And someone's going to rent a room *from* a complete stranger? Who are the freaks on both sides of that transaction? When you have an idea like that—which is so far outside conventional understanding of how things work—very smart people will tell you: There's no there there. But they may very well be wrong.
>
> So if you're pitching a contrarian idea—an idea that questions the status quo, that imagines a different and better way of doing things—brace yourself to withstand and learn from a string of rejections. And when you hear that chorus of "Nos," start looking for other signs that you're on to something.

"The squirmy no": Or the magic of "Yes, but . . ."

"No" comes in many forms, each with its own type of useful information. You just have to know how to recognize what's in the "No"—even when people are saying "Yes" and "No" in the same breath.

Every entrepreneur has an underlying theory on human nature that informs their work. **Reid**'s is this: What gives people the most meaning and joy in their life is *other people*. We're social animals. Sure, some of us are introverts and some of us are extroverts (Reid considers himself a "six-person-or-less extrovert," by the way), but the vast majority of us draw deep meaning and joy from the people we're connected to.

When he set out to launch LinkedIn in 2002, Reid knew he wanted to build a platform that leveraged the connections between people in order to give their lives more meaning and satisfaction. And he felt certain that our real identities—and our real networks—would become the platform by which we'd find opportunities. Of all the ways people might connect online, our work lives—and specifically the job search—felt the most urgent. Because when people are job searching, they're motivated enough to try something new.

Reid was looking for the biggest, most transformative version of this idea he could imagine—the kind of contrarian idea that would draw a polarized reaction from investors, where some would say, "I see it!" but many would say, "You're nuts."

LinkedIn turned out to be exactly that. Its value was totally clear to Reid. But as he began talking about it with his network, no one got it. People would literally tell him, "I have no idea what you're talking about." And so he got an astounding number of "Nos." It turns out, for one thing, that the whole idea of networking is a turnoff for a lot of people. He'd hear, "Is this a service for people who intrinsically like networking? If so, it's not for me. Networking is like flossing—I know it's important, but I don't like doing it, and want to do as little as I can."

In 2002, people didn't fully understand how a social platform like LinkedIn could help improve the dreaded networking experience by making it easier to create real-life connections. And yet, everyone seemed to think the LinkedIn approach to networking was a great idea—*for someone else*. Again and again, LinkedIn was met with a resounding "It's not for us." Young people thought it could be a valuable service for experienced professionals. And experienced professionals would say, "That could be a good service for young people." Technologists saw it as a service for the traditional industry; old industries thought it was for the newfangled tech industry.

Reid and his co-founders had to decide how to act on the range of neutral to negative reactions they heard. "Should we fold our hand, or play it?" they wondered, as they listened closely to the various objections and ambivalent reactions.

For example, the LinkedIn team themselves had been hotly debating whether their network signups should be *closed*, where you could only join by referral, with LinkedIn facilitating connections (and where the initial group of LinkedIn members were all known, in some way, by the founding team), or *open*, where you could sign up yourself and then send your own invitations to connect. The fact that neither a strong pro nor a con had emerged from the ambivalent feedback was a sign that people didn't have a clear picture of the value of LinkedIn. This gave them the courage to chance the more radical route: open up the network.

You lose the initial exclusivity of the club with an open network, but it has the advantage of building the fastest possible path to the set of users who will say, "I believe this network could be valuable . . . for someone else"—and then share it with them.

So Reid and his team went all-in on building a service where users could share their professional details openly and grow their professional networks. By doing so, LinkedIn created a viral loop that kept people coming back and bringing their friends, over and over. With the viral loop in full swing, LinkedIn grew to half a billion users and more

REID'S ANALYSIS | Look for a polarized reaction and "the squirmy no"

When I present an idea to my partners at Greylock, and they all say, "That's great! We should do that!" my response is: "Uh-oh." When you have a group of hyperintelligent, sophisticated investors and no one's saying, "Watch out for this!"—that's when I know it's too easy. The idea is so obviously good, I can already hear the stampede of competitors trampling over my hopeful little startup. So unanimous consent is always a concerning sign.

On the other hand, I don't exactly want every person in the room to say, "Reid, you're out of your mind." If everyone I talk to thinks it's a terrible idea, I'll start wondering: Am I drinking the Kool-Aid in a very bad way?

What I want is for some people to say, "You're out of your mind," and some people to say, "I see it." I want a polarized reaction.

Take my decision to invest in Airbnb as an example. David Sze, a partner of mine at Greylock Partners, thought I was making an epic mistake with that investment. I remember him saying to me, "Well, Reid, every venture capitalist has a deal that doesn't work, which they learn from. Airbnb can be yours." To be clear: David Sze is a super-smart VC. He invested in LinkedIn, Facebook, and Pandora. He personally returned two and a half billion dollars to Greylock's funds. So I weighed his objections carefully. If someone as smart as David disagrees with me, I worry. But I also get excited—because I just might be right.

The other thing I look for with the biggest ideas: "the squirmy no." As you take your idea out to potential investors, you want to see at least a minority of them squirm. You don't have to get them to a "Yes," but you're hoping to detect some friction as they reason their way to a "No." This "squirmy no"—the space between a "No" and a "Yes"—is a clue that you may be on to something truly big, because the best ideas make people want to say "Yes" and "No" in the same breath. It's an emotional roller coaster for everyone, including the investors.

And as for that Airbnb investment? Not a bad bet, after all.

than $6 billion in revenue. In 2016, LinkedIn was acquired by Microsoft for $26.2 billion.

"The telling no": When a "No" tells you exactly why you're right

"My problem was an addiction to diet soda," says **Kara Goldin**. "I was drinking diet soda and I couldn't lose weight. I was working out thirty to forty-five minutes every day. I had terrible acne, had no energy." When Kara gave up the diet soda and started drinking plain water, all of those things changed for the better.

After almost a year of drinking plain water, she felt better than ever, but was tired of the taste—or rather, the lack of taste. So to convince herself to drink more, she started throwing fresh fruit into a glass of water. She wondered: *Why couldn't someone bottle that?* She looked for such a product on market shelves and couldn't find it.

She decided, *I'm just going to go and develop this product and see what happens.*

Kara went to work on a recipe for a flavored drink with no sugar or preservatives, and she also started taking meetings with potential partners and investors. During one fateful meeting, a bigwig in the beverage industry gave Kara a definitive and dismissive "No." But he also unknowingly gave her the best advice she received.

After Kara gave him her pitch for an all-natural drink with just a splash of flavor, his response was, "Sweetie, Americans love *sweet.*" Setting aside for the moment just how inappropriate it is to call anyone "sweetie" in a business context, these four careless words gave Kara an aha moment. She realized that this patronizing executive at this major soda company was operating on the assumption—correct or not—that Americans weren't interested in a bottled beverage product that wasn't sweet.

Some might see this as a simple dismissal or an outright rejection, but Kara recognized this "No" as a gift—one that imparted a vital piece of information: His company was going to stay in its "sweet" lane, giving *her* the chance to own the "not sweet" category. "I saw the fork that they were taking in the road," she says, "and that *I* needed to put the gas on and grow this business before they decided to come down my fork as well."

It turns out that Kara's critic was wrong to the tune of $100 million a year. That's how much revenue **Hint Water**, now lining aisles in grocery stores big and small, takes in annually from Americans who *supposedly* have incurable sweet tooths. His careless dismissal of her idea was an "affirmative no"—the kind that tells you exactly why you're right. The lesson: Don't always believe the naysayers. But listen to them closely, for they may inadvertently speed you along your path.

"It's amazing how many entrepreneurs I meet along the way who will say to me, 'I'm really frustrated. I spoke to so-and-so in my industry and they really think this is a bad idea,'" Kara says. "Just because a large company is saying you're wrong or that it's a bad idea—that doesn't mean it's a terrible idea. The reality is that you can actually gain some knowledge from these executives and industry that will prove you're doing something different. Take that information and really go run with it."

Of course, it isn't only entrepreneurs who encounter this kind of naysaying from experts. It's anyone with an idea that's out of the ordinary. Take **Andrés Ruzo**, a National Geographic Explorer and a geologist who studies natural sources of energy.

In 2010, Andrés began to search for a legend that had never been documented. His Peruvian grandfather had told him stories of the Spanish conquest of Peru: fantastic tales about giant snakes that can swallow men whole, spiders as big as your hands that eat birds, fierce warriors with poison arrows that can kill you with a single nick. Of all the legends Andrés heard, it was the story of a single river that most captivated him.

"Every company that I'd work with, every geologist I could get my hands on, I'd ask, 'Hey, have you heard of a boiling river, a large, big, thermal river in the middle of the Amazon?'" Most people would respond skeptically. But Andrés had grown up between Peru and Nicaragua. He was fascinated by the Amazon. And he believed, as a scientist, that the boiling river could exist—and that finding it could mean access to a clean, naturally recurring source of virtually carbon-free energy.

After giving a presentation at a mining company, Andrés was chatting with an older geologist sitting in the back. "I asked him if he knew about the boiling river. His response was, 'Andrés, your geothermal work is very interesting, very innovative, but don't ask stupid questions.' I walked out of that meeting with my tail between my legs," he recalls.

Andrés spent a full two years asking experts of every stripe the same question, and he heard every variation of "No" we talk about in this chapter: *That's crazy. That's stupid. That's a fool's errand. Don't waste my time.* But he pressed on, and ultimately, he did discover that boiling river of legend. (You can read about it in his book *The Boiling River*.)

Today, Andrés is studying that river to understand the hydrothermal system that powers it, and the unique microbes that grow within it. He's also engaged deeply in efforts to preserve the rapidly disappearing Peruvian rain forest—and the human cultures that depend on it—from the encroachment of clearcutting and logging.

One of the many things for entrepreneurs, and anyone with an outlier idea, to take from Andrés's dramatic story: Remember that many people will tell you you're crazy, and make you doubt what you know in your bones to be possible. But you can't let rejection rule you. Instead, let it fuel you. In the case of "the telling no," the naysayers are teaching you more about their own assumptions than about the truth of how the world actually works. To your keen ears, their "Nos" should sound like, "Yes, conventional wisdom is overlooking this opportunity."

"The honest no": When a "No" tells you exactly what you're doing wrong

It's the classic entrepreneurial hero's journey: You have an idea, you toil to bring it to life, you endure endless "Nos," and then you ultimately secure funding, scale a successful business, and prove your critics wrong.

But what if you're pitching a truly terrible idea? What if the people saying "No" are right? Like, *really* right?

One afternoon in 1996, Mark Pincus and his business partner Sunil Paul were standing outside a Tower Records in New York City, offering free computers to passersby. It was a clever if unconventional way to pitch New Yorkers on an idea for their next startup: a computer with built-in internet access.

Mark was convinced that the internet was "too hard for consumers," and he had an idea for an all-in-one device that would get people online with zero fuss. Fast, frictionless internet access via a free computer. Who could say no?

As it turns out, *everyone*. Mark didn't get a single taker. Some turned down the free PC because they thought Mark was a scam artist. But others refused it for a more basic reason: They weren't interested in getting a new computer at all. "The number one thing stopping people from getting a new PC was this fear of moving their software and having to reinstall their kids' games and everything else," Mark says. "I thought, *huh, that's a solvable problem.*"

But addressing that particular problem would require Mark to acknowledge that his all-in-one internet idea wasn't viable. So he killed it.

His idea might have been dead, but his gut feeling—that there was a big opportunity in users' desire for a more frictionless experience—was very much alive, prompting him to create a piece of software he called Move It, which helped people switch easily and seamlessly to a new PC. And that led to the core technology that became the basis for his *next* big idea, Support.com—a pioneer in tech support and cloud services. But none of that would have happened if Mark hadn't listened to criticism—and used that information to iterate his way to a successful idea.

This wasn't the last time Mark would learn a tough lesson about the value of listening to "No." It happened again at the startup he launched after Support.com—the early social network called Tribe, which he launched in 2003—the same year that brought the world MySpace, and a year ahead of Facebook.

"I was in my early thirties and I thought, *Okay we're all living in these urban tribes, let's codify that online,*" Mark recalls. So he asked himself, *What would it look like if we could connect with our tribes and then use those tribes to find apartments and jobs and couches and cars?*

While it wasn't initially aimed at any particular section of society, Tribe turned out to be very popular with certain subcultures—the most famous of these being people who attended Burning Man, the annual gathering in Nevada's Black Rock Desert known for its countercultural creativity.

While Tribe was a hit among this small but loyal user base, it failed to appeal to a more general audience. Looking back at it, Mark sees the exact moment he might have turned things around, if only he'd listened to a fateful and emphatic "No."

"My girlfriend at the time was completely turned off by Tribe," Mark says. "When she was on there, she got lots of unsolicited messages and interest and it freaked her out. She said, 'This isn't for me.'"

It's worth noting that an honest partner is almost always your best source of ideas and critiques. But Mark ignored this feedback, writing it off as a focus-group-of-one. He was unwilling to retool Tribe for mainstream appeal, and eventually the network foundered.

This bitter experience with Tribe highlighted an important lesson for Mark: "Part of the journey that we entrepreneurs are on is learning how to separate our winning instincts from our losing ideas. I think, as a rule of thumb, if you're a good entrepreneur you can assume that your instincts are right 95 percent of the time and your ideas might be right 25 percent of the time."

Out of this realization came the mentality of "I'm not wedded to any idea," Mark says. "Whether it's mine, yours, someone else's. I'll try anything and I'll kill anything and I'll kill it quickly. And I'm not going to let killing an idea kill a winning instinct."

The ability to both recognize a winning instinct and kill or refine a losing idea is an essential part of succeeding as an entrepreneur. **Time is your most precious resource; don't waste it on a bad idea.** When you realize the naysayers are likely to be right, their "Nos" can help you switch from a failing Plan A to a more promising Plan B.

"The discouraging no": Or the wrong "No" at the wrong time

For every good theory, there is a countertheory.

As much as it's important to listen to the "Nos" and harness the constructive, honest criticism within them, there will invariably be exceptions to the rule.

Sara Blakely's journey as an entrepreneur began when she cut the feet out of her pantyhose. As she leaned into the idea that would become **Spanx**—fabricating them, iterating on them, patenting them, and pitching them—there was just one thing she *did not* do.

REID'S ANALYSIS | The time I said "No" when it should have been "Yes"

Every investor, no matter how smart or skilled, has an "anti-portfolio"—the list of companies they didn't invest in that went on to monumental success. The times they said "No" when they should have said "Yes."

Etsy is one of these for me. Caterina Fake, the co-founder of Flickr, brought it to me as an angel investment, in Etsy's earliest days. And I've always regretted passing on it.

In my defense, it was pitched as handmade goods—and handmade goods are literally the opposite of scale. The way I saw it, you can either create the corner bookstore, or you can create Amazon. You can be a gourmet chocolatier, or you can be the new Godiva or Nestlé. My reaction was, "Well, Etsy is cool, but it isn't really a good investment." After all, you can hire a bunch of people to make handmade goods, but then you wonder: How many can they make? How do you grow that business? How scalable is that?

My mistake was not realizing that once you get to a network-connected world, the talent pool is so much bigger than I realized. Because Etsy wasn't at all like the gourmet chocolate store in San Francisco. It was more like an online marketplace where you can order from any gourmet chocolate store or any at-home chocolate maker in any city. If I'd realized that, I could have said, "Oh, an early-stage investment in that could be great."

Caterina called this one right, because she was looking for different markers than I was. She saw in Etsy the start of a countercultural movement—a scaling movement that placed value on the homemade, the artisanal, the local.

Also, when Caterina took a close look at those first two thousand Etsy sellers, what she saw was not just willing merchants but passionate community members. Etsy showed all the signs of a community that could thrive.

I looked at Etsy and saw it as . . . knickknacks. I didn't see the network behind it. It's one of my regrets.

She didn't tell friends or family about her idea for a whole year.

And there's a wisdom to that. While it's true that embracing feedback—and negative feedback in particular—is an essential ingredient in scaling an idea successfully, not all feedback is equal. And sometimes you're better off getting early constructive feedback from outside experts rather than people in your inner circle, who may inadvertently throw cold water on an idea in an effort to protect you from the risk of failure.

"I didn't want to tell friends and family, because I didn't want to invite ego into the process too soon," Sara says. "So I kept it a secret from everybody in my life and didn't seek validation. But I did share it with manufacturers and patent lawyers and people who could help me move it along. And by doing that, I didn't spend my first year explaining it and defending it. I just spent it pursuing it."

It's not that Sara didn't get *any* input. She just figured out where to get the most *useful* input—from people who knew the ins and outs of the business—and shielded herself from the kind of criticism that might have undermined her.

"An idea is at its most vulnerable in its infancy," Sara says. "That's also the moment in human nature we want to immediately turn to our co-worker or friend or boyfriend or boss and say, 'I have this idea.' And out of love and concern we hear a lot of things that stop us right in our tracks: 'Well, sweetie, if it's such a good idea, why doesn't it already exist?' And 'Even if this idea does take off, the big guys will knock you out of the water in six months.'"

You can hear this in **Linda Rottenberg**'s story, too. Today, Linda is the CEO of Endeavor, an extraordinary organization that builds entrepreneurial communities all over the world. But twenty years ago, she was a recent graduate with a dream—a dream that was about to be crushed.

"My parents freaked out," Linda says. "They overheard my co-founder and me plotting this global organization to support high-growth entrepreneurs in emerging markets. And my mother looked at my father like, *You've got to stop this.* My dad gently came over and reminded me that I needed to be financially independent, that I didn't have anything to fall back on, and this didn't sound like job security."

Linda refers to this as her kitchen-table moment. "It's really scary to tell your family that you're going to do something unconventional," she says. "And you have to make this choice: Do I do what's safe and expected, or do I venture into the unknown?"

Linda, of course, ventured into the unknown. "I just had this sense that I would never forgive myself if I followed the conventional path and was miserable ten or twenty years later." And she remains convinced that the first—and one of the most important—hurdles for entrepreneurs involves simply getting past their own "kitchen-table" moment.

REID'S THEORIES OF "NO"

"The lazy no"

Potential investors may completely miss the point of your idea or simply be ignorant. Either way, once it becomes clear that they aren't trying to gain a better understanding, you need to move on from these naysayers—quickly. Their "No" gives you no additional information.

"The squirmy no"

The best, highest-potential ideas make investors want to say "Yes" and "No" in the same breath. This signals that the idea might be great, although of course it might be a very attractive disaster.

"The affirmative no"

Sometimes an expert's "No" is proof you're on the path to something big and different. The key: You should have an active theory about why you are right and the experts are wrong—more than a gut feeling or simply grit, but another signal for a potentially great idea.

"The honest no"

Frequently, the experts *are* right. You have to be ruthless about killing your own bad ideas along the way—and an honest "No" could be a lifeline to turn a bad idea into something good, or to help you move on to a better idea.

"The unhelpful no"

If you're the kind of person who might get easily discouraged or talked out of your idea, you need to keep your idea away from people whose opinions you have an emotional investment in.

2

Do Things That Don't Scale

The meeting definitely did not go as he expected.

In 2009, **Brian Chesky**, a young entrepreneur with a big idea, was meeting with Paul Graham, co-founder of Y Combinator, the renowned Silicon Valley startup accelerator. Brian's company, **Airbnb**, was partway through the Y Combinator program, and he was ready to wow Paul with his vision of a bright future for an unconventional new business that enabled people to rent out their spare rooms or sofa beds to total strangers.

Airbnb was already up and running, but at this early stage not many people seemed to know about it. The number of hosts offering up a room or a couch was tiny. But no matter: Brian had ambitious plans and rosy projections that he was eager to share with Paul.

Paul is not your typical investor. He is, however, a provocative thinker and the author of a prolific series of essays on topics ranging from economic inequality to why nerds are unpopular (one journalist dubbed him "the hacker philosopher").

When meeting with entrepreneurs, Paul has little use for spreadsheets and projections, relying mostly on instinct and a battery of his own counterintuitive theories on scaling a business. He's famous in Silicon Valley for his Socratic style, asking pointed, sometimes perplexing questions. The exchange with Paul, as Brian recalls it, went something like this:

PAUL: "So . . . where's your business?"
BRIAN: "What do you mean?"
PAUL: "I mean, where's your traction?"
BRIAN (*sheepishly*): "Well . . . we don't have a lot of traction."
PAUL: "But people must be using it."
BRIAN: "Well, there's a few people in New York using it."
PAUL: "So your users are in New York."
BRIAN: "Yeah."
PAUL: "And you're still here in Mountain View."
BRIAN: [silence]
PAUL: "What are you still doing here?"
BRIAN: "What do you mean?"
PAUL: "Go to your users. Get to know them. One by one."
BRIAN: "But that won't scale. If we're huge and we have millions of customers, we can't meet every customer."
PAUL: "That's exactly why you should do it now."

As Paul saw it, the projections, the spreadsheets, the grand marketing plans were all secondary. First, you had to build something that a tiny cohort of users would love. If they loved it, presumably millions of others would, too. And since love tends to be shared, your product or service would have the best kind of marketing, the kind money couldn't buy—and it would grow and grow.

Paul's point was that in order to build something Brian's core user would truly love, he needed to meet them where they live—literally. He had to talk to them, listen to them, watch them, and try his best to understand them. And as Paul told Brian, *this* was the moment to seize that opportunity. "It's the only time," Paul said, "you'll ever be small enough that you can meet all your customers, get to know them—and make something directly for them." In 2013, Paul would codify this advice in his famous essay "Do Things That Don't Scale," which also serves as #6 of my Counterintuitive Rules of *Blitzscaling*.

In this chapter, we'll dig into what happens—or *should* happen—during the critical early days of launching your product, a pre-scale moment you won't ever get back. It's an opportunity to define and refine your product, based on direct feedback, until you've handcrafted something that people love. Some of the world's most successful founders, including Brian, look back on this stage of development as a golden period, though of course it may not have seemed that way at the time.

When you're building a product, or laying the groundwork for a successful, scalable company, you're inevitably going to get your hands dirty. You'll find yourself doing things that, at the time, seem insignificant and labor-intensive: coding, designing, serving customers, onboarding users, answering the customer support line. Yet these could be the very things that determine how far your company will go in years ahead. As Reid notes, "This poses an almost Zen-like riddle for entrepreneurs: **The first step to scale is to renounce your desire to scale.**"

Why a hundred beats a million

The power of "handcrafting"—the slow, painstaking work of getting every detail just right—is a concept that every artisanal maker of small-batch goods grasps instinctively. It's precisely what distinguishes chef Dominique Ansel's pastries from the baked goods found on grocery store shelves. Artisans understand why they need to handcraft. But scale entrepreneurs? Not so much.

When entrepreneurs think about scaling, they usually think in terms of high impact and visibility; they think of marketing blitzes or viral growth. And it's logical, in a way—to *be* big, you gotta *go* big. By this line of thinking, the subtle details of a product or customer experience matter less than just finding some way to make a splash and get on the radar. Handcrafting? Most MBA students will tell you, "That doesn't scale."

But ignoring those details won't work—not in the long run, says Y Combinator's president from 2014 to 2019, **Sam Altman**. An acolyte of Paul Graham's, Sam adhered to the core Y Combinator dictum: *It's better to have one hundred users who love you than a million users who just kind of like you.*

It's counterintuitive. You may be thinking *If a million people "kind of like" my product enough to buy it, isn't that better for business than a hundred obsessive oddballs?*

To which Sam would say . . . definitely not.

Y Combinator has incubated more than fifty companies that have reached $100 million in value or more—so they have a fairly good sense of what does and doesn't scale. "If you look at the companies that have gone on to become most valuable," Sam says, "they tend to have fanatical early users." Fanatical users are in it for the long haul; they stand by you, they stick with you—and importantly, they tell their friends.

In contrast, there are endless new flash-in-the-pan offerings that receive early attention that doesn't sustain. You can get a lot of people to try your product with a clever growth hack, but unless they fall in love with the product, that clever tactic eventually stops working. This is "the illusion of scale"—the one million users who show up and then quickly disappear, simply because, as Sam notes, "People don't stick with products they don't love."

This is why it makes sense to super-serve your early users, to really understand what they want and what they *love*. When you build loyalty with a core group of early users, they become a narrow but deep wedge—a solid base for expansion. When Facebook launched, for example, it was available only to students at Harvard. Those first students invited their friends, who invited their friends, until the entire student body was comparing status updates. Facebook then expanded from Harvard to Columbia to Stanford, and to other universities across the country, and eventually to the wider world. Had the social network not been so beloved by its early users, it couldn't have spread so far and wide.

Sam recalls that after the success of Facebook and Twitter, everyone wanted the quick copycat kill. Entrepreneurs were saying, "I'm just going to make another photo-sharing app."

Y Combinator instead became interested in startups that were trying something more ambitious, what Sam calls "bits-to-atoms companies, where you had software, but you also had to do this very complex thing in the real world." Because these companies were trying to do something hard, and potentially game-changing, they didn't have as much competition as all the copycat startups.

One such company was Airbnb.

When Brian Chesky and his partner, Joe Gebbia, got to New York, at the urging of Y Combinator's Paul Graham, they had a clear mandate: Go to your users. So they contacted their local hosts and offered to send professional photographers to take pictures for the Airbnb listing. Who were the photographers? Brian and Joe.

One particular visit stands out in Brian's memory.

"It's winter. It's snowing outside and we're in snow boots," Brian recalls. "We walk up to the apartment and we went there to photograph the home. We're like, 'I'll upload your photos to the website. Do you have any other feedback?'"

The host disappears into a back room, then returns. "He comes back with a binder and he's got dozens of pages of notes." The binder was filled with pages and pages of written suggestions, for all the changes that the host wanted to see on Airbnb. "It was like he created a roadmap for us," Brian recalls. Some entrepreneurs might have interpreted those copious suggestions as a critique from a hater. But Brian understood that it was actually a good sign. This kind of detailed feedback is a clue that someone is really passionate about what you have to offer, and they want a deeper, stronger relationship with the product. "I think that always stuck in our mind," Brian says. "The roadmap often exists in the minds of the users you're designing things for."

Ultimately, these home visits became Airbnb's secret weapon in learning what people loved. "It's really hard to get even ten people to love anything," Brian says, "but it's not hard if you spend a ton of time with them. And if you keep asking, 'Well, what if I did this? And what if I did this? And what if I did this?'" These conversations went long and deep, with questions like *How would you like to see peer reviews work?* And *What do you need most from customer support, and when?*

"We didn't just meet our users, we lived with them," Brian says. "I used to joke that when you bought an iPhone, Steve Jobs didn't come sleep on your couch, but I did."

As he was doing his home visits, Brian developed a clever method for extracting valuable feedback. Instead of just asking what people thought about the product as it existed now, he'd ask what they thought about the product he *might build*. "If I ask, 'What can I do to make this better?' they'll say something small," Brian explains. So instead, he'd ask bigger, bolder questions, like "What can we do to surprise you?" or "What would it take for me to design something that you would literally tell every single person you've ever encountered?" In doing so, he invited users to join him in imagining a bigger, bolder version of Airbnb.

The secret to a great brainstorm: Design an "11-star" experience

To succeed as an entrepreneur, you don't need any particular degree or knowledge set; what you need is the right mindset. Nonetheless, the vast majority of tech CEOs have degrees in business or computer science. Brian, however, has a BFA in Industrial Design (from the Rhode Island School of Design). And design thinking is one of his superpowers.

But just in case you think "design" means "making things pretty," Brian would like to shift your thinking. "We have a different definition of 'design.' Steve Jobs had a famous quote: 'A lot of people have the fallacy of believing design is how it *looks*. Design is how it *works*.' Another way of saying that is: 'Design is what it *is*.'"

And Brian knows how to use design thinking to reimagine what something is—or could be. He can turn a commonplace conference-room brainstorm into an elevated exercise in inventing the future. Here's one of his best techniques. It's been used hundreds of times by our team at *Masters of Scale* alone, and we can't recommend it highly enough.

It starts by forcing you to imagine things you could *never* actually do. Why? Because that's how you win. "The core thesis is if you want to build a massively successful company, you need to build something that people love so much *they tell each other*. Which means that you must build something worth talking about. And if you want to build something worth talking about, you have to go back to things that don't scale."

You start by abandoning the ordinary. "If you want to build something truly viral, you have to create a total mind*&%# experience that you tell everyone about. So as an exercise, we took one part of our product and we extrapolated: What would a 5-star experience be?" Meaning: What kind of product or service would inspire a 5-star review? "Then we went crazy." Let's follow Brian as he moves from a guest's disappointing 1-star experience checking in to an Airbnb to the current standard-bearer for 5 stars all the way to an imaginary check-in process that might earn 11 stars.

"So a 1-, 2-, or 3-star experience is you get to your Airbnb, and no one's there. You knock on the door. They don't open. That's a 1-star. Maybe it's a 3-star if you have to wait twenty minutes. If they never show up, and you need to get your money back, that's a 1-star experience. You're never using us again."

"So a 5-star experience is: You knock on the door, they open the door, they let you in. Great. That's not a big deal. You're not going to tell every friend about it. You might say, 'I used Airbnb. It worked.'

"So we thought, *What would a 6-star experience be?* You knock on the door, the host opens. 'Welcome to my house.' On the table would be a welcome gift. It would be a bottle of wine, maybe some candy. You'd open the fridge. There's water. You go to the bathroom, there's toiletries. The whole thing is great. You'd say, 'Wow, I love this more than a hotel. I'm definitely going to use Airbnb again.'

"What's a 7-star experience? You knock on the door. Reid Hoffman opens it. 'Welcome. I know you like surfing. There's a surfboard; I've booked lessons for you. By the way, you can use my car. And I also want to surprise you. I got you a table at the best restaurant in the city of San Francisco.' And you're like, 'Whoa. This is way beyond.'

"So what would an 8-star check-in be? I would land at the airport, and there would be a limousine waiting for me. It would take me to the house, and it would be a total surprise.

"A 9-star check-in: I would show up at the airport, and there'd be a parade in my honor. I would have an elephant waiting for me, as in the traditional Indian ceremony.

"So what would a 10-star check-in be? A 10-star check-in would be the Beatles check-in, in 1964. I'd get off the plane and there'd be

REID'S ANALYSIS | Passionate feedback is the foundation of scale

Over the last twenty years, I've worked on or invested in many companies that scaled to one hundred million users or more. But here's the thing: You don't start with one hundred million users. You start with a few. So you actually have to stop thinking big, and start thinking small. Hand-serve your customers. Win them over, one by one.

Now this may sound like odd advice if you're an entrepreneur with global ambitions. Sergey Brin and Larry Page didn't hand-serve two billion people search results. They built a great product, and the users just poured in. Right? Not exactly. The most successful entrepreneurs with the most beloved products pay obsessive attention to their users—especially their early users. They watch what they do, they listen to what they say, they answer their customer service calls and fix the things that are going wrong.

It's worth dwelling on these early days of handcrafted work, because most entrepreneurs tend to have a funny reaction to these experiences. They may laugh about it later. They may call the work unglamorous. They may celebrate the day they could hire a helping hand or automate these chores out of existence. But thoughtful founders will never say, "What a complete waste of time." They'll often look back on this period as one of the most creative phases of their careers.

And one of the things to keep a watchful eye out for is the kind of superfan who will almost write your product roadmap for you. It's typical, in fact, to get very detailed feedback from some of your early users. Ones who produce a binder full of suggestions, like the super-host that Brian Chesky met on one of his early customer visits. In fact, if you're *not* coming across customers who say, "I love this product. It's super important to me. I really need this to work well," it usually means you're off track. Passionate feedback is a clue that your product really matters to someone. And one passionate user can turn into many, if you listen to them carefully.

It's essential, though, to get this kind of feedback as early as you can, while you're still defining the product. It's like setting a foundation as an architect. You wouldn't build a skyscraper before you've built a solid foundation. User feedback ensures you won't build a dozen floors on an unstable swamp.

This advice may seem paradoxical to readers of my book *Blitzscaling*, in which I articulate the counterintuitive rule, "Ignore Your Customers." The common thread between "engage one-on-one with passionate customers" and "ignore your customers" is this: Find and focus on the customers who represent your scale opportunity, and ignore the others. Spending precious time and resources on responding to requests from the loudest of your current customers can distract you from the work that will win you millions of loyal, passionate future customers.

five thousand high school kids cheering my name, with cards welcoming me to the country.

"So what would an 11-star experience be? I would show up at the airport and you'd be there with Elon Musk and you're saying, 'You're going to space.'"

Obviously, those higher stars are imaginative and whimsical. But they serve a serious purpose. "The point of the process is that maybe 9, 10, 11 are not feasible," Brian explains. "But if you go through the crazy exercise, there's some sweet spot between 'They showed up and they opened the door' and 'I went to space.' That's the sweet spot. You have to almost design the extreme to come backward."

Scale, and the beginner's mind

Brian no longer knocks on hosts' doors or sleeps on their couches. Airbnb today is a public company that hardly resembles the scrappy little startup in the stories above. But handcrafting still matters to Brian. He relies on close contact with longtime hosts and customers for input on design and strategy. And any time he considers a bold new product direction, he instinctively imagines it through the eyes of a single user.

For example, when they first conceived Airbnb Trips—an extension of Airbnb's core business offering curated end-to-end experiences—Brian and his team began by handcrafting a vacation experience for a single customer. Literally. So they posted a flyer: *"Seeking a traveler. We'll photograph your trip to San Francisco if you let us follow you."* Ricardo from London was happy to volunteer.

The trip Ricardo had planned for himself was not exactly a dream vacation. He went to all the typical tourist spots but never got beyond them. "He'd go to Alcatraz by himself, put on the headset; go to Bubba Gump Shrimp. He'd stay in a budget hotel that was $300 a night. And he'd go to a hotel bar by himself, sitting with a bunch of dudes at the bar. And he doesn't talk to anyone because he was introverted."

In the course of the whole trip, "he was either in line, or alone, and always doing things that people who live in San Francisco would never do."

Afterward, Airbnb contacted Ricardo and invited him back, saying: "We want to create the perfect trip to San Francisco for you." In the meantime, Brian's team worked with a storyboard artist from Pixar to literally script, scene by scene, how a transformative travel experience might unfold. And it's worth hearing Brian's thought process here. What creates transformative travel? Connection—and leaving your comfort zone.

"When you first go to a city, you need a welcome event within the first twenty-four or forty-eight hours where you're around people," Brian begins. "By day two or three, you need to have a challenge out of your comfort zone. If you do not leave your comfort zone, you do not remember the trip.

"If you *can* get out of your comfort zone and something new happens to you, there's going to be a moment of transformation—where the person you *were* in a small way dies, and a new, better version of yourself is reborn. This is the narrative of every movie you've ever seen: A main character starts in an ordinary world. They leave their ordinary world, they cross the threshold. They call it the hero's journey."

So when Ricardo came back to San Francisco, he had a hero's journey, of sorts, awaiting him. The team booked Ricardo a stay with a top-notch Airbnb host; took him to dinner parties; booked seats at a couple of the city's best restaurants; even brought him on a midnight mystery bike tour.

At the end of the trip, Brian met up with Ricardo so he could personally ask how it had gone. By the time they were done talking, Ricardo was in tears. "This is the best trip I've ever had," he told Brian.

Clearly, the Ricardo experiment doesn't scale, as such. Airbnb couldn't possibly handcraft every trip for every customer. But the lessons learned from these experiments shaped the Airbnb Trips model—showing them the most important elements to emphasize. "We applied this to Trips and spent the last couple of years figuring out how to scale it."

Brian is determined to keep redesigning the Airbnb experience by experimenting at the individual scale and then applying the learnings to larger programs. But it gets harder and harder to handcraft as your company grows. As Brian often tells entrepreneurs who are still small and in the designing stage, "I miss those times. Yes, it's great to have a company that *has* traction—but the biggest leaps, the greatest innovations you're ever going to get, will happen when you're small."

Onboarding, one by one

Growing up in Perth, Australia, **Melanie Perkins**'s first job was the epitome of handcrafting, in the literal sense. At age fifteen, she started hand-knitting scarves. "I sold them at women's boutiques around Perth, my home city, which happens to be the most isolated city in the world. I would get incredibly nervous and call up these shops to sell these scarves that I'd hand-made."

Melanie's mother had nudged her on her entrepreneurial path. "My mom had a very good theory. She encouraged all of her kids—all three of us—to start our own teeny little businesses. And even though it didn't make a lot of money, I learned, firstly, that I could take on something that was really scary and then succeed. And it also meant that I could make a business myself rather than having to just purely work for someone else."

Melanie was also learning another, more subtle lesson about how to position an imperfect product. "I put little 'handmade NWA' tags on [all the scarves] because I thought if I had a tag, it would help them to forgive any of the little errors that I'd made."

This kind of beautiful imperfection—which the Japanese might call "wabi-sabi"—embodies the appeal of truly handcrafted items. We love them for their individuality and their humanness. But ironically, the kind of "handcrafting" we're talking about here means almost the opposite. It's less about offering users a product with many tiny charming flaws, and more about working with users one by one to identify and then polish over those rough spots—to smooth out all the small stumbles and scrapes that trip users up.

And this is exactly what Melanie set out to do when she launched **Canva**, the online design platform. The inspiration came from her second job, during college—teaching other students how to use design programs like Photoshop. She was struck by how user-unfriendly the programs were. "They were really, really complicated," Melanie recalls. "They would take a whole semester just to learn the very basics of how to use the software. It would take an absurd number of clicks to learn to do the most simple of things."

Melanie found herself asking: "Why is it so complicated to create a design? Why do people have to study for such a long time to be able to do the basics?" Facebook was gaining popularity at the time, and the contrast between the two was stark. "People could just jump on Facebook and start using it straightaway without having to have gone through this incredibly long period of learning," Melanie recalls. "So we really wanted to take that same simplicity but apply it to design, and make design accessible to everyone, rather than just people who could afford it, rather than people who had the educational background."

Melanie could imagine the path forward from an idea to a company. "I had this very big plan of how to take on the entire world of design and integrate it all into one page and make it accessible to the whole world. But at that point in time, I was nineteen and I had very little business experience other than my scarves."

Melanie and her partner, Cliff Obrecht, launched their first company, Fusion Books, which eventually evolved into Canva. Canva's online tools are meant to make attractive, shareable digital design as easy as drag-and-drop. And from the beginning, they were intent on personally ensuring that everyone could use the product with ease. And they really meant *everyone*.

"Every time we would give someone a new account, I'd actually call the customer and give them a walkthrough, or my partner, Cliff, would do the same," Melanie says. "We spoke to hundreds and thousands of people, and got a deep insight into what they needed, what questions that they had, a button that didn't make perfect sense the first time they saw it."

They battle-tested every button, every click-and-drag action, by watching their users make mistakes during onboarding. They wrangled every major usability challenge they encountered, and then took on another onboarding hurdle—creative shyness.

"People had been told their entire lives that they weren't creative, that they didn't have a design bone in their body," Melanie says. "They were put with this tool, and they were scared to actually use it."

The answer? Turn Canva's customer onboarding into a game. "When people first jumped into the product, within a couple of minutes they were having fun, they felt playful, they felt that they could actually do this. And then, very important, they would share it."

This playful approach revolutionized the design experience for Canva's users, but Melanie and Cliff wouldn't have known where to add clarity and where to add whimsy if they weren't watching individual users as they struggled, strained, and eventually triumphed in their efforts to use it. By smoothing out the edges of the experience, one user at a time, they removed any friction that might stop users from trying, succeeding, and sharing their service.

And it worked. The online design platform now draws fifty million monthly active users, with over three billion designs created—that's eighty new designs every second.

Frame your constitution

If you've ever shared a photo, followed someone online, or tagged a #selfie, then Caterina Fake has shaped part of your life. As co-founder of Flickr, the first photo-sharing platform, Caterina pioneered many of the features that later became conventions. She's like the Noah of social media—she was there just before the Flood. And while she's quick to denounce much of what social media has become, she did realize early on, well before Flickr scaled, that what her company did in its early days would *beget* much of what followed.

As Caterina sees it, the founders of a company are creating their own civilization. They need to model the rules and standards they want to promote—not just within the company but throughout the entire community of customers and users.

As founder Caterina says, "You are the framer of your own constitution."

And that constitution gets written in the days *before* you scale.

It doesn't necessarily involve writing rules of law on parchment. It can be expressed through small everyday actions by the company's founders. In Flickr's early days, for example, Caterina volunteered to greet each and every new user on Flickr . . . personally.

"Flickr was an online community, and all of us participated in it," she remembers. But as the leader, "you are the person who everybody is taking the lead from for whatever values, whatever the mores of the platform and the community are—as in, 'We say this, and we don't say that.' Or, 'We have a custom of greeting people here.'"

Flickr's small startup team, just a half dozen people, were each posting fifty times a day to communicate directly with early users. Many successful founders have similar stories of intense personal contact with customers during pre-scale days—tales of taking calls on personal cellphones, at all hours of the day or night. It's labor intensive (and can intrude on your personal life at times), but it's also a key edge startups have over larger companies that often try to automate all contact with customers.

Moreover, if you use that early contact to establish a certain kind of relationship and code of conduct with your first one hundred users, it will spread to the next five hundred, then five thousand, then five hundred thousand.

As the framer of your new world, you may be challenged and tested early on. It happened with Caterina and Flickr. Like many websites and services, Flickr instantly attracted a global community and users who represented many cultures, languages, and expectations, which didn't always align with each other. For example, many of Flickr's earliest users were from the United Arab Emirates, a predominantly Islamic country where extremely conservative dress was the norm. At the same time, images of the pop star Britney Spears, known then for her revealing clothes and bare midriff, were all over Flickr. "These two things were incompatible," Caterina says.

When complaints arose about Spears's photos, Flickr had to make a decision, and it cost them a significant number of community members.

"We came down on the side of the bare midriff," says Caterina. "This bare midriff issue may sound trivial, but decisions like these are the lifeblood of your community. It isn't that any one decision is the right decision. But you do have to know your company's values and decide."

She adds, "If you're not grappling with decisions, then you're living with a false sense of neutrality." And that may mean your most extreme users could end up making the decision for you.

This lack of clarity remains a problem for social media platforms today. "They don't know who they are. They don't have a clear moral compass or things that they believe."

The pre-scale days are the time to figure all of that out. No site or platform can 100 percent control what its users do—particularly when they run in the millions to billions. Some of them will run amok. But that's all the more reason to put guardrails in place, before it's too late. As Caterina says—quoting her Flickr colleague Heather Champ— **"You are what you tolerate."**

The handcrafter's tale

You'd be hard-pressed to find more than one founder whose origin story begins with: "I wanted my students to read *Little House on the Prairie*."

But that's exactly how **Charles Best**'s story begins. An elementary school teacher in the Bronx, he had almost no budget even for basic supplies, much less for books. So, he says, "I would go to a Staples . . . at like 5:00 every morning and photocopy that day's section of *Little House on the Prairie* to give to each of my students."

Like so many committed teachers across America and the world, Charles and his colleagues were used to spending their own money to make copies and buy school supplies—pencils, crayons, posterboard. They all had long wish lists of bigger things they wanted for their students—things that are standard issue at schools in wealthy neighborhoods, but beyond the realm of possibility in the Bronx: "My colleague wanted to take her students on a field trip to the Museum of Modern Art. The art teacher wanted to do a wall-to-wall quilt with her students and she needed fabric and thread and sewing needles."

One early morning in 2000, while making photocopies at Staples, Charles thought, *All right, I'm gonna put pencil to paper and draw out this website where teachers can post classroom requests and donors can choose projects that they want to support.*

The idea for **DonorsChoose** was born. It was the first site to sup-port what we now call "crowdfunding," and here's how it worked: Any public school teacher could submit a class project for donations. Charles and team would vet and authenticate the project, then post the listing to the site, where users could learn about it and make a donation. Rather than just sending the collected donations directly to the teacher, DonorsChoose would purchase the materials or pay the vendors, then deliver the supplies directly. "Even if it's a field trip," Charles explains, "we're paying the museum, we're paying the bus company to take them to the museum."

This process is labor intensive, but Charles believed it would cre-ate an important layer of integrity assurance. They would show donors exactly where each of their dollars was going, and they would reinforce this trust by sending donors handwritten thank-yous from the kids and a full financial report.

But first, Charles would have to find some donors—and some projects. To populate the site before it launched, Charles asked the teachers at his school to add projects for their own classrooms. And he did something that definitely did not scale: He bribed them.

"My mom made a famous roasted pear dessert," Charles says. "So I asked her to make eleven of those roasted pears and I brought them into the teachers' lunchroom. As my colleagues got ready to pounce, I said, 'Hold up, there's a toll. If you eat one of these pears, you have to go to this new website called DonorsChoose and pro-pose the project you've always wanted to do with your students.' My colleagues scarfed the eleven pears and then posted the first eleven projects on our site."

Now Charles needed some donors to fund the projects. He ended up funding most of that first batch of projects himself, anonymously ("which I could afford to do," he says, "because I was living at home with my parents and they weren't charging me any rent").

To be clear, self-funding your growth definitely does not scale. But this act of generosity was a shrewd initial maneuver. Charles's col-leagues assumed there were donors just hanging out on the site wait-ing to fulfill teachers' classroom dreams. As that rumor spread across the Bronx, teachers started posting hundreds of projects.

But now that he had more teachers coming to the site, Charles needed *real* donors. To help out their teacher, a group of Charles's students volunteered to spend time after school, every day, handwriting letters to two thousand potential donors. "I think they could see the potential of this experiment to enrich their lives. But," he admits, "I also think they felt really bad for me."

Each of the student letters contained a modest but specific ask: "Give $10.00, and become a classroom hero!" The teacher and his students sorted the mail themselves to get the cheapest postal rates, then carted those batches of letters to the post office, fingers crossed.

Their efforts paid off. Thirty thousand dollars later, the donor side of the flywheel was up and running.

In 2003, a small item in *Newsweek* caught the eye of Oprah Winfrey's producers. When she shined her spotlight on DonorsChoose, "she crashed our website," Charles recalls—not that he was complaining. It put them firmly on the path to scale.

This next part of the story, after the Oprah-effect server crash, is where it gets really interesting. As DonorsChoose grew, Charles opted over and over again to hold on to the personal touches that set it apart. They scaled not just despite their high-touch ways but also because of them.

Take the example of Charles's labor-intensive approach to buying and distributing all those school project supplies. "In those early days we sent each teacher a disposable camera to take photographs of the project in action. We sent them a stamped envelope for sending us back the student letters," remembers Charles. "Early funders heard about this model and thought, 'That is insane, inefficient, unscalable.'"

But Charles didn't want to compromise the integrity of the system. Hence, "much of our quest over our first decade," he says, "was taking all of those pieces of integrity assurance and trying to make each of them scalable."

One big piece was the advance vetting of all DonorsChoose projects. Initially, the nonprofit had been paying college students to review each teacher's project request. But as the organization grew, Charles realized he needed a more cost-efficient way to do that.

Whereas previously he'd turned to students for help, now Charles approached teachers: He asked those who'd had more than twenty projects funded on the site to give back by volunteering to be a project screener. It was an inspired idea. In addition to costing less, "it turned out the teachers were more rigorous and much faster at doing it," he says.

One area that Charles admits has always been hard for DonorsChoose to scale is one of the most valued, handcrafted aspects of the donor experience: the student thank-you letters. There's simply no substitute for the emotional power generated by receiving a letter handwritten by a child.

So even as DonorsChoose has grown into a global phenomenon over the past two decades, the organization proudly continues to do some things that simply do not scale—those letters being one of them. They're still written, one by one, by the students. And they all pass through Charles's office on the way to the donors—"and it does make my office look like Santa's workshop," he jokes, "with burlap bags full of letters everywhere."

It's hard to imagine burlap bags as an ingredient to anything that scales. But the handwritten notes, in particular, turned out to be a stroke of genius. They strengthened the bond between the kids and the donors—with a force that's hard to measure.

As Stephen Colbert, a board member, says: "The whole idea of DonorsChoose puts you and the people who you are helping directly in contact with each other. And I found that very powerful." It was handwritten letters in particular that turned Stephen from a onetime supporter to a committed board member. "Those letters from the children, the letters from the teachers made it very real for me. And I didn't want that to end."

Many leaders who aspire toward impact and growth have a hard time with the handcrafted mindset—they often have a list of objections about why the process won't work, why it won't scale, won't operationalize. But the smartest founders never fully abandon the labor-intensive, hands-on mindset—at least in selected areas—no matter how big they get.

Sleeping with the frenemy

When he first launched his online music-sharing startup **Spotify**, **Daniel Ek** didn't quite anticipate that there would be nights like this. "I slept outside of conference rooms, waiting for an executive to turn up. I slept in these $30-a-night motels where the wallpaper falls down on you and there's all sorts of things in the bathroom," Daniel recalls. "It wasn't a very nice time."

In those years, music pirating was rampant in Sweden, and it had devastated the local music industry, which lost 80 percent of its entire revenue base. So Daniel made a bold move. He went directly to top Swedish record industry executives and made them an offer they couldn't refuse: "I guarantee you one year's worth of revenue if you enable this business model."

Record companies were being assailed from all sides by music-downloading services like Kazaa, BitTorrent, and Pirate Bay—and Spotify, with its free subscriptions, was seen as just another online threat. So Daniel was de-risking the deal for the record industry, even if that meant Spotify had to take a painful short-term loss itself.

It's the kind of move that builds trust—something Daniel knew he had to do with this potential adversary, because he understood that his business couldn't succeed without the music business on its side. And he also understood that "doing things that don't scale" can be as much about building critical early relationships and partnerships as it is about building a better product.

Daniel's "Swedish experiment" gradually proved that the music industry and Spotify could coexist. And not only did this begin to earn the trust of record companies in other markets, it also drew the attention of investors—who now saw the possibility of a viable online music business that wasn't a bunch of outlaws and were eager to back Spotify.

But Daniel wasn't out of the woods just yet. To achieve the level of scale he imagined, he knew he'd have to solidify his company's relationship with industry gatekeepers beyond just Sweden. So once again, he relied on the personal touch. Determined to meet with key record company decision-makers to share the results of the Swedish experiment and get their buy-in, Daniel went wherever he had to go—even if it was halfway around the world—just to be in the room where it happens.

Taking that time to cozy up to the music industry gatekeepers paid off. "This is a community where people have known each other for twenty years," he says. "Gradually, I started getting included in the conversations—and that's when acceptance started happening."

In hindsight, many of the things Daniel did—covering the revenues for the record companies, spending his precious founder's time schlepping to meetings in other countries, having his editors curate playlists by hand—were not scalable in and of themselves. But they built the critical early relationships, established the trust, and created a competitive advantage that made it possible to scale later—something Spotify certainly did, to the tune of 345 million active users and more than $2.5 billion in venture funding.

While Daniel Ek needed to establish trust with an old-school industry that viewed him as a threat, **Anne Wojcicki**, founder of the DNA testing and analysis company **23andMe**, faced even more formidable hurdles as she launched her business. She had to take on both the entrenched healthcare establishment *and* the U.S. government agencies that regulated it.

Anne's big idea was born out of a passionate belief that people have a right to know more about their genetic history—so they can use that information to make more informed and empowered decisions about their own health.

But that noble calling didn't make it any easier to sell her unusual product: an at-home DNA testing kit. "We launched the company and sold one thousand kits those first couple days," Anne recalls. "Then we saw it trickle down to ten to twenty kits a day. It was sad. In those early days, people would say, 'Wouldn't my doctor pay for that? Why am I paying for it? What would *I* do with the results?'"

As the 23andMe founders grappled with the problem of reaching consumers, Anne's marketing team suggested a messaging pivot. Instead of emphasizing a health-information angle, 23andMe began playing up the joys of discovering and sharing your ancestry. Bingo—customers warmed to the idea of getting closer to their roots. And if they could also gain more information about their health, well, that was a nice bonus.

The next hurdle was unexpected pushback from physicians. They suddenly had patients coming in saying, "Look what I've learned about my health risks from DNA testing—what should I do?" Doctors were used to being the gatekeepers of that type of information. So 23andMe began an ongoing effort to convince physicians that it was a good thing for patients to be proactively asking more questions about their health.

But the biggest challenge for 23andMe was dealing with state and federal regulators. One particularly challenging gatekeeper was the U.S. Food and Drug Administration. Anne and her team had been meeting with the FDA since early days, but because 23andMe was a first-of-its-kind company, government regulators didn't know how to classify it. (Note to readers: Occasionally, being a first-in-field, ground-breaking innovator makes you *very* annoying to regulators.)

First, the FDA classified genetic tests as "medical devices," requiring federal approval. Later, a new team of FDA regulators sent a cease-and-desist letter to 23andMe, claiming it was offering medical advice and was thus a "healthcare product." Anne was frustrated: "It was the first time in my experience where the problem was not solvable. I really had to shift mentality."

With her back against the wall, Anne's first instinct was: *fight*. Her thinking was: "I represent the consumer, and the consumer has a First Amendment argument here. It's the *consumer's* information."

But then, Anne had a revelation, sparked by an encounter with one of the very regulators she was preparing to do battle with. "I had one wise regulator who asked me, 'What do you want to do? If you really want to change healthcare, just sit down with the FDA and do the hard work. It may take years. And you've got to be ready for that. At the end of those years, you will have really changed society. But you've got to know that you're committed to doing that.'"

Anne's response: "I'm not going anywhere. What else do I have to do? I'm committed."

Anne and her 23andMe team decided to slow down the rollout of new products. Usually this is the last thing a founder should do. But in 23andMe's case, no one else was going to swoop in and grab market share—the FDA was a hard barrier that someone would need to break through. Anne decided it would be her.

Although working with the FDA would prove slow and sometimes painful, it would build the trust that allowed 23andMe to grow in the long term. "Our work with the FDA changed our company a lot," says Anne. "Our engineers, the way we develop, the way we do quality control—it's a very different process now. We had to really prove out to the FDA that the product is accurate, which is something that we always felt confident in." The company also had to convince the FDA that 23andMe was providing consumers with enough information to

REID'S ANALYSIS | How to build trust fast

Entrepreneurs often have to build trust fast—with partners, with investors, with customers, or with colleagues. And the first thing you need to understand is that "fast trust" is almost an oxymoron. Trust typically builds over the course of a long relationship. In fact, my favorite definition (courtesy of Jeff Weiner) is:

Trust = Consistency Over Time

When you're very consistent in following through on your promises—and when you do this over and over again to establish a deep, unbroken pattern—that creates trust. That consistency allows people to say, "Right, we trust you. We know you'll do what you say. We know this will work."

But as an entrepreneur, you often don't have time. And so you need to find shortcuts—or bridges. And there are three great ones I know of.

One effective bridge to trust: Get someone that people already trust to endorse you, or to be the articulator of your value proposition. This is trust by the transitive property. So that people say, "Well, if this person who I trust endorses this, or agrees to it—then it's trustworthy."

A second bridge might be making a substantial and costly commitment or guarantee—as Daniel Ek did when he enticed the music industry to try out Spotify by putting the industry's monetary interests ahead of his own. You want your commitment to show that you're really putting something on the line—that you not only have skin in the game, and not only are putting their interests ahead of yours, but stand to lose big if you fail them: "If we break trust in this way, then in each instance we'll pay you X dollars or we'll donate Y dollars to charity."

A third bridge is to be radically transparent. You might share all of your code. Or post an online bulletin board that all of your customers can use, and that everyone can see. Or offer to do an "Ask Me Anything" interaction and be completely open to any question.

When you need to build trust fast, those three bridges can be key. And they can work even in sensitive circumstances. But bridge building is never easy, and it doesn't happen overnight. And remember: Lasting bridges must be built from both sides.

fully understand their DNA test results, so they hired a dedicated regulation consultant to help guide them through this long process.

It has taken years to work through the issues with the FDA—and it's still ongoing. But in the meantime, 23andMe has steadily built its consumer base, while helping the FDA to understand the value and benefits of enabling more people to do genetic testing. "There were days where I had to point my people to the shiny object in the future and say, 'There is a vision,'" Anne says. "My end goal is I want to meaningfully say I made people healthier. And I really feel like we're just at the beginning."

REID'S THEORIES ON DOING THINGS THAT DON'T SCALE

Focus on the few

When you're building your company, it's more important to have one hundred people *love* your product than a million people kind of like it.

Shoot for the moon (while you still can)

Use the early days to come up with amazing ideas to improve your customer experience.

Get in the trenches

Before you scale is the time for direct contact with your customers and doing whatever's necessary to build that relationship.

Handcraft your way into their hearts

By customizing and adding personal touches to everything you do, you can use the early days to forge a strong connection with your users or customers.

Sleep with the frenemy

Take the time to embrace and build trust with gatekeepers and other unlikely bedfellows.

Set the standards

Now is the time to establish guardrails and model behaviors that will shape the new world you are creating.

3

What's the Big Idea?

"Sometimes the best time to start a business is when you're broke."

It's not necessarily the advice you associate with **Mark Cuban**, *Shark Tank* investor, owner of the Dallas Mavericks basketball team, and self-made billionaire who advises the U.S. government on occasion. But in the early '80s, he was indeed broke.

Mark was a recent college graduate, living with five roommates in Dallas, wearing two-for-$99 suits, just trying to find his path.

He loved to sell, he loved to learn, and perhaps most of all, he loved to toss around business ideas. In his job at a computer software store, he was one of the only salespeople who knew how to program—and who actually read the manuals for the software they were selling.

He had an idea for improving sales that he was sure his boss would love. His boss said no. Mark did it anyway, and it worked. And then he got fired. Someone else might have started looking for another company to work for, but Mark started looking for a company he could *start*. (To this day, he describes that boss as a "negative mentor" because he learned so much from him on what not to do.)

And in retrospect, to him, the timing seemed perfect.

"When your back is against the wall, when you're broke and you have to come up with something, you've got nothing to lose," he says now. "If you try and you fail, you're back where you started. You haven't lost anything—so why not try?"

Mark started hunting for the big idea he could launch a business around. He wasn't looking for a Dallas Mavericks–sized idea or a Broadcast.com–sized idea. He wasn't looking for an idea that could get picked up on *Shark Tank*, if *Shark Tank* had existed then. He was looking for an idea to pay the rent. He asked himself: What do I know? And who do I know? Mark's nonstop reading and conversations with his old clients pointed him toward a clear big idea: computer networking. PCs were just making their way onto company desktops, and Mark knew there were two things business owners were going to want: first, to connect all the computers inside their company to share files and messages; and then, to connect that network with the outside world to do things like, say, replace paper purchase orders.

His new company, MicroSolutions, was built around these twin ideas. And it was powered by something Mark had learned about himself by this time: "I like to be first."

As he tells it: "We were one of the first local area networking integrators, and one of the first to write software for multi-user networks and wide area networks. I wrote the first purchase order system that Walmart ever used, I wrote the first video integration that Zales Jewelers used to use, because I knew about all these things."

Being first with a good idea isn't enough to carry a business, of course. In fact, it can make the climb steeper—because there are so many unknowns. To tackle that uncharted terrain, Mark knew he needed the right team—or his highly technical, high-touch, labor-intensive idea would die on the journey. And the first thing he needed to do was balance out himself. He knew that his grit wasn't enough.

"You want to have that vision and you want to have that push, right? You want to have that relentlessness. But you also have to be very self-aware. And that was one of the things that I was fortunate to recognize early on." Mark chose a co-founder—and made *him* CEO.

"I'm not exactly organized," Mark says. He's a "messy desk" kind of leader, given to following his instincts with quick decisions. And he needed to complement his own skills with the ones he didn't have. "Every single one of my partners or first hires has always been incredibly anal, incredibly detail-oriented," he says. "Because I'm 'ready fire aim'—and I need a 'ready aim fire' person to partner with me and complement my skill set. You gotta be brutally honest."

Mark and his co-founders helped pioneer the first wave of PC networking—from one just-got-fired salesman in a $50 suit to $30 million in annual sales in only seven years. MicroSolutions was acquired by CompuServe at the dawn of the 1990s, leaving Mark with a payout that would allow him to retire from business at thirty. (Which he did, for a time. But as we know now, it didn't stick.)

Long before Mark founded and sold Broadcast.com, long before he became a legendary investor on prime-time TV, he had the entrepreneurial mindset—a mindset not just for business but for finding big ideas and making them work.

And as you can see in his story, you don't need any of the traditional ingredients to make a great idea succeed. You don't need an MBA, you don't need access to capital, and you definitely don't need lightning to strike. What you need is the right mindset.

You need *curiosity*—so you're always asking: Could this work? Could this be a business? Could this be *the* idea?

You need a *bias to action*—so when you spot an idea with potential, you move on it.

You need to *collaborate*—to tap the ideas and strengths of other people, so you can improve your idea and actualize it.

And finally, you need *grit*—to persist through the inevitable failures along the way. And there will be failures.

"We've all had failures. Even when you do all the things you need to do, you're still going to have failures and mistakes," Mark says. "What I tell people is **it doesn't matter how many times you fail, you only have to be right one time.** Just one time. Then you're going to be called an overnight success—you're going to be called 'lucky.'"

REID'S ANALYSIS | The myth of the lightning strike

There's a myth among entrepreneurs of the lightning strike or the aha moment, when a big idea just comes to you—drops right out of the sky, lands in your lap, and transforms you into a billionaire the next day.

This almost never happens.

The most successful entrepreneurs are likely already on the hunt. They aim for big ideas, and they track them. They keep their eyes open for clues. They put themselves in situations where inspiration is most likely to strike. And often they surround themselves with a team of people who can help surface those ideas. They are constantly searching through the eyes of their network for opportunities and insights. To find a big idea, you have to be actively looking for it.

You also must be able to rebound from dead ends and false discoveries—you need unwavering persistence and grit to push through the inevitable failures, setbacks, and naysayers, using the network of people around you to find ideas and solutions (and to avoid fatal and costly errors).

Great entrepreneurs know: **Not every idea is going to succeed.** But even if your first idea doesn't take flight, it may just land you at the doorstep of your next big idea.

In this chapter, you'll hear dramatically different stories of how great founders found their great ideas. And you'll see that every business you've ever admired has a hero's journey behind it. The details might vary, but the plot points are the same. It starts with a spark—an idea!—but that's inevitably followed by endless toil, dramatic setbacks, magical people who arrive to help just in time, and the breakthrough that carries you to scale.

But it always starts with that idea. And with someone in the right place at the right time, with the right mindset to bring it into the world.

The idea you hunt for

Sara Blakely was having a bad day. The kind of bad day that makes you question everything. She was twenty-six years old, selling fax machines door-to-door for a living. During a cold call that day, she was escorted out of a building, "my business card ripped up in my face."

"I literally had a moment where I pulled off to the side of the road and thought, *I'm in the wrong movie. This is not my life.*" Right there on the side of the road, Sara's despair led to a clarity of purpose. She went home that night and wrote in her journal, "I want to invent a product I can sell to millions of people that will make them feel good." As she puts it, "I asked the universe to give me an idea that I could bring to the world."

Different people have different ways of expressing how ideas came to them. Sara will tell you that she asked the universe, and the universe answered. We might observe that Sara kept asking herself the same set of interesting questions, starting with "Is this my big idea?" And one day, inevitably, the answer was going to be "Yes."

And that day—or evening—arrived as Sara was getting ready to go to a party. "I wanted to wear my cream pants that night, and I had no undergarment to wear under them that wouldn't show," she says. So Sara took matters into her own hands: "I cut the feet out of my own control-top pantyhose so I could wear them under my pants and wear any kind of great strappy heel. And it worked beautifully—except they rolled up my leg all night at the party.

"I came home that night, and was like, 'This should exist for women.'"

Sara uttered the three words that flicker like a neon flashing light over a truly big idea. Those three words: "This. Should. Exist." They're your clue that you've stumbled onto something with real potential. If you feel, as a consumer, that you need it, if you can imagine a crowd of others nodding with emphatic encouragement, this just might be your idea.

And Sara had spent years scanning the horizon for that neon sign pointing to her big idea. When she saw it, she followed the sign. And it's worth asking: How many other women had mutilated their pantyhose in exactly the same way? The answer, apparently, is: plenty.

"I meet women all the time that have been cutting the feet out of their pantyhose for years trying to solve undergarment issues for them-selves. And they're always like, 'Why didn't I do Spanx?' And I really just think it's because I had been looking for this and was prepared in my mind to go for whatever idea presented itself."

For an idea to become a business, you have to be prepared to execute it. And Sara was prepared. When the idea struck, she was ready. All the other women who had the same thought simply went to their party and back to work the next morning, leaving the neon sign "This should exist" behind them in the night.

And this gets to the heart of a major misconception around entrepreneurship. There is a myth that big ideas drop out of the sky, land in your lap, and transform you into a billionaire the next day. Nope.

Yes, Sara did have a key moment of inspiration—in her bedroom getting ready for a party—and that matters. But you have to look at what happened *before* that moment. Sara had already oriented herself squarely in the direction of a big idea; she'd been on the hunt for the last ten years. And you have to look at what happened *after*. . . .

When Sara declared, "This should exist," it was a pivotal moment in her trajectory. She calls it the moment that Spanx was born. But here's the thing: It wasn't born just because Sara came up with an idea. It was born because she decided to do something about it.

Sara could have just kept cutting the feet off pantyhose every time she had a party to attend. She could've just tolerated her makeshift contraption rolling up her legs all night. Instead, she saw an opportunity—and she acted.

She immediately went to work building a prototype, so she could see and feel and explain what it was she was trying to create. Mind you, Sara had no background in fashion design or clothes fabrication. But that didn't stop her. "I tried to make the prototypes myself. I went to fabric stores and bought elastic and tried to paper-clip it to the end, and then I tried to sew it. It was through the iteration of the prototype that I really started to love what it could do for my wardrobe."

But Sara soon hit the limits of what she could do on her own. So she started talking to people about it. She actually did not talk to her family or friends—because she didn't believe they'd be *useful* (and in fact, anticipated that they'd be *harmful*, as we read in Chapter 1). Instead, she talked to everyone who could make her idea better, and she listened to what they told her.

To learn about the competition? She asked. "I went to Neiman's and Saks and asked: 'You know, what do women wear under these white pants?' And the salesladies would always say, 'Well, we don't really know,' or they'd point me in the direction of the shapewear that did exist, and it was really thick and dreadful."

To learn about production? She asked. "I cold-called all the manufacturing plants. No one took my call. Every single person thought this was the craziest idea. They didn't get it—but I ended up getting one manufacturer in North Carolina that called me after I did my cold-calling round begging all of these people to try to make my product. He said, 'Sara, I've decided to help make your crazy idea.' He said the only reason why he gave me the chance was my enthusiasm for the idea. He still didn't think it was a good idea."

And to learn about patents? She . . . well, she didn't ask anyone, because patent lawyers are so expensive. In this case, she read: "I immediately went and researched patents at the Georgia Tech Library, and I wrote my own patent."

Sara's story of persistence and grit continues—through her pitch to Oprah Winfrey and her appearance on that show; her application to Sir Richard Branson's show *Rebel Billionaire* and her appearance with him. But what is now a $400 million company started with that single sentence: "This should exist."

To find a "this should exist" idea, Sara has a suggestion: "Go home and look at fifteen things in your life and write them down on a piece of paper. Then write down how and why they could be better. You'll have probably a big idea right there on that sheet."

But next, you have to actually *do something* about it. As Endeavor's Linda Rottenberg puts it, "The best ideas don't die in the marketplace or in the laboratory—they die in the shower. People don't even give themselves permission to walk out of the shower and write it on a napkin and take it into the world. Because they're afraid of what others are going to think about them, or that people might say, 'That's just a crazy idea.'"

To which Linda says: *Embrace the crazy.* "If you're starting something new and people don't call you crazy," she says, "then you're probably not thinking big enough."

The simple idea

When **Kevin Systrom** arrived in Florence, he had a very clear vision of how his semester abroad would unfold. He would indulge his passions: "I love coffee and art and art history." And he would photograph everything he encountered with his brand-new, top-of-the-line camera—an exquisite instrument that was "an embodiment of my personality of perfection. The exact lens you'd want to use with the sharpest glass that you could get."

His photography professor had something else in mind.

"My professor looks at me with my expensive camera," Kevin says, "and he was like, 'No, no, no. You're not here to do perfection. Give me that.'" Kevin reluctantly handed over his fancy camera and his professor took it away, replacing it with a cheap plastic camera called a Holga. "He said to me, 'You're not allowed to use your camera for the next three months.' And I had, like, saved for this thing! So he gives me this camera and I'm just looking at it. If you haven't seen a Holga, it's like a toy camera. It's got a plastic lens. And the light leaks into the side of it if you're not careful." Kevin was horrified, but his professor's point was clear: "You have to learn to love imperfection."

Armed with his "toy camera," Kevin immersed himself in the art and café culture of Florence. And much to his own surprise, he soon embraced the simplicity of the Holga. "I started taking pictures on the go and I would bring them back and he would show me how to develop the photos. They were square, first of all, but they were also slightly blurry and slightly artistic. And then he showed me how to add chemicals to the development bath so that it could tone the black-and-white photo with different colors."

Kevin was learning a lesson in the power of constraints—how *limiting* yourself as an artist can be the secret to unlocking your best work. The technique sometimes works for entrepreneurs as well.

Square photos . . . color filters . . . perfectly imperfect images . . . Hold those ideas in your mind, as we fast-forward to Kevin's post-college career.

After graduating from Stanford and working briefly for Google, Kevin launched an app called Burbn. Burbn was a simple app. **Sometimes, simplicity is intentional. Other times, it's foisted upon us by limitations**: in time, in resources or, in Kevin's case, his own abilities. He had set out to create a location-based gaming app, but scaled it back to a check-in app, similar to Foursquare. "It turns out, I wasn't good enough to build all of the gaming features. So it was just a check-in service and I gave it to my friends and they started using it."

Kevin started to look for investment to build a company around Burbn. He got one offer, but it came with a critical condition. "One of the VCs told me, 'Hey, I'll give you money to do this, but you have to find a co-founder.'" Kevin resisted at first. "I was like, 'I can do this myself!' And he said, 'No, no, no, like, companies I fund, you have to have a co-founder.'"

It was solid, proven advice. As Reid likes to say, two co-founders are almost always better than one. And Kevin soon found the perfect match in Mike Krieger, an old college friend who brought the engineering heft to balance Kevin's product development credentials. They built out the app together but were struggling to get it off the ground. "Our friends liked it, but no one else did," Kevin recalls.

Burbn had three popular features: Users could check in at locations, coordinate visits to those locations with other users, and upload photos when they checked in somewhere. Desperate to shake things up, Kevin and his partner decided to streamline their idea by focusing on one of the three features. To Kevin, they had to have a simpler story to tell about the product. "Mike and I said to each other, 'Let's focus.' So we wrote out on the whiteboard the three things that we thought were best about Burbn." They decided to choose just one and make it great.

"We just looked at all the things our product did and said, 'What's resonating, what's not?' Pick a beachhead—like in Geoffrey Moore's

Crossing the Chasm. Don't do all the things, do one thing really, really well."

Of course, they chose photos.

"That's when the pivot to Instagram happened," Kevin recalls. "We got rid of all the other features, and it just focused on sharing a photo of what you were doing. We made the check-in optional."

Once his focus was trained on the "photo" part of the app, Kevin began to zero in on ways to make that special. He was days away from launch when he got a critical insight from a close advisor: his wife.

Kevin's wife, Nicole, had been watching the photo-app idea begin to take shape when, on a trip to Mexico, she had decided to offer her husband a piece of candid feedback.

"I don't think I'm going to ever use this app," she told Kevin.

"Why not?"

"Well, my photos aren't good.'"

"They're good *enough*," Kevin said.

Nicole then pointed out that her photos were "not as good as your friend Greg's," to which Kevin replied, "Well, Greg *filters* all his photos."

"And my wife looks at me and says, 'Well, you should add filters then.' And I was like, 'Ah. You're right. I should add filters.'"

Kevin learned two important lessons in that moment: An honest partner or spouse can be your best source of feedback. And a single insight can result in a defining feature.

Filtering became one of Instagram's most distinctive elements—perhaps *the* killer feature, enabling users to add the blurred edges, color wash, and light leaks that gave even mediocre photos a rich and warm nostalgia bath.

"Any person we gave it to, their reaction was, 'Oh, my photos seem so much better now,'" Kevin recalls. "And that was when we realized, 'We might have something.'" Within ten weeks, Instagram had a million users.

Big ideas are often based on formative experiences from your past—though as Kevin points out, "you never know exactly what parts of your past will come together to complete that puzzle and be a product that you want to build for the world."

REID'S ANALYSIS | Ask, "What's wrong with my idea?"

One of the most persistent and damaging myths in business today is the myth of the lone genius. We tend to tell the heroic story of innovation. This is a story that credits a single inventor: the founder, the creator. A genius has an idea. Everyone else executes on the idea. And then everyone waits for the genius to have another idea.

But that's a false story of innovation. Very rarely do ideas spring from our brains perfectly formed, like Athena from the brow of Zeus. To turn a good idea into a great product or company, you have to talk about that idea—to a lot of smart people. Because great ideas come from networks, not individuals.

In my book *The Alliance,* I wrote about how one of the most valuable and underutilized sources of information is your network. Both your personal network and your organization's collective network can provide rapid feedback and insights, if you take the right approach to tapping them.

One of the biggest mistakes I see would-be founders make is holding too tightly to their idea for too long. Rather than standing in a closed dark room and waiting for the genius idea to occur to me, I've learned to choose a few people in my network who I know will give me strong feedback, then talk to them. This is the single most important thing you can do to refine your idea. But you can't just go in search of encouragement; you have to also actively invite good criticism. Otherwise, you'll mostly receive polite praise from people who don't want to hurt your feelings. And praise might make you feel good in the moment, but it doesn't actually help you succeed.

I do my best thinking when I'm around people who challenge me, who poke holes in my ideas, and who can tell me where the land mines are. This is one of the advantages, in fact, of seeking investors for your company. Each time you pitch your company, you get valuable feedback. Even from the "nos"—especially from the "nos."

I usually ask people to tell me all the reasons why my idea will fail. This lets me take a spark of an idea and shape it into something that can win. This gives me an edge when it comes to spotting land mines and roadblocks, even before I act on my idea.

And so the advice I always give founders is: Don't ask people, "What do you think of my idea?" Ask them, "What's wrong with my idea?"

The idea hiding in the closet

For **Jenn Hyman**, the idea was hiding in her sister's closet. While on break from Harvard Business School, visiting family for the holidays, Jenn found herself scolding her younger sister for buying a dress that was *way* out of her budget. "I told her she should return that dress she just bought and wear something that was already in her closet," Jenn recalls. "Everything in this closet is dead to me," her sister complained. "I've been photographed in everything. The photos are up on Facebook. I need to wear something new."

Inside that closet, a lightbulb started flickering for Jenn as she realized that, for many of us, our closets are filled with relics of our sartorial past—or as Jenn put it, the typical closet is "a museum to who we once were." It was a universal truth for a certain demographic. A problem in need of a solution.

Jenn started asking herself a series of questions. "The clothing itself, the closet, was dead. *What if the closet was a living thing?* What if this closet could adapt to changes in the weather, changes in our mood, changes in our lifestyle, changes in our size?" What if I could simply *rent* all my clothing, instead of owning it?

When she returned to Harvard Business School after the holiday break, Jenn shared the notion of a "living closet" with HBS classmate Jenny Fleiss.

And in this one move, she did two things that set her apart from so many would-be entrepreneurs. First, she recognized the idea, asking: *Could this be a business?* But what she did next mattered more: She told someone about it.

When you suspect you're on to a big idea, you may be so concerned about protecting it that you keep it to yourself. But you can't scale an idea that lives in your head. In fact, you can't even know for sure if it really *is* a scalable idea. You always need input—but not from just anyone: from someone, experienced or not, who's willing to help you improve it.

Jenn and her soon-to-be co-founder Jenny agreed it made sense to get a perspective from someone in the fashion world. They decided to start at the top by contacting Diane von Furstenberg, who was not only one of the most famous designers of her generation but also president of the Council of Fashion Designers of America. There was just one problem: They didn't actually have von Furstenberg's contact information. So, even though they knew it was a long shot, Jenn sent cold emails to twelve different iterations of her name at dvf.com. Luckily, one of those email addresses was correct.

She got a meeting with the designer, and it yielded the first refinement to Jenn's big idea. Diane liked the idea of using rental as a way to introduce her brand to younger women. But she wanted to do it if other brands did, too. Another entrepreneur might have seen that as an impossible hurdle. But for Jenn, it meant she was on to something. Boom. **Rent the Runway**'s first industry contact had inadvertently provided them with a new business model. Why be the rental service for one brand when you could do it for twenty brands? Or fifty?

This was a turning point for Jenn and Jenny. "In a sense, Diane kind of gave us the permission in that meeting to go off and build our own 'Rent the Runway' site and become our own retail company," says Jenn.

Jenn and Jenny left the meeting and decided to go into business. But they didn't look for external reinforcement; instead, Jenn went straight to someone who would challenge the idea. "I thought, *Who is apt to hate this idea the most? It's going to be a traditional department store.*'" The second person she cold-called was the president of Neiman Marcus. She got the meeting.

When Jenn met the president at his office, she said she was planning to start renting the same designer dresses Neiman Marcus sells—and that she would do it for less than 10 percent of what Neiman Marcus charges. "Oh, women have been 'renting the runway' at my stores for decades," he told her. "It's called 'buying a dress, keeping the tags on, and returning it to the store.'"

"How often does that happen?" Jenn asked.

"About 70 percent of the time."

He went on to explain why they put up with it: That same customer "borrowing" from the dress department was also often buying ten pairs of shoes downstairs—so the store was willing to tolerate the former in order to get the latter.

After hearing similar stories about the pervasiveness of dress borrowing at Macy's and Saks, Jenn knew she was on the right track. There was already a large market of women who wanted to wear designer dresses but didn't want to buy them. An affordable, convenient, and *ethical* way to "borrow" dresses should definitely exist.

Rent the Runway launched in 2009 and grew to a billion-dollar valuation by 2019. But borrowing designer dresses was just the first of many evolving ideas that propelled it to success. The original rental business evolved into a subscription service—a "closet in the cloud"—and along the way, Jenn built different businesses to support the evolving idea. She built a data team to analyze trends and maximize investment; she built partnerships to build inventory. And perhaps least expected, she built the world's largest dry-cleaning service—complete with expert seamstresses—to ensure the customer experience matched expectations. "The customer experience of Rent the Runway is not the website or an app. That is easy," Jenn says. "The customer experience is receiving back millions of units of worn clothing, capturing data on those units, restoring them to perfect condition, dry-cleaning them, repairing them, reassembling them with new units and shipping them out—often with a zero-day turnaround time."

Jenn hadn't anticipated any of that process when the idea first came to her. "We've had to build all of our underlying logistics technology from scratch," she says. "I really did think that we were going to be able to outsource part of our technology stack. I thought that we'd be able to outsource, potentially, our dry-cleaning at the very beginning." But then she realized: "Wait, that *is* the business."

Because your first big idea is just the spark. The truly scalable business may emerge several ideas later.

The idea born out of an annoyance

"I just wanted to stop carrying a thumb drive around."

That was the motivation for **Drew Houston** as he began to think about launching his now-thriving data storage company **Dropbox**. And it's typical of the kind of everyday annoyances that can light up that flashing neon sign.

Drew certainly didn't start out dreaming of becoming a data storage mogul. At the time, he was developing an online SAT prep course called Accolade. But his need to keep moving files between computers forced him to use a less-than-reliable USB drive for that sensitive job. His thumb drives contained the source code to Accolade, which meant he was always one careless step away from disaster.

"I can't count the number of times I bent the connector," he says. He worried about the drives going bad, as they tend to do without warning. Or about losing them. Or (and this was his biggest fear) about putting his pants in the washing machine with that little drive in the pocket.

Now, it is technically true that in 2006, online data storage already did exist—in the sense that there were companies offering some version of it. But as he looked into them, Drew noticed these companies' user forums were swamped with complaints. "Visiting their user forums was like walking into a battlefield infirmary," recalls Drew. "People were writing, 'Hey, you destroyed all my Excel spreadsheets' or 'I lost my tax returns' or 'I really wanted those wedding photos. I don't see them anymore. Can you help me go get them?' Just disaster after disaster in these forums."

Was it too much to ask that an online storage company safely store your data? Drew didn't think so; he decided that he could build a better cloud storage system that would actually keep data and files safe.

He and his co-founder, Arash Ferdowsi, had little to lose: "Worst-case scenario, we build something awesome and we solve this interesting problem," says Drew. "Other people will come knocking, we sell the company, build something else." That sounds pretty good to a twenty-four-year-old living in an apartment with four dudes.

Things didn't quite go "worst-case scenario" for Dropbox. Drew built the system, launched the company, scaled it (didn't sell it), conquered the category—and finally freed himself from that gnawing anxiety about his thumb drive ending up in the washing machine.

The twist on an existing idea

"No one was thinking of the consequences," says **Whitney Wolfe Herd** about the first startup she co-founded, the immensely popular dating app Tinder. Famous for letting users "swipe right" on potential matches, Tinder was an undeniable success. But pretty soon, the brand also became synonymous with meaningless hookups, and the platform was reported to be rife with misogyny and harassment.

This was why Whitney decided it was time for her to move on. Looking back, she says, "I think what I learned there was, the minute you encourage someone to use a piece of technology, you are inherently responsible. And that lingered with me as I left the company."

REID'S ANALYSIS | Notice a pattern and build toward it

As you're trying to find ideas, it can be useful to look at how some of the best business minds find theirs. In Silicon Valley, for example, many of us have an engineer's mindset, and so we look for patterns: patterns of success in other companies, patterns by which new technologies open markets, and also patterns in the broader culture that might lead to a different kind of world.

Some entrepreneurs find their initial ideas by observing the innovations and advances around us, and asking ourselves, "What businesses does this open up?" As in, "Now we have mobile phones—what business opportunities does that create? Now we have cloud storage—what businesses are now possible? Now we have artificial intelligence—what businesses could exist?"

Other entrepreneurs key in to a single long-term trend and imagine the future it will create. Melanie Perkins imagined a world in which design and publishing tools enabled non-designers, instead of intimidating them. She turned that picture of the future into Canva, an Australia-based company currently valued at $6 billion. Ev Williams read an article in *Wired* magazine on the idea that technology could eventually connect all the brains on the planet; he turned that single underlying vision of the future into three culture-shaping companies: Blogger, Twitter, and Medium.

Another way that entrepreneurs find their ideas is by noticing a more abstract pattern or trend and building toward it. As in, "I can see this model for how these components can come together. And even though there's no initial, explicit demand for it in this way, I can build to that." LinkedIn is one of those, and so is Airbnb. There were some signs of demand for Airbnb, in that there were a lot of young people who wanted to travel, and needed to do it cheaply, and were happy to sleep on someone's couch; "couch surfing" was a thing. And there was also a trend at the time toward collaborative consumption—with companies like ZipCar pioneering shared car ownership. But the idea of renting someone else's room in their apartment for a night—that was definitely new.

The translation of patterns into business ideas is at the core of what it means to be an entrepreneur. And no matter how quickly you translate those patterns into ideas, chances are other people will be doing the same thing. Whether you or your competitors win will depend on how quickly and decisively you act. (I write more about the importance of speed, and what you can do to outpace your competition, in my book *Blitzscaling*.)

Her concerns about the dark side of online interactions only deepened after word of her acrimonious breakup with Tinder got out—and she found herself under online attack by strangers. "So I was on the other end of what it can feel like to be exposed on the internet," she says. As she thought about all the young girls and women out there being exposed to similar types of cyberbullying behavior, "that really started to shape 'the next thing' for me," she says.

Whitney wanted to change the way people talk to each other online—to, in her words, "rethink social media in the context of kindness." She initially set out to start a social network she called Merci. It had one small but important distinction from all the other social networks that had gone before, she says. "You couldn't just leave random comments, they had to be *compliments*." It was an effort to engineer a twist in online social discourse—just a slight turn, in the direction of kindness.

As she was starting to pursue this idea, a different—but related—opportunity came her way. Because of her background at Tinder, she was offered a chance to help launch a new online dating service. Her initial reaction: *No way. Swipe left. Next!*

But as Whitney politely tried to decline the opportunity, she also began thinking about an intriguing possibility: *Might there be some way to create a dating app that could offer a safer, more respectful experience for women?*

Whitney agreed to consider coming on board as leader of this new dating app if it could be aligned with her vision of creating a safe digital ecosystem for women and girls online. The challenge, she believed, had to do with control: Women simply did not have enough of it in the world of online dating.

"All of a sudden," Whitney says, "I had this hurricane moment in my mind. What if we take the standard dating platform but there is a catch—only the *woman* can initiate conversation?"

The idea of the "woman speaking first" is counter to the expectations set by the past hundreds of years of dating, says Whitney. "Women are taught not to speak first, never to send the first message, never to initiate. And men are taught to be very aggressive and really beat down that wall until she says 'yes.' And that creates an imbalance. And so the whole effort is to take some of that pressure and that aggressive nature away from the man—and to lift the woman up. It really balances things out."

The more Whitney thought about it, the more she saw the potential to rewrite the rules not just of online dating but of online interaction in general, by putting more control into women's hands. "This is going to reduce harassment," she remembers thinking. "It is going to reduce bad behavior. And women will be empowered and encouraged to actually be in the driver's seat."

The resulting app—**Bumble**—became a sensational success, thanks to a single tweak to the way dating apps worked. Or as Whitney puts it, "We weren't trying to reinvent the wheel. We were just trying to reverse it."

The idea you were born to do

After two decades on Wall Street, **Sallie Krawcheck** knew that something was missing—and that she might be just the person to create it.

As an investment analyst, Sallie became aware of an issue she called "the gender investing gap." Everyone knows about the gender *pay* gap, but this was something altogether different, and within it was an opportunity.

A woman making $85,000 typically keeps 71 cents of every salary dollar in cash—which means she is investing far less than her male counterpart. "This can cost a woman a million dollars over her life," Sallie notes. "That's 'start my business' money, or 'buy my dream house' money, 'take your friggin' hand off my leg' money, or 'leave the job you hate' money. So I realized there was this gap there that the investing industry simply wasn't closing."

Sallie began her career at Salomon Brothers, the firm made infamous by the book *Liar's Poker*. If Wall Street was a frat party, Salomon Brothers was its Animal House. "It was this very, what we today call toxically masculine culture," she remembers. "And of course, at the time, there was sexual harassment. I would come into the office and there would be a Xerox copy of male genitalia on my desk, which was, for a young lady from Charleston, a little horrifying. Like they were trying to run me out for the sport of it."

But Sallie held her ground at Salomon, and eventually found her way to the asset management firm Bernstein, where she wrote investor reports. Her first report for Bernstein was a "negative," she recalls—a recommendation *not* to invest in the company she wrote about. Why? Their business was making subprime loans. Some in her company discouraged her from publishing the report; she did anyway. When she turned out to be right, her star began to rise. Five years later, as CEO, she bucked the status quo a second time when she took aim at a common Wall Street practice that troubled her. At the time, many financial analysts were doing investment banking and research for two different sets of clients, which created clear conflicts of interest. "It meant an investment bank could advise their clients to do one thing, and then turn around and bet against that same advice," she says. Sallie decided to end that practice at her firm by pulling them out of the investment banking business—even though it meant sacrificing millions of dollars in revenue.

Sallie's timing could not have been better. In just a few months, the NASDAQ crashed as the dot-com bubble burst. And when that happened, Bernstein stood out, in a good way, because it didn't have the same conflicts of interest as many of the other firms. That's when Sallie landed on the cover of *Fortune* magazine with the headline, "In Search of the Last Honest Analyst."

This attention vaulted Sallie to a top position at Smith Barney, one of Wall Street's biggest banks, where she again challenged con-

ventional practices—and this time it cost her her job. After it became clear that the bank she worked for had given bad advice to
clients, Sallie recommended reimbursing those clients—and the
CEO did not agree. Not only was she fired, but her firing made front-
page news. The "last honest analyst" had been shown the door.

The good news: This incident freed her up to try to right one more
wrong on Wall Street—the gender investing gap. "It just lit a fire in me
that I *needed* to do this, that I couldn't leave this Earth if I wasn't helping women close these money gaps," she says.

With women controlling some $7 trillion in investable assets and
90 percent of all women managing their money on their own at some
point in their lives, creating investment offerings and services aimed at
this market felt like a big opportunity.

Not everyone agreed.

And even after years spent on the receiving end of Wall Street
misogyny, the reactions to her idea still shocked her—variations on a
persistent theme: "But don't their husbands manage their money for
them?"

Up to this point, Sallie hadn't planned to launch a startup—she
hoped an existing financial services company might adopt her idea.
But the responses she got made it clear: *Okay,* she thought, *if this is
going to get done, then I've got to do it.*

Wall Street had taught her how things *shouldn't* be done—which
helped her envision how to do it differently. So she began to design
something that was fundamentally different from all the investment
products currently available: **Ellevest**, an investment platform designed for and marketed exclusively to any woman, anywhere, who has
been overlooked by the financial industry, who has earned her own
money and is confident in all areas of her life—*except* when it comes
to investing.

The Hail Mary idea

Caterina Fake and Stewart Butterfield were more than a little bit worried. Their innovative online role-playing game was not growing the
way they'd hoped. *Game Neverending* had a small loyal following. But
growth had stalled and they couldn't find investment.

"This was right after the dot-com crash, a bleak-looking point in the history of financial markets generally," Stewart says. "Anything as frivolous as a game was not going to get funded. I had tried everything—put all of my savings into it, tapped out friends and family. We had more or less worked through the very small amount of angel investment we were able to get. We were looking for a Hail Mary."

During this dark time, Stewart and Caterina took a trip to New York for a conference. And that's when things went from bad to worse. "I got food poisoning on the plane," Stewart says. "We arrived and I was throwing up on the Van Wyck Expressway into New York, and then at the hotel I was just sick all night." And in the middle of all that—Stewart figures it was around 3 or 4 in the morning—the idea for Flickr came to him, "like a fever dream."

It grew from a feature in the game. "In the game, you had an inventory where you could pick up objects," says Stewart, "and we made that inventory a shoebox full of photos. You could do interesting things, like drag photos into group conversations. They would pop up on the other person's screen, and you could annotate them in real time."

Flickr, the groundbreaking photo-sharing community, laid the foundation for so much of what is done today on Facebook, Instagram, and Twitter: tagging, sharing, following, memes. It was an important early experiment in modern social media—a test bed for innovations. And it helped change the paradigm of social interaction online.

But it started as a feature buried inside a game that wasn't very popular. You could say that Caterina and Stewart owe their success with Flickr to their ability to spot the idea within the idea, with some help from excellent timing. But there was something else that pushed them to go all in on Flickr—desperation.

"Flickr wasn't coming from a grand vision of what photos could be and how you could build social interaction around them to make them more searchable. All that stuff came later. At the time, it was just: *Can we not go out of business?*"

• • •

You can find similar origin stories for so many of the companies profiled in this book. Sara Blakely "being escorted out of a building, my business card ripped up in my face" just before she had the idea for Spanx. Sallie Krawcheck being fired from her high-profile Wall Street job, her firing splashed on the front page of *The Wall Street Journal*, when she came up with her idea for Ellevest. Kevin Systrom holding on to a failing check-in app, before turning it into Instagram. Whitney Wolfe Herd enduring an episode of online harassment . . . then, the idea for Bumble arrived. Mark Cuban being flat broke in a cheap suit.

Sometimes a big idea sprouts from hard circumstances, like a rose from concrete. Often it's the case that a big idea is actually *embedded* in hardship—and only as you experience that hardship firsthand (painful as it may be) do you get close enough to glimpse a possible solution.

Put simply, *resistance causes friction, and friction creates sparks.*

Moreover, a crisis can sharpen focus and strengthen resolve. It can cause you to go from thinking *It would be nice to come up with a big idea*, to: *I'm finding a big idea, dammit!* And then having found that idea, a crisis provides the sense of urgency that compels you to actually throw the Hail Mary pass.

Of course, in the end, launching a big idea and building a business around it is not as easy as making one great throw. It is more of a steady, relentless march downfield, obstacles—of which there will be many—notwithstanding.

The beautifully "bad" idea

Tristan Walker was in search of an idea. If you read Chapter 1, you already know what happens next—he'll run an epic gauntlet of "nos" from potential investors, before funding, building, and ultimately selling the company. And you also know what happened first: He helped build Foursquare from the ground up—helping to take the company from zero merchants to over a million.

But in 2012, Tristan was between things. He was ready to "go out and build ambitious things myself." All he needed was an idea. And to find ideas, you have to go where ideas will find you. You have to talk to

REID'S ANALYSIS | Go where ideas will find you

As an entrepreneur, you should intentionally create the time and space—every day—to open yourself up to new ideas. This means you have to put yourself in situations where your great ideas are likely to strike.

I ask every guest on *Masters of Scale* about their favorite place to think big, and what I've learned is: There is no one perfect way. Some people do their best thinking in solitude; some need the active presence of a creative team; and some need the electricity of crowds around them. Some need a familiar, regular place; and some need the novelty of a new experience. Some look to nature; some to city streets.

Spanx founder Sara Blakely told me that her best thinking happens in the car. And since she lives really close to the Spanx headquarters, she created what her friends call her "fake commute." She gets up an hour early and drives aimlessly around Atlanta, so she can let thoughts come to her. She thought of the name "Spanx" in the car.

The intentionality is critical. By creating the time and space—first thing every day—to open herself up to new ideas, she actively cultivates her best thinking. And every great entrepreneur does the same. Netflix's Reed Hastings thinks best in his own living room in Santa Cruz. For Airbnb's Brian Chesky it's the Walt Disney Family Museum. Bill Gates gets in his car to drive; Zynga's Mark Pincus gets on his surfboard; and ClassPass's Payal Kadakia hits the dance studio.

Caterina Fake, co-founder of Flickr and internet pioneer, has one of the more unusual go-tos. She tends to wake in the night and use the span of time between 2:00 A.M. and 5:00 A.M. to do a lot of thinking. So for her, it's a "when," not a "where," that drives her best ideas.

For me, I do my best thinking when I'm around people who challenge me and who poke holes in my ideas. And while some people think more expansively in familiar places, like the shower or their favorite running path (which makes sense—familiar spots let you go on autopilot, while your mind wanders), my favorite thinking spots are ones that are new to me. I do my best thinking in cafés and other places with a little bit of bustle. That's where I can really focus on a purely blank page.

Finding your idea is a combination of your unique capabilities, your ideas for the future, and the markets around you. In my first book, *The Startup of You,* I have a chapter on how to find your path by mapping your assets, aspirations, and the market realities.

Above all, even if you are an introverted inventor, never forget your network. Talking through your idea with challenging people, creative people, skeptical people, and other entrepreneurs: These conversations can accelerate your pace to finding the next big idea in time.

people who will challenge you, in the right ways, to find the biggest and best version of an idea that's right for you. So Tristan went to a place where ideas are not only in the air but bouncing off the walls—the iconic venture capital firm Andreessen Horowitz. Recognizing Tristan's eye for innovation, Ben Horowitz, a founding partner there, invited Tristan to "hang around the office and think big," naming him an Entrepreneur in Residence.

While Tristan cast about for his big idea, Ben shared an insight that confirmed what Tristan had first intuited about Twitter, back at Stanford: Sometimes, what look like bad ideas are good ideas—and what look like good ideas are bad.

As Ben explained it, people tend to chase "good ideas"—ideas that seem to make a lot of sense, almost to the point of being obvious. But there's not much value in the obvious. They're either incremental ideas, or they've been done, or there's a sound reason why they *can't* be done.

But the so-called bad ideas? That's where the gold might be hidden. *Airbnb? Who would let strangers sleep in their homes? Uber? Who would want to get a ride from a stranger in an unmarked vehicle?* Tristan thought about it for a minute and decided: "Definitely, I want to chase the bad ideas."

Most of Tristan's ideas were good ideas. Or good enough, anyway. But his single-blade razor idea? Too small a niche. Too big an industry, with massive players that could crush new competition. Too counter-intuitive (but *more* blades is better, right?).

Tristan figured—and Ben agreed—the "bad" idea was the one to pursue. He sensed that prevailing assumptions about this "niche" were wrong, and the opportunity was bigger than people realized. He also knew, in his heart, that *he* was the right person to pursue it: "When I think of my experience of not having products that worked for me, and my ability to potentially raise money for this thing—I don't think there's anyone better on the planet to do this one thing than me. And the day I came to that realization, it was the most freeing moment for me."

Today, as his company continues to develop new products for the Walker line, Tristan still relies on the "bad idea" test. "Now, whenever we come up with ideas, we're asking ourselves, 'Why is that a terrible idea?' And if we can't answer that question, it's probably not worth doing."

REID'S THEORIES ON FINDING THE BIG IDEA

Chase the bad idea

When everyone is telling you, "That's a good idea," it can mean lots of other people are likely already pursuing it. Instead, look for the beautiful idea disguised as a bad one—the idea whose potential value is unseen or misunderstood.

If not you, who?

When you take a penetrating look at your history and passions, your destiny idea may be staring right back at you.

Pay attention to the flashing neon sign

If you believe that something should exist—and you can imagine many other people nodding in agreement—it may just be an idea worth pursuing.

You don't have to reinvent the wheel

When searching for a big idea, don't discount the "slight twist" that can have a major impact.

The Hail Mary

Never let a crisis go to waste. Desperate times can sharpen focus, strengthen resolve . . . and yield killer ideas, while also creating the urgency to act on them.

4

The Never-Ending Project: Culture

Before he brought Blockbuster to its knees with his innovative DVD-by-mail service, and long before he transformed that DVD delivery company—with its trademark red envelopes—into the streaming network/studio that conquered Hollywood, **Netflix CEO Reed Hastings** was a programmer. And a good one, it seems: Along with two of his colleagues at the time, Reed invented a debugging tool for other programmers. They called it Purify, and it was a hit.

That's when things got messy.

At this point in his career Reed was by no means an experienced executive, yet he quickly found himself not only managing a growing staff but overseeing the acquisition of new companies—which meant new teams of employees were arriving overnight. At one point, Reed's company, now called Pure Software, bought three new businesses in a span of eighteen months. They were moving so fast that integrating these new teams into the company's culture—to the extent they even had one—was hardly even an afterthought.

"I was coding all night, trying to be CEO in the day, and once in a while, I'd squeeze in a shower," Reed recalls. "At the time I thought if I could just do more—more sales calls, more travel, write more code, do more interviews—that somehow it would work out better."

It didn't.

Reed was trying to do it all himself—a common mistake among founders, and one that tends to create more problems as a company grows. Instead of leveraging his employees' capabilities, Reed tried to work around them. Not trusting his employees' abilities to problem-solve on their own, he tried to solve problems for them.

"Every time we had a significant error—sales call didn't go well, bug in the code—we tried to think about it in terms of what process could we put in place to ensure that this doesn't happen again," Reed recalls.

But **in trying to "dummy-proof" all the systems, Reed ended up dumbing down the culture of his company.** "The intellectual level of the company fell," he says. "Then the market changed as it inevitably does—in this case it was C++ to Java, but it could have been anything. And when change came, we were unable to adapt." Reed had unwittingly created a culture in which people were good at following processes, but not so good at thinking for themselves.

Reed never was able to fix the culture at Pure—company culture is hard to fix retroactively, because it gets cemented during the formative years—but once he sold Pure, he was determined to do things differently with his next venture.

In this chapter, we'll explore the mysteries of culture—a term that, when applied to organizations, can seem maddeningly vague. What do we mean by culture? And does it really matter—or is it just a buzzword? Can it actually be shaped and guided by a company's leaders, or is it something that develops of its own accord?

While there may not be a simple foolproof formula for a winning company culture, what seems clear is that certain qualities and characteristics are at the beating heart of one.

Culture is a living, breathing thing—the context you set for your employees to work at their best. It should be grounded in a shared sense of mission—the thing your company is actually trying to accomplish. It should be understood by everyone, and *built* by everyone; in fact, it fully emerges only when every employee feels a sense of personal investment and ownership. And the work of creating that culture—through thoughtful, intentional design and action on the part of a company's founders—should begin at the earliest moments of a startup.

But it's no easy task. It requires a delicate balancing act to get everyone across an organization to share a common set of values without stifling diversity or hiring only in your own image. And it can be particularly hard to protect and strengthen those values when you're scaling up—and hiring new employees en masse.

So how do you create a culture *today* that will serve you well *tomorrow*? One that can somehow anticipate, and be ready for, and drive the changes that may be years away from happening?

If you foolproof your culture, you'll have a culture of fools

It's easy to forget just how radically Netflix upended the video rental business. Reed co-founded and seed-funded Netflix in 1997, using some of the money he earned when Pure Software was acquired for $750 million that year. The premise was elegantly simple: DVDs by mail. No late fees. No return shipping charges. No getting in your car to drive to the store. Lose a DVD? You get a new one in the mail, no questions asked.

Blockbuster tried to follow suit, matching service for service, but they didn't move quickly enough, and they filed for bankruptcy in 2010. But even as Reed's audacious startup was upending how movie rentals had worked in the past, he kept an eye fixed on the future. And what he saw was an enormous threat to his young company, not from the old dinosaur Blockbuster, but from the first glimmers of online streaming.

With broadband internet making its way into households across the United States, it seemed inevitable to Reed that streaming entertainment would soon eclipse DVDs. Remember: This is in the late '90s, when broadband internet had reached fewer than one in ten households. But he felt it coming.

So while on the one hand Reed needed a team to develop a first-rate logistics operation for shipping DVDs, he knew that soon enough that same team would need to completely shift gears—and focus on building an online streaming service from scratch.

Finding engineers to build a pioneering video-streaming service was going to be a challenge. Reed looked for "first-principle thinkers." First-principle thinking is the idea that everything you do is underpinned by foundational beliefs or first principles. Instead of blindly following directions, or sticking to an established process, a first-principle thinker will break down a problem to its most basic assumptions, test or question those assumptions, and then re-create them from the ground up. And rather than do things in a habitual way, such a thinker will wonder, "Couldn't we do it this *other way* instead?" These are the kinds of inquisitive minds Reed Hastings wanted in the room. And to lure them he devised an unexpectedly effective tool: the Culture Deck.

The Netflix Culture Deck is a now-legendary document consisting of about one hundred slides describing what the Netflix culture stands for, who it seeks to hire, and what to expect upon going to work there. As Reed admits, the Culture Deck "is not very pretty, it's not highly designed—it doesn't look like an external marketing piece."

Indeed, it began as an internal document, but then Netflix started posting the slides on SlideShare—"just to be able to send a link to job candidates." Soon it was being passed around online. And before long, it had over ten million views on SlideShare.

To this day, founders study the Culture Deck for clues on how to understand (and perhaps emulate) the Netflix culture. And more important, the Culture Deck has become a magnet for first-principle thinkers who want to work in a culture like Netflix's, which promises a balance of freedom and responsibility.

Looking at the Culture Deck, one learns, for instance, that there is no set vacation policy at Netflix. "We say, 'Take what you want,'" Reed explains. "And, during the day we don't have a nine-to-five policy. People just work as they see appropriate." The Culture Deck also emphasizes the company's transparency and honesty. For instance, people working at Netflix are encouraged to frequently ask their manager, "Hey, if I were leaving, how hard would you work to change my mind to stay?" Reed calls this the "keeper test," intended as a way of letting employees know exactly where they stand at all times.

Reed eschews phony corporate-speak about employees being like family. At Netflix, the analogy is not to family but to a sports team. "Ultimately, it is about performance—unlike a family, which is really about unconditional love," Reed explains. "What we're about is collectively changing the world in the area of internet television, and that takes incredible performance at every level. We're also about honest feedback all the time, so you can learn and be the best you can be."

This distinction between a family and a sports team is so insightful that Reid Hoffman made it the core of his book *The Alliance,* which explains why managers should treat employees like allies trying to accomplish a mutually beneficial mission, rather than trying to pretend that their company is a family.

Today, Netflix is filled with first-principle thinkers, whose mindset permeates company-wide decision-making on everything from entertainment content to spending on business-related travel. "With all those decisions, we ask people to think about what is best for the company," Reed says. "We don't give them any more guidelines than that." But of course that kind of agency isn't for everyone—some people want to be told what to do. "Those people are not a good match for Netflix," he says.

By building a culture of flexible, adaptable, first-principle thinkers, Netflix was able to evolve as quickly and dramatically as any company in recent memory. The company went from shipping millions of DVDs by mail to producing original creative content, scouting at film festivals, and curating a library of streaming entertainment available worldwide. It's a remarkable reinvention.

When Reed thinks about the transformation Netflix has gone through and tries to imagine his old company, Pure Software, dealing with similar challenges, he is convinced Pure would not have survived. That's because Pure had a culture built for process; Netflix, on the other hand, has a culture built to scale.

As Netflix evolves, so the culture will evolve with it. "We try to constantly encourage employees to figure out how to improve the culture, not how to preserve it," Reed says. "Everyone is trying to add value by saying, 'Here's a place we can improve what we do.'" The Culture Deck is "not the golden tablets. It's a constantly evolving, living document."

REID'S ANALYSIS | **A culture is always under construction**

Many founders misunderstand company culture, and there are two major mistakes I see over and over. The first and most common mistake founders make is to ignore company culture, or to delay thinking about it. These founders think their most critical problem is to solve for product or revenue. In my own case, as a young entrepreneur, I prioritized strategy over culture. To these entrepreneurs, as to me then, culture seems squishy and secondary, perhaps even occurs naturally.

But culture actually underlies everything a company will achieve, and it's critical to start thinking intentionally about this when your team is small and the culture is still malleable. A company's culture cements very quickly—and sometimes invisibly—as it spreads from person to person. You have to be very careful about the beliefs, practices, and rituals you're scaling. If you don't get it right among the initial set of people, it won't be right anywhere.

If you allow a broken culture to take root, there is no reliable path to fixing it. It may take much longer than the market realities and competition allow. Depending upon how your culture is broken, it may make establishing your new culture impossibly difficult. For example, if your employees fear political retaliation, it will likely be very difficult to establish a Reed Hastings–style first-principle culture. Or, if your culture tolerates verbal abuse (usually by "high-performance" employees), then it will likely be very difficult to establish a kind, collaborative culture like the one built by WaitWhat, the company that produces *Masters of Scale*. In shorthand: If you have a C culture, you can revise it to a B+. But a C culture will never become an A culture. The only way you get an A company culture is by creating it at the beginning and preserving it.

But that leads to the second, very common misconception about culture. Many people talk about culture as if it's etched in stone, like the Ten Commandments. But a company culture can't be constructed by edict, and it isn't static. Like anything involving humans, culture is always evolving. It's shaped and molded by the individuals who carry it forward on the team, and it will necessarily change as you grow. But you can keep the same solid foundation that you established intentionally and institutionally.

That doesn't mean there can't be mistakes and misunderstandings as the culture is being established. Actually, part of the growth and evolution of culture can be acknowledgment and correction for missteps along the way. Such corrections can make people and relationships much stronger.

Earlier in my career, I thought that you could take a hard turn with a company culture—that a "new sheriff" could come into town, lay down new laws, and turn everything around. But culture doesn't work this way. Whether you're in the building stages of a company or amid a turnaround, culture has to evolve.

Another thing to understand about culture is that we all work in the service of our mission, and the culture defines how we work together to accomplish that mission. In other words, culture is owned, built, and improved upon by everyone in the company. So it's a joint project—and an ongoing one that never ends.

Culture underlies everything that you do as a company: hiring talent, building and executing strategy, shaping customer engagement. Hence, in my book *Blitzscaling*, I outline many entrepreneurial business challenges that can be solved later—even challenges as extreme as business model or operating financial model—but make the point that culture is something to establish now, always.

What's in a name?

"The food in Rome was the great discovery of my life," says restaurateur **Danny Meyer**. As the son of a travel agent, "I would visit Europe every few years as a kid. These early trips are filled with delight—and the delight is always connected to discovery. I've come to believe that this sense of discovery can be as nourishing as the food itself."

And it wasn't just the food in Rome that captured Danny's imagination. It was the way Roman trattorias *felt*. "In Rome, I discovered the way the restaurant itself can transform a meal: the earthy terracotta floors, the checkered tablecloths, the domed brick ceiling, and a warm glow of table lanterns. The tables are closer together than I'd ever seen in St. Louis. In the trattorias of Rome, no matter where you sit, you feel the buzzing energy of everyone around you."

When Danny opened his first restaurant, Union Square Cafe, he knew exactly how he wanted it to feel. "I wanted to create a restaurant that—if only it existed—would be my favorite." And Danny had an unconventional idea about what would make that restaurant truly great. Food would not be the star attraction. It would be about the experience, first and foremost.

"I knew how I wanted to be treated, and that was the big deal," he says. "I knew how it felt to not be treated well in a restaurant, and I was picking up lessons about what not to do as much as what to do. Union Square Cafe was like a grab bag of all the design elements, food elements, wine elements, value elements, and above all hospitality elements that I wanted in my favorite restaurant."

Danny made *feeling*—not food—his guiding principle. This belief in how to treat people led all his decisions in the crazy early days. "I didn't know anything except how to treat people," Danny remembers with a broad smile. "The first bookkeeper I hired didn't know how to balance his own checkbook. And the first waiter I hired, I found him trying to open a bottle of champagne on opening night with a corkscrew—that is a dangerous thing to do."

But Danny's empathy for his diners made up for Union Square Cafe's initial failings.

"We couldn't get drinks from the bar. We couldn't get food out of the kitchen, but dammit . . . I had this ability from the beginning to figure out how people were feeling and to figure out what it was going to take—whether it was going to be via food or alcohol or caffeine or remembering their favorite table—whatever it was going to take, I had a desire and an ability to figure out how to make sure people would leave a little happier than however they came. And that became really the bulwark for the restaurant."

With those early kinks behind him, Danny brought his vision to life each day at the restaurant. And it wasn't long before Union Square Cafe became one of New York's most beloved and innovative dining spots. It topped the then-powerful Zagat ratings; it appeared on every critic's list of must-visit spots. Everyone wanted Danny to open a second restaurant. Everyone but Danny.

Having watched his father twice grow a business, expand it—and then go bankrupt—Danny had deep misgivings about growth. He waited ten years before opening his second restaurant, Gramercy Tavern. He made a deal with himself: "I'll open a second restaurant if it can satisfy these three things: It's even better than the first; the first one gets better in the process; and I'll actually have a more balanced life in the process of opening this."

If you've ever doubled your business, or even your team, you already know that this isn't exactly how it played out. Any time you double anything—whether you're going from one million to two million or just one to two, like Danny did—you're going to feel growing pains.

"I opened Gramercy Tavern and the very first year that it opened, we got horrible reviews. Union Square Cafe, for the first time ever, dropped in the Zagat survey, and my life was a mess. So I was 0 for 3. I wasn't even 1 for 3, I was 0 for 3. And it was bad. It was really really hard. I didn't know how to be in two places at once."

In opening Gramercy Tavern, Danny had gone against his own personal received wisdom. This was his fear: that if he scaled his restaurant business, it would all come crashing down. And now, it looked like that fear had been justified. Danny was hit by two clear signs in one day. The first came from his bookkeeper, but it wasn't to do with the finances.

"On his desk I noticed two sets of keys, and one of them had a yellow smiley face, like you used to see in the '70s, and one had a yellow frowning face. I said, 'What's that?'"

"Well, I think you know," the bookkeeper replied.

"I said, 'No, what are you talking about?'"

"He said, 'Well, the smiley face is Union Square Cafe and the frowning face is Gramercy Tavern.'"

"I said, 'Why?' And he said, 'Because Gramercy Tavern doesn't feel like one of your restaurants.'"

The next wakeup call came from a loyal, longtime Union Square customer who gave him an earful one afternoon after eating lunch at Gramercy Tavern. She informed him that her salmon had been overcooked (which might sound like a small complaint, but at a Michelin-starred restaurant, customers expect precision). What was worse, no one on the staff had noticed as she politely picked at it with a frown on her face. Instead, they just asked her if she'd like to take it home with her. "At Union Square Cafe, they would have noticed!" she told Danny. "They would have asked me if I'd like to have it recooked. They would have brought me something else, compliments of the owner. But here, no one noticed. What's going on?"

"That was the day," Danny says, "that I finally, in addition to relieving that particular manager of his job, came up with a name for what really mattered to me. I called it 'enlightened hospitality.'"

"Enlightened hospitality" is what Danny had already been doing for years. But the simple act of *naming it* now enabled him to express it to his growing staff. "My leadership style was basically, 'Watch me: If I'm doing it, this is what I expect of you.' So I'd never given language to anything."

Danny immediately started sharing these new tools with his team. "We had an all-staff meeting at Gramercy Tavern and I said, 'Instead of making you guess what matters to me, I'm going to tell you, right now.' I had never done that before. I'd *been* it, but I hadn't taught it."

Danny told his staff, "I'm going to give you the best recipe you've ever had. And it only has two ingredients. It's forty-nine parts performance and fifty-one parts hospitality. And that's what you are going to be judged on. That's how you're going to get paid. That's how you're going to get your bonus."

Then Danny dropped the real bombshell, the linchpin of his guiding philosophy: "In this business, the customer is going to come second."

If you've been paying attention to the story, that probably wasn't how you expected that sentence to end. His staff did a double take. Was Danny *actually* telling them that the customer was no longer at the top of the food chain? This is close to heresy in the restaurant business. Danny clarified: "In this restaurant, from this day forward, the staff comes first."

Initially, some employees interpreted "the staff comes first" as "what can Danny do for us?" To clear up that misunderstanding, Danny hammered home his message: "It's not my job to take great care of you. It's your job to take care of each other." Danny had a reason for putting the workplace culture above all else: He knew that if he created the right kind of culture, the customers would get even better service than before.

And he rewarded the "culture carriers," employees who exemplified those most-valued attributes. He even implemented something called "Caught Doing Right" pads—small preprinted Post-it notes that list the four core values that employees are accountable for—*excellence, hospitality, entrepreneurial spirit*, and *integrity*. When one employee caught another expressing a core value, they circled that value on the pad, wrote in the employee's name, and posted the note publicly—so that "the team is in a competition to do thoughtful things for others."

Did all of that thoughtfulness translate to the bottom line? Well, in terms of growth, Union Square Hospitality Group eventually expanded to 20 flourishing restaurants, including the beloved, fast-growing, fast-casual chain Shake Shack, which went public in 2015 and expanded to 275 locations before the 2020 pandemic. Perhaps more important, each of those restaurants embodies the "enlightened hospitality" of Danny's vision—such that, at one point, literally half the list of New York's top ten restaurants were from the Union Square Hospitality Group.

And it all started once Danny began verbalizing and teaching his ideas on culture. "Once I had this sort of secret way of talking about our culture with our team, it changed everything," Danny says. "Each time we opened a new restaurant, it would just zoom right to the top of New Yorkers' favorite restaurants. This helped me to understand that you *can* actually scale culture."

The cultural manifesto

Before she was CEO of **ClassPass**—before she was even in kindergarten—**Payal Kadakia** was a dancer. "I started dancing when I was three years old. My parents immigrated here in the '70s and dance is a very big part of the Indian culture. Most girls in India—and even here now—are put into dance at a very young age. One of my earliest memories would be waking up on Saturday morning and going to one of my friends' houses. We would dance together with a group of ten girls and learn Indian folk dances, which really connected me to my culture, it connected me to my ancestors."

By the age of five, Payal's family would ask her to perform on demand. "Every family event we would go to, people would ask 'Payal, can you dance? Can you perform?' I was like this mini roadshow of a performer since I was really young." Dance taught her responsibility (remembering her costume, and her cassettes), and it also gave her a sense of self. "I remember being really quiet when I was younger. But dance made me come alive. It was my way of sharing with the world something that was inside me."

And she stuck with it. Through her years in school, getting her MBA at Harvard, even as she became a management consultant, Payal never left her love for traditional Indian dance behind. "Dance is absolutely a lifelong thing for me. I had to fight to keep dancing in my life, because it's not easy. It's not easy as we get older and we have other commitments, other responsibilities, to keep these passionate things at center, that ground us, that give us confidence in our lives."

Payal's founding vision for ClassPass, spurred by her lifelong passion for Indian dance, was that everyone should discover a fitness routine that doesn't feel like a chore. She believed you shouldn't force yourself to go to exercise class because you know it's good for you; you should feel inspired by the experience itself. "I always say, I created ClassPass because I wanted other people to have what I had in dance in their life."

This vision eventually led to a $12 million Series A fundraising round, followed by a growth spurt during which ClassPass doubled in size in a span of just a few months.

So far, so good—but then Payal noticed that her newer employees didn't seem to share her personal passion; the "why" behind ClassPass wasn't fully embedded in the culture. This was partially because of the breathtaking speed at which they grew. "We were completely out of our space. We were exploding at the seams. People were in the hallway—our neighbors would be like, 'Can you guys stop doing calls in the hallway?' People would be in the elevators taking calls."

At one point, Payal stopped and thought, *Oh my god, does everyone here know the vision and mission?* She says, "A lot of these people were sort of hired so fast, so I felt like I had to course-correct for that after."

Payal realized she had never really articulated ClassPass's mission. "The 'why' is clear in my heart and in my head, and I live it all day— but that doesn't mean the team does," Payal says. "It's important to give them that purpose and that soul."

So Payal wrote a manifesto that spelled out, in effect: *This is what*

I believe; this is why ClassPass exists; this is the future we're trying to create. The manifesto reinforced the ClassPass values, what Payal calls the five pillars: *growth, efficiency, positivity, passion,* and *empowerment.* It was her philosophy, in writing.

Not everyone bought into it—which is often the case with strong visions. And that's actually what you want. You want to open the door to a conversation about why the vision matters—and why people should ultimately stick around only if they can see it and believe in it. As Payal came to realize, the vision is not a negotiable part of the company. It's the foundation of your company's culture.

Startups are similar in some ways to a cultural movement—you're trying to get others to join it, believe in it, and rally around it. **Articulating who you are and what you stand for is how you let people know what they're signing on to. Not just a job—but a belief system, too.**

Hang it up

Certain moments stand out in the history of a company—captured forever not only because they represent a milestone but because they encapsulate a key piece of learning. For **Kevin Systrom** of **Instagram** it was the day when former U.S. vice president Al Gore stopped by their office for a visit.

"He was the first big influencer to visit our offices," says Kevin. "And I really look up to him." Instagram had recently been acquired by Facebook and had moved into their headquarters. "At the time we hadn't really customized it to make it look like us—or like anything. It just looked like a co-working space. He looked around, and he was like, 'So . . . this is Instagram?' And I said, 'Yeah. This is Instagram.'"

It was as if Kevin looked up and *saw* the office for the first time. He decided right then that the whole look and feel of the place had to change. Instagram got their own space and invested in renovating the offices to reflect the personality and stories of the company. For instance, they named all of their conference rooms after iconic Instagram hashtags, like #FromWhereIStand.

"All of that adds to the experience of your culture," Kevin says. "The moment we customized our space, we realized that not only were employees much happier because they were living their values and living the brand, but also when we had guests over, they didn't look at me like I was crazy. Which was a nice side effect."

Establishing the physical environment can be a key reinforcement of company culture. At PayPal, when Reid was one of the five senior executives, every conference room was themed and named after major national currencies. At Airbnb, where Reid was a board member, each conference room was designed, named, and decorated after one of the amazing Airbnb host properties.

Hire your co-founders (all five hundred of them!)

Aneel Bhusri didn't have much experience with company cultures back when he was first starting his career. But he recognized a good one when he walked into it: the very first day of his first job after graduating from business school, at a company called PeopleSoft.

Aneel noticed how friendly everyone was as soon as he walked through the company's doors. "People immediately took me under their wing to teach me the ropes," he recalls.

Among those extending a warm welcome was the boss, David Duffield, who was the founder of PeopleSoft—and who later became Aneel's co-founder at **Workday**. "That first day, Dave took me out for a beer and I thought, *Wow, the CEO's taking me out for a beer! I'm twenty-six years old, I don't know why he's doing it; but I want to work for this guy.*"

When Dave hired Aneel, who'd just finished business school, he didn't have a specific position for him in mind. He wasn't clear on exactly which of Aneel's skills he'd put to use, but he knew that Aneel would be a good fit with PeopleSoft.

And he was. Aneel quickly rose up to a top position. When Oracle acquired the company in a hostile takeover, Aneel and David left and formed Workday.

Their idea was to leverage advances in technology that made it possible to manage human resources and accounting in the cloud: a radical and contrarian new way of doing business at that time. To make it happen, they needed a strong team. And here's where Aneel started to act on a belief that first began to take hold earlier at

PeopleSoft—that assembling the right culture, with just the right mix of people, was central to building a great company.

With that in mind, Aneel decided that he, personally, would interview the company's first wave of employees. It's not unusual for a founder or CEO to personally interview their first ten or twenty employees. But Aneel just kept going . . . all the way up to employee number five hundred.

That's an astonishing number of job interviews for a CEO of a rapidly growing company. And it's not even counting the inevitable dozens (or perhaps hundreds?) of people he interviewed who *didn't* get the job. But Aneel and Dave invested the time because they understood that the first people you hire are not just your employees but your "cultural co-founders." They set the tone; they imprint behaviors and values; and they will draw—or repel—others to you. As such, they can make or break the culture, and the business.

So what was Aneel looking for in all those people he interviewed? To be clear, skills and experience were assessed in the earlier stages of screening candidates. By the time Aneel and Dave got involved, they were looking for more intangible qualities. "We would then interview the individual purely on cultural fit," Aneel says.

Cultural fit is a slippery concept. Different companies have different ideals, and one company's "Perfect 10" will be another's "0." Some companies look for free thinkers; others look for employees who will follow direction. Some prize directness, and others want diplomacy. But whatever attributes matter to your company, it's up to you, the founder, to screen for them.

A mistake that early founders frequently make: They interview for cultural *fit*, an exact match between the employee and the culture as it is, versus cultural *growth*, the idea that this employee will help grow your culture, building upon your established foundation. Understand cultural fit as cultural growth; this approach allows you to focus on such essential initiatives as reinforcing diversity and inclusion as part of your corporate culture.

And some of the most important qualities to look for are the ones that are hard to measure and cannot be taught. "You can train someone on technical skills, but you can't train somebody on what they believe or what they don't believe," says Michael Bush, CEO of the workplace consultancy Great Place to Work. "They have to have shared beliefs about the importance of work. They have to have shared beliefs about the customer and what it means to satisfy the customer. And about what happens when people disagree with each other."

So how does that translate into effective hiring? The closest thing to a formula might be this: Articulate for yourself what kind of company you want to build; detail which qualities your employees should have to achieve that; then design specific questions to screen for those qualities.

In Aneel's case, he already had a clear picture of the kind of company he was building, and how he wanted it to feel: friendly and open—just as Aneel felt on his first day at PeopleSoft. That was the personality of a company that could serve its customers well. To get there, Aneel knew his ideal candidates had to be team players, and he perfected, over time, a way to screen for that trait. "You have to figure out if they're 'I people' or 'we people.' You start by asking them to talk about their accomplishments. If they talk about 'We did this' and 'We did that' as a team, you know you've got a pretty good fit there."

David and Aneel strongly believed that hiring "we people" wasn't just good for the culture; it would also have a direct impact on how well they served their customers.

And they were right. Over the past decade, Workday has consistently had customer satisfaction above 95 percent; more recently it has reached 98 percent. The reason is simple, or so it seems when Aneel sums it up this way: "We hire great employees. Great employees take care of your customers."

You are who you hire: Get the blend right

Leaders have a lot to learn from bourbon. Ask **Joyce Nethery.** She's a chemical engineer turned master distiller. And she understands that with bourbon—as with many things in business and life—what you get depends on what you put in.

Joyce and her family run Kentucky's Jeptha Creed Distillery, a "ground-to-glass" distillery where they carefully oversee the entire ecosystem that supports a world-class product. "We grow our corn. We literally put the seed in the soil, and nourish the ground, and then I distill it, and we make a beautiful product."

The bourbon-making process begins with the corn grown on their own land. "Bourbon has to be at least 51 percent corn, so we grow a beautiful heirloom varietal of corn called Bloody Butcher," Joyce explains. But it isn't the only grain in the mix, and Joyce has thought carefully about how each ingredient will react with the others. "We use rye, it gives you some spiciness—whereas wheat is a smoother, calmer grain."

Water matters, too, but not just any water. They use limestone-filtered, iron-free water sourced from a local creek. As for the whiskey barrels? They have "literally been put on fire—and that little bit of nuttiness you taste, that comes from that toasting."

The whiskey sits in those barrels for two to three years before it's ready for bottling. But Joyce knows that—setting aside the slings and arrows of fortune—the choices she made on her initial ingredients will determine everything about the whiskey's ultimate success.

If you're a company founder, then you're also a master distiller, responsible for selecting the right mix of ingredients to take your company to scale. But instead of artisanal grains, the key ingredients are the people who make up the essence of your culture.

How do you strike that delicate balance of finding talented, diverse people who will also "mix" well? The answer will always depend on the kind of company you're building—and its ultimate size. But its fate is set in the mix of people you hire early on. You have to articulate for yourself the human qualities that are central to your culture, and then figure out how to *identify* them in an interview. The answers are different for different founders. . . .

Arianna Huffington considers **"compassionate directness"** to be the most important cultural value at her company, Thrive Global. Arianna defines this as "being able to have tough conversations, being able to disagree—including with managers and executives of every rank—and being able to speak out when you're upset about something or have a complaint." When interviewing, Arianna asks candidates to give an example of a tough conversation they recently had with a colleague or a manager to get a sense of how they handle dissatisfaction. "Because there is no workplace where you're going to be happy all the time. That Garden of Eden does not exist."

For former **Google** CEO **Eric Schmidt**, the winning combination is **persistence** and **curiosity**. "Persistence is the single biggest predictor of future success," Schmidt says. "And so at Google, we would look for persistence. And the second thing was *curiosity*—as in, what do you care about? The combination of persistence and curiosity is a very good predictor of employee success in a knowledge economy."

It's not surprising that **kindness** heads the list of attributes sought out by **Shake Shack's Danny Meyer**, as he strives to build cultures of "enlightened hospitality." But the list doesn't end there. Danny also looks for people who are *curious;* have a strong *work ethic;* display *empathy;* are *self-aware;* and finally, have *integrity.* Danny's team heads into every interview with those six cultural ideals in mind (alongside the technical skills of cooking or serving, of course). "It's frustrating because sometimes there are really good performers who suck for your culture," he says. "And sometimes there are extraordinarily awesome people who just can't get the job done."

Bill Gates values **deep knowledge, different from his own,** an attribute he says he didn't have enough respect for back in his early years leading Microsoft. Then, he respected engineers and engineers only. "The notion that these intelligences were as specialized as they are—I didn't get it," Bill admits. "I thought, *Hey, I can learn sales. Do you need to go to business school? I don't think so.* I didn't have enough respect for good management."

An awareness of the gaps in your own knowledge is especially important for growing companies. Two key transitions you'll need to manage are the shift from generalists to specialists, and from contributors to managers to executives. In the early days, you need people who can roll up their sleeves and work on whatever is necessary that day. The ideal team member is a jack-of-all-trades (the generalist) that gets stuff done (the contributor). But as the company scales up, you need to change the mix to include more specialists (who are only good at one thing, but are really, really good at that thing), managers (who make contributors more productive), and experienced executives (who can lead massive teams). You can read more about "Generalists to Specialists" and "Contributors to Managers to Executives" in my book *Blitzscaling*.

· · ·

As important as it is to hire the right people, it can be just as important to consider who you *don't* want to hire. The psychologist and Wharton School professor Adam Grant, who has written extensively on business culture, says, "As a founder trying to build a culture, the first thing you do is say, 'It is nice to have the right people on your bus, but it is even more critical to keep the wrong people off your bus.' Every founder, when it comes to hiring, should be asking, 'What are the qualities that I am absolutely unwilling to let into the organization?'"

CEO and consultant **Margaret Heffernan** advises: *Don't hire people who can't name anyone who ever helped them.* You can figure that out by simply asking who has helped most in a candidate's career. "If they can't remember anyone, that's a pretty bad sign."

Margaret recalls how she once shared this observation at a business conference. "When the next speaker, a chief technology officer, came onstage, somebody in the audience asked him, 'Who helped you in the course of your career?' He couldn't think of anybody. And there was this sort of stunned, horrified silence."

Another *don't* is from **Mark Zuckerberg** of Facebook, who says: *Don't hire someone to work for you unless you would work for them in an alternate universe.* "Which doesn't mean that you should give them your job," Zuckerberg adds, "but just imagine if the tables were turned and you were looking for a job—would you be comfortable working for this person?"

A common refrain among founders: Beware the soloist who never learned to play with an orchestra. The lack of a team spirit can be toxic, especially in the early days. In PayPal's early days, despite an ideological focus on high-performing individuals, Reid and other executives added some interview questions about team sports in order to capture each candidate's insight on team play, mutual help, and "we" behavior.

And one last *don't*, from Arianna again: *Don't interview or hire people when you're tired.* "I can trace back all my hiring mistakes to being tired—which has the impact not just of impairing your cognitive abilities to make the right decisions but also subconsciously of making you want to say yes," she says. "So now at Thrive, having learned from my mistakes, we have a rule that nobody should interview while tired."

REID'S ANALYSIS | Your early hires are your "cultural co-founders"

I'm a huge fan of shortcuts. I wrote an entire book (*Blitzscaling*) on the importance of speed, and company-growing hacks are practically the guiding spirit of *Masters of Scale*. But there are a few times and places where I encourage founders to exercise caution that might slow you down—and one of them is your early hires.

Here's why: When you're starting a company, the people you hire first are more than just team members; they're your cultural co-founders. Their skills and capacities will not only determine what your company can do, they'll determine who your company can be. The genetics of your company—its culture—is set by those first employees.

Scaling up a great company requires you to build a strong culture that makes clear to employees what really matters and how things are done. A strong culture isn't always a "good" culture; strength is a measure of how much a culture shapes employee behavior, for good or ill. But if you establish a strong, bad culture, I doubt you'll want to work for the company that culture allows you to build.

It's really hard to recover from an early bad hire; my friend Mike Cassidy of Apollo Fusion told me, "A bad hire in the first fifteen is fatal to the company," and most often he is right.

But your cultural co-founders go well beyond the first fifteen employees. The exact number varies based on your company and your industry. You may bring on cultural co-founders later as well, such as when starting an important new project or opening a new office. Whenever they board the bus, it's up to you, the founder, to make the right choices.

What does this mean? Well, if your first set of hires will make or break your business, that means you, the founder, should sit down with every qualified candidate and decide whether they're a strong cultural match. Or you'll have to develop a strong system for establishing the cultural fit.

Those early hires will not only set the cultural norms, they will also ensure that those norms are self-perpetuating. And cultures self-perpetuate in two ways: by assimilation and by association. An additional point: Those early hires will determine which other employees you hire and which you fail to hire. They will shape customer engagement. They will establish how you make decisions together, and which decisions you prioritize.

Adaptation happens when each person who joins the company absorbs and upholds the culture. But adaptation is a two-way street. Each person who joins can also add to and improve the culture with their own unique contribution. In this way, the culture continues to evolve.

But then, too, there's the way cultures self-perpetuate by association. When you hire a person, you also hire their network. When a new job opens, they'll refer their friends. When you need partnerships, they'll open doors. The powerful connection of that initial group of hires shouldn't be underestimated. If that initial cohort isn't right—or if it isn't diverse—it can be extraordinarily difficult to correct later.

Cognitive diversity: Solving the Rubik's Cube

With all the dos and don'ts, and all the questions and techniques designed to ferret out just the right qualities in a potential hire, it may seem as if the goal is to identify the ideal employee and then replicate that process until you've assembled an army of identically ideal employees. But even if that were possible, it would be a recipe for cultural disaster.

The goal is not to hire a bunch of look-alikes or think-alikes. **If your company is dominated by one type of person, your collective blind spots will add up to tunnel vision.**

Sallie Krawcheck understands this, and built her company Ellevest accordingly, puncturing and deflating some deeply ingrained biases about women and money in the process.

"I grew up in an industry, Wall Street, that calls itself a meritocracy, but it has given poor returns to shareholders through the course of a cycle for a long, long time," she notes. And yet, we're all supposed to believe "that 90 percent of traders should be white men because they're just better at it, and 86 percent of financial advisors should be white men because they're just better at it. So it's supposedly a meritocracy at work—oh, except for that financial crisis. Except for that."

Sallie is on the front lines of creating a diverse work culture, not only in terms of gender and race but also cognitive diversity. The idea is that you need differing perspectives that can inform each other and lead to deeper insight.

Sallie's strong belief in cognitive diversity is partly rooted in her experience working in one of the least cognitively diverse cultures there is. But in truth, her experience battling the conformity of a monoculture goes back even further—to her days at an all-girls school in Charleston, South Carolina, where Sallie was the odd girl out. "Glasses, braces, I'm not really sure I had corrective shoes, but in my mind I had corrective shoes," she recalls. Sallie vividly remembers what it felt like to eat lunch by herself every day. "Working your way through that, you've got to put your armor on, and go back into the field of battle. Later, I liked to say, 'There's nothing they could do to me on Wall Street that was worse than seventh grade.'"

Sallie wanted the culture at Ellevest to be the exact opposite of the Wall Street monoculture—and, for that matter, the all-girls-school monoculture. So her first step was to look for a co-founder "as different from me as that individual can possibly be." It would be reasonable to assume Sallie would hire another woman—after all, her product is aimed at women, and her mission is to correct some of the gender imbalance in the financial world. But instead, she hired a man, Charlie Kroll, with a tech background that complemented her finance experience, as well as a work style and personality that couldn't be less similar to her own. Sallie says they rarely agree on things—which is how it should be.

She wanted to ensure Ellevest was inclusive in other ways, too, and she put systems in place to ensure that diversity of race, ethnicity, and gender was vigorously maintained. "Today, we're two-thirds women at the company, we're 40 percent people of color, our engineering team is half women," she says. Any time the company moves off those diversity levels, there's a pause in hiring so that the company can focus on rebalancing.

This gets to a larger point about diversity—it isn't just about gender and ethnicity. It's about all dimensions of human experience and personality—age, height, language, sexual orientation, religion, background, education, personality type. You should think about extroverts and introverts; people who are open-ended versus people who are precise. "It's also about, you've got X number of optimists—how many pessimists do you have?" Sallie says. "It's almost like solving a Rubik's Cube."

Caterina Fake, tech entrepreneur and co-founder of Yes VC, believes the work begins on day one. "If you have women in the founding team, if you have African Americans, if your team includes Latinos, it will continue to naturally evolve that way." Diverse people will tend to bring in other diverse people, and the process will be more organic. Whereas, when companies try to "graft on" diversity initiatives years later, that tends to be more difficult, Caterina says. "That's because the culture has already been formed. The culture is very, very hard to change once it has been established."

And don't just "delegate diversity" to one person at the company and then assume the issue is covered. "It's not just who we hire, it's who do we do business with, what do our suppliers look like," says **Shellye Archambeau**, the former head of the software company MetricStream, and one of the first Black female CEOs in Silicon Valley. "What markets are we targeting, where are our offices? It's all of these things." So don't think of diversity as a challenge that has a quick fix, something you can check off in the "problem-solved" box. True diversity is a continuous, long-term commitment. And casting a wider net when you hire is key.

Robert F. Smith, CEO of Vista Equity Partners, pays little attention to résumés, per se: where someone's gone to school, or what companies they worked for. Instead, he focuses on aptitudes, capabilities, and personality types, an approach that tends to bring in people from varying backgrounds.

Vista calls their new hires "HIPEL hires," for high-performance entry level. Once they're in the door, HIPEL hires take Vista's proprietary aptitude exam, which yields a personality profile that identifies things like patience or assertiveness. These attributes, not schooling or economic background, help determine where people are placed within Vista's various organizations and how they're developed. "With data from the last twenty years and earlier, we have many examples of how people with a certain sort of profile perform," says Robert. "We can say, 'You may be better suited for a services group than sales or development. Why don't you try that?' Essentially, we're skewing the composition of the functional groups and laying aptitude on top of that to get a higher-performing business organization."

By relying on aptitude tests, Robert's companies have seen diversity hires go up by as much as 50 percent. But it takes a leap of faith, Robert says. "And most people don't have the courage for that, because you tend to hire what you know."

One last point on diversity: If you want a wide range of perspectives, don't allow your company to be fenced in, geographically. There's a strong movement now, accelerated by the COVID-19 pandemic, toward remote offices or distributed companies. This trend may prove to be a boon to cognitive diversity, according to **Wences Casares**, founder and CEO of **Xapo**, the digital currency company.

Xapo is not huge—only about three hundred employees—but they are spread out in sixty-two locations around the globe. That means key people at the company not only come from different backgrounds, they are also immersed in different local cultures and lifestyles. In order to truly scale globally, companies must have this kind of geographic and cultural diversity, so that they can reach beyond customers who are like them and connect with the much larger global market.

REID'S THEORIES ON DESIGNING YOUR CULTURE

Build a culture that's smart enough to evolve

In technology businesses—and all large businesses are increasingly becoming technology businesses—people your culture with "first-principle" thinkers. Instead of blindly following directions, or sticking to a tried-and-true process, a first-principle thinker will constantly wonder, "What's best for the company?" Or, "Couldn't we do this another way instead?"

Put your customer second

If you can create the right kind of employees-first culture, one where employees model for each other what it's like to be great at what you do, that will in turn lead to customers getting increasingly better products and services.

Find ways to manifest your culture

Your vision, your values, and even your unique company heritage matter more than you think in defining your culture. Don't assume everyone knows what's in your head and heart—say it loudly and proudly from day one.

Think of early hires as your co-founders

Your early hires will set the tone for your company. Early on, define the human qualities that are central to your culture (as well as the qualities you *don't* want) and then use those as guides when interviewing people for cultural fit.

Solve the Rubik's Cube of cognitive diversity

Without cognitive diversity, you will miss opportunities. You will perpetuate fallacies. And you will be lost in a monotonous haze.

5

Growing Fast, Growing Slow

It was opening day for **Tory Burch**'s startup—her big opportunity to debut her new clothing line at her new store during New York Fashion Week. Tory was ready. She had found an affordable downtown (*way* downtown) space. She had racks of clothes she'd designed herself—lots of them. She had family and friends milling about, as well as members of the press. And most important, she had customers starting to show up that morning. The only thing missing was . . . a front door.

What happened was this: Tory had designed a beautiful, custom-built door, painted her trademark bright orange. But as she was setting up the space in the days leading up to the opening, "the doors just didn't arrive," Tory says. "It was cold out. It was *February*."

Tory could have hit the pause button and delayed her opening until she could receive customers with the kind of dramatic entrance (and reasonable temperature) she had imagined. But like most entrepreneurs, Tory has a bias for action. She knew she had a moment in time during Fashion Week when she could capture attention—and if she hesitated, it might be gone forever.

So she went full speed ahead. She literally opened the doors of her business without any doors. The result: explosive. "It was amazing," Tory recalls, "almost as if we were giving the product away. I started seeing people changing clothes in the middle of the store. We sold through most of our inventory that day. So we kind of realized that we were on to something."

It's a classic entrepreneurial story: products launched with a hope and a prayer and the bugs not quite worked out; businesses opened with no one there to answer the phones; websites launched with a single groaning server that quickly becomes overloaded.

Why not just wait a little longer, until a few more pieces are in place? Because for startups, speed is of the essence. By definition, startups are racing the clock—to gain customers and build their business model before their competitors can, or before they run out of money. Sure, if you have a bottomless bank account and no competition, you can afford to take your time. But for the vast majority of entrepreneurs, a slow-moving startup is dead in the water.

In the consumer internet business, Reid is well known in Silicon Valley for saying: "If you're not embarrassed by your first product release, you've released too late." The point of this aphorism is the importance of speed and accelerating the learning curve by engaging with customers via your launch.

But speed is not the same as haste. And as important as it is to move fast, it can be just as important to know exactly when and why to be patient. Note: Patience doesn't mean slowness; it means strategically choosing the right moment.

For Tory, Fashion Week 2004 was *the* moment to launch her eponymous clothing line. But that isn't the whole story. When Tory first hatched the plan for her fashion company, hers wasn't the typical entrepreneurial dream. She imagined an organization with two complementary sides: one for profit, and one not-for-profit. "I wanted to start a company in *order* to build a foundation—that was my business plan," she says. Making money and giving back were intertwined from the start.

Specifically, she wanted to build a nonprofit to support women-owned small businesses. But when she tried to raise money for her business and soon-to-be foundation, "I was basically laughed at and told never to say 'business' and 'social responsibility' in the same sentence," she says.

Tory was equally passionate—and equally convinced—about both halves of her idea. But after hearing consistent, immovable feedback from funders, she changed strategies. She moved full speed ahead on her idea for a business offering distinctive, casual, yet stylish clothing at affordable prices, and selling direct to consumer. And she set the idea of the foundation aside—for the moment.

But she never lost sight of the goal that was integral to her original idea. She just waited for precisely the right moment. And that kind of determination is key for any patient strategy. In 2009, five years after the famous "day of no doors," Tory quietly launched her foundation. Ten years later, Bank of America committed $100 million to the foundation's Capital Program, which connects women entrepreneurs to affordable loans, and creates a virtuous cycle with the business that's made her a billionaire.

In this chapter, we'll focus on why it's so important to strike that balance between aggressive, rapid growth and strategic, watchful patience. It can be a factor in how much money you raise (and who you choose to take it from), and a factor in which early growth opportunities and partnerships you pursue. And it can impact how you structure your organization and develop your culture.

Maintaining that fast/slow balance can be tricky: It's risky to go too fast, but going slow is often even more dangerous for a startup, as it can starve you out of the resources you need to grow. And sometimes, especially in intense competition, it's important to take extraordinary risks to move as fast as possible.

To envision the specific kind of patience we're talking about, picture a great blue heron: that elegant, stately bird with impossibly long legs and a dagger-like bill. A heron will stand perfectly still in a marsh. It will stand so still for so long that it almost looks painted into the landscape. And it might appear to be quite lazy—until . . . it spots a fish. Then it strikes, with incredible speed and precision.

• • •

If you're not familiar with Tory Burch's fashion brand, the style brings together modern and classic—it has been dubbed "preppy-chic." But Tory doesn't come from a suburban country club background. Her childhood was more "Huck Finn meets Andy Warhol."

"I think people have this vision of how I grew up, and the opposite is true," she says. "I grew up on a farm in the middle of nowhere with three brothers. We spent our entire time outside. Our parents would travel and we were left to ourselves a lot." But at the same time, "my parents would have all of these random people to dinner. We never would know who—it could be the plumber, it could be a poet, it could be an artist. It was always insightful, and we were always intellectually curious to understand all different kinds of people."

As a kid, Tory had no interest in fashion. "I was a tomboy and didn't put on a dress until junior year for prom," she recalls. In fact, she landed in fashion quite by accident. When she graduated from college, Tory had no idea what she wanted to do with her life. But she *did* know she wanted a job—any job—that would allow her to live in New York. So she cold-called a designer (not easy for someone who is "incredibly shy," as Tory described herself) who told her she could have a job, as long as she was willing to start the following week. No problem: She graduated on Friday, moved to New York that weekend, and started a job on Monday.

After years working for other designers—and a stretch as a stay-at-home parent—Tory finally hatched a plan for her own venture. It was a contrarian plan with many ideas that were ahead of their time, like selling direct to consumers with retail stores and a website (back when most fashion lines would begin in department stores). But it was also a relatively "patient plan"—conservatively aiming to open three stores in her first five years. And this made sense until an unexpected opportunity presented itself in year one. Oprah Winfrey discovered Tory's clothing line and featured it on her show. The three-store plan was torn up. Tory opened seventeen stores instead.

International opportunities soon beckoned. Again, Tory remained purposefully patient, particularly with her entry into China. "We never want to be the company that goes in with a bang," she says. "We always want to learn our markets, and be respectful, and understand cultures. We've been very careful that way. Often when we go into a new country, we'll partner with someone from that market." But once Tory's ready to move more aggressively, she does: She now has thirty stores in China.

Throughout these years of rapid growth, Tory relied on her instincts to tell her when to push ahead and when to slow down—which, in some cases, meant saying no to growth opportunities, or at least putting them on a slower track.

Take outlet stores, for example. These large-scale discount stores have massively grown in popularity and sales in recent years. "The outlet business is like a drug," Tory says. "It's a very easy fix, but it's not a long-term solution. It can be very dilutive to your company." She would only open outlets when the time and place seemed right—at a pace that would allow her to protect her pricing and her brand image.

"Everyone needs to have an outlet business in our industry. But to me it's not a business strategy," Tory explains. "We need to do it in a careful way. We want to protect our full-price selling, but use the outlet as I feel it should be used. That's very different from what a lot of people are thinking."

She also watches carefully how her brand is treated in the major department stores, and on at least one occasion pulled her entire line out of a major store—an extreme move that's seen as unthinkable by most designer labels. "When you're not treated in the way that you think your company should be treated—with the right assortments, the right adjacencies, if they put [your products] on sale before you're ready to—and you can't have that conversation, you just have to move on," she says.

Tory's approach on this front—long-term brand first; short-term revenue second—can be befuddling for those on the outside looking in. She describes it with a smile: "I had lunch yesterday with a journalist, and she said, 'You're known for protecting your brand to the point where it must be annoying to your investors.'"

In truth, Tory's investors are quite thrilled with her decisions. With more than $1.5 billion in annual sales—as a private company—it's hard to argue with her results. And she thinks her balanced approach to growth might be more common among women business leaders. "The women I know in business have a long-term view," she says. "They tend to think about how each thing they're doing will affect the business five and ten years out." Tory believes that women know, instinctively, when it's time to be patient—and when it's time to speed ahead.

Watching for the signs

In May 2017, Lehua Kamalu set sail from Tahiti to Hawaii in a traditional Polynesian double-hulled canoe. The stakes were high. It was Lehua's first time sailing as the solo navigator, leading a crew on an epic journey spanning twenty-five hundred miles of open ocean. And Lehua's vessel was "designed just like the ones my ancestors sailed," she says, with no backup engine, no electricity, no kerosene, no computers on board, and no modern instruments—not even a compass.

Lehua is the first female navigator with the Polynesian Voyaging Society—and every time they sail, they're not only navigating treacherous routes but reliving their ancestors' experience, and keeping their ancient wisdom alive. The first time this route was sailed in modern times, it overturned centuries of assumptions: The Tahiti-to-Hawaii route was once believed to be impossible without modern instruments.

The first week of the trip was smooth sailing. Then the crew hit the doldrums—literally. The doldrums are the flat, calm area at the equator that are known for deathly stillness, punctuated by violent and unpredictable storms. When Lehua's boat arrived there, the stillness was unnerving. The winds and current dropped away; the sky was socked in with clouds. "When you're in the doldrums, it's easy to lose faith," Lehua says. Remember, this is a sailing vessel with no engine—and a limited supply of food. The crew relies on wind and currents to stay on course. Here's where patience is needed—"but it isn't a lazy patience," she explains, "it's a vigilant, watchful patience."

The crew searched for signs—currents, winds, a single glimpse of the sun, moon, or stars—to identify their location and get a sense of what might be coming next. "On our second day in the doldrums," Lehua recalls, "there is a layer of clouds so thick that the sun can't shine through at all—it's pitch black. You can't see the waves, but you can feel them. I feel the force of each wave as it punches the side of our canoe, this rhythmic pounding."

The pounding waves and total darkness continued for the next five days, and all they could do was "look and wait, look and wait." As

Lehua explains, "The job of the navigator is to see as far into the future as you can, to protect your crew and your vessel, and to make sure you're going on the right path." Lehua hunts for a sign that may appear only for a moment: "And then, we must be ready to move."

Finally, on the fifth day of darkness, the sun pierced through the darkness for just a moment, in a flash of intense red light, like "a dragon eye," as Lehua describes it. It was the sign she'd been awaiting, as it told her the exact position of the setting sun and where it would touch down. Once she knew the direction of the sun, she could calculate her position and figure out everything she needed to resume her journey.

"I can take stock of my entire horizon—the wind, the ocean, the waves—as they relate to this sign," she says. "Everyone is really excited now, because we've all been looking for this." The crew adjusts course, homing in on the latitude of Hawaii on the east side of the Big Island. "I'm confident now and I'm getting continuous signals that I'm on the right path. We've held steady in these uncertain waters, waiting patiently—but now it's time for speed."

Lehua's story is a perfect metaphor for leadership. Great captains and great CEOs both know you can't move fast every minute of the journey. **If you're going to go the distance, you have to recognize that the conditions around you are always changing.** You have to be strategically patient, but that doesn't mean sitting back and waiting. It means leaning in and being prepared for the moment to step on the gas.

But when that breakout moment first arrives, your first steps out of the starting gates should be fast. In fact, they should be explosive. The whole idea is to generate enormous early momentum behind your idea—before anyone else can steal your thunder.

Achieving escape velocity

If you start fast enough out of the gate, you may be able to not only outpace your competition—but leave them behind altogether. That's the philosophy of one of PayPal's co-founders, **Peter Thiel**.

Peter is a controversial figure in Silicon Valley, known for his provocative statements and unpredictable politics. But his track record as an entrepreneur and an investor is undeniable—and rooted in an extreme "seize the initiative" approach.

Peter doesn't believe in *beating* the competition, he believes in *escaping* it altogether—either by entering an emerging field with no natural competitors or by moving so quickly and decisively that competitors have no hope of catching up.

In the early days of PayPal, Peter knew that to escape the competition, they'd have to acquire as many customers as possible—and fast. So he ran a costly experiment. Most companies, to find new customers, set aside a budget to pay for advertisements. But PayPal took a more direct route: paying the customers themselves. If an existing PayPal customer referred the service to a friend, they each got $10 in (online) cash, on the house. It's not that Peter *wanted* to give away all that money—but he felt it was the best, surest strategy to get off to a fast start.

The logic was solid. First, by paying users this way, it demonstrates PayPal's use case, the easy transfer of money. Second, while this might seem expensive, it turned out to be a much cheaper and more direct route to user acquisition than the advertising programs that almost every other consumer internet company was using.

"We had to get to scale as quickly as possible," Peter says. "If we didn't, maybe somebody else would beat us, and we wouldn't achieve escape velocity." It turned out PayPal would later keep growing even after the referral bonuses stopped, but Peter couldn't be sure of that at the time. "You have to race really hard to scale fast—but the benefit is that you're achieving escape velocity from the black hole that is hypercompetition."

At this point, PayPal didn't even have a business model fully worked out. "I thought that we either could get to scale or figure out our business model," Peter says. He opted to get to scale first and worry about the business model later.

While Peter was exponentially growing PayPal's users, he was also exponentially growing the company's costs. "We had a burn rate north of $10 million a month," Peter says. "That was pretty uncomfortable."

But plenty of businesses defer profitability, sometimes for years. Amazon ignored gripes from Wall Street investors for almost two decades, while diligently breaking free of their competition in one retail sector after the next.

Even as PayPal was zooming out of the gate, there was no point at which the company could rest easy. **Escape velocity is not a fixed speed. It's always relative to competition.** Your fastest competitor determines how hard you hit the gas. And PayPal had a fierce competitor in eBay, which was itself rolling out a new online payment system.

Here's where nimble startups have an advantage over established companies, which tend to move slower. Reid (who was on PayPal's founding board, and then became COO) explains: "The reality is, your most dangerous competitors are rarely the big guys, like eBay. They are hesitant to storm the field and take the risk alongside you. A fumble for PayPal [at that time] risked blowback from a few thousand users. A fumble for eBay, however, could anger users in the millions, and draw the watchful eye of government regulators."

And even if eBay were willing to take those risks, Reid says, "why would they burn so much creative energy on the online equivalent of a cash register? After all, they were building the full store—a global marketplace for online commerce. So what if a little company is hijacking the checkout counter? So while we were wringing our hands over eBay's new payment system, we also were encouraged to see that they took more than a year to roll it out."

Meanwhile, PayPal was growing and growing, locking up a large user base. Peter understood that even when you start out in a very competitive situation, over time, escape velocity can get you to a place where fewer and fewer challengers remain.

But how do you know you're hitting escape velocity? Peter had a formula.

"I used to have this equation written on the PayPal whiteboards," he says. He can still rattle it off: "$u_t = u_0 e^{xt}$—where u sub 0 is the initial users, u sub t is the users at time t, and e to the xt is the exponential growth factor. And if you get x up, the exponent rises even more quickly."

Got that? No worries if not. Suffice it to say, PayPal's "x" was such that its user base was growing up to 7 percent per day, leading to the kind of growth you get when your users and/or revenue are consistently doubling—the kind that creates a hockey stick on your growth charts. PayPal started with twenty-four users and very quickly reached one thousand; a month after that, thirteen thousand; then a month or so later, one hundred thousand; within three months of launch it had a million users.

"There's an Einstein quote that may be apocryphal," Peter says, "but it's to the effect that compound interest is the most powerful force in the universe." (Note: There is no evidence—and, we believe, no chance—that Einstein actually said this, but it's still a smart point.)

Peter predicted that paying early users to sign up would allow PayPal to tap into the power of compounding from the outset—and he was right. "It made for a very crazy ride," he says.

This underappreciated rule of compound growth is why Silicon Valley seems to spawn so many overnight successes. "It's why investors pour hundreds of millions into a wisp of a company," says Reid. "So long as your startup is hitting escape velocity, anyone who understands the power of compound growth will keep funding you."

And as long as they keep funding you, you can keep growing. But be aware that sustaining escape velocity—the force that enabled you to secure huge sums of capital in the first place—may also require you to spend at an alarming rate.

In the end, PayPal secured such a dominant position in the online payment sector, and did so at such warp speed, that the larger, slower eBay was left with no choice—it stopped trying to compete with Pay-Pal and instead bought it, in 2002, for a staggering $1.5 billion. Perhaps even more telling is PayPal's $247 billion market cap at press time.

Decide, decide, decide

Eric Schmidt was realizing that he'd made a very big mistake. After fourteen successful years at Sun Microsystems, he decided: "It was time for a change. It was time to be a CEO somewhere." He was offered the job leading a networking software company called Novell. On paper, it sounded perfect. "But in the typical way I operate, I did not do enough due diligence.

"The reality hit on the first day, because I was presented with different numbers for revenue for the quarter than I'd been told when I was interviewing. And by that Wednesday—third day on the job—we were in a real crisis." Things went rapidly downhill. "Later that summer, we had a month which we called 'the worst month,' where every-thing was failing. And there was a moment in that month where I remember saying to my colleague, 'I just want to get out of here with my integrity intact.' When you face those kinds of challenges, you learn what really matters."

In the midst of this crisis, Eric set out to learn something else entirely. He became a small-plane pilot. And while that may sound inconsequential, it turned out to have a profound influence. A friend said to Eric: "You need a distraction. And if you're flying planes, you won't be able to think of anything else."

"It was the best advice ever," Eric recalls. "Because in aviation, they teach you to make rapid decisions, over and over again: *Decide. Decide. Decide.* It's better to make a decision and just accept the con-sequences."

"That discipline helped me in the hard times at Novell, when I was in a real hard-core turnaround," Eric recalls. But this habit of rapid decision-making also served Eric well at Google, historically so.

Rapid decision-making has been key to Google's explosive growth, for at least two reasons. The first is that it allowed them to outpace com-petition in the fast-changing ecosystem of online search. The second—and less understood—is that **fast decisions fuel innovation. Nothing kills creativity like running into bureaucratic red tape.** "Most large corporations have too many lawyers, too many decision makers, un-clear owners—and things congeal."

To avoid such clotting, Schmidt baked rapid decision-making into the company's early rituals. "We adopted a model of staff meeting on Monday, a business meeting on Wednesday, and a product meeting on Friday," Eric says. "The agenda was that everybody knew which meet-ing the decisions were made at. Today at Google, decisions are made quickly in almost every case, even at its current scale. And that's a legacy of that early decision."

The $1.65 billion acquisition of YouTube is a perfect example. "We made the decision to purchase YouTube in about ten days. Incredibly historic decision but we were ready. People were focused. We wanted to get it done," Eric recalls.

And Susan Wojcicki also recalls the speed. Susan is YouTube's current CEO, but at the time of the acquisition, she was a longtime Googler, then working on a new program called Google Video, a direct competitor to YouTube.

"YouTube launched a few months after us, and they very quickly grew and were very soon bigger than us," Susan recalls. "And we realized that we were losing. It was first a moment of incredible highs—while we found this great area that we could develop and build product around—and then soon afterward, realizing *Wow. We were failing.*

"For me one of the big factors was, I was tracking the number of videos uploaded—how many new people were uploading to YouTube or to Google Video. And they were already significantly larger than us. And even though we made changes, it was just too late. So that for me was the defining moment. I knew it'd be very hard for us to catch up.

"YouTube at the same time realized that they needed to have a lot more investment; they were going to have huge capital needs. And so they were going to need either significantly more investment—which at the time I don't think the market would have really understood"—or they would need to be acquired.

"So they quickly realized they needed to sell and started shopping it around. It was clear to me this was just a huge opportunity in terms of future video, and I was a big advocate along with Salar Kamangar, who ended up being my predecessor as YouTube's CEO. We got together and we had a good conversation with Sergey and Larry. I produced a model. I did a model in like fifteen minutes to show that this actually had huge potential in the future—not just in views, but in revenue, too. We didn't have a lot of time."

Eric had dismissed an earlier suggestion to buy YouTube for $600 million. He was told it would probably cost more than that if he waited, but he insisted that it still wasn't worth it. Then came word that YouTube might be talking to Yahoo about a sale.

Now he was ready to talk.

Eric found himself sitting across a table with YouTube's founders—at a Denny's restaurant. Because where else would you want to do a billion-dollar deal?

"Actually, we met at Denny's because we were quite sure that we wouldn't see anyone else there—we did not want this to leak," Eric says.

Within days they settled on a price. The YouTube team was invited to a Google board meeting, the board voted, and just like that, YouTube was part of Google. And it's a good thing Eric moved as quickly as he did. "I found out later that they met with Yahoo the day after us—at the same Denny's!"

"We purchased it for $1.65 billion," Susan recalls. "And so the first direction that we got was, 'Don't screw it up.'"

Those words would ring true a few years later, when Susan was given another high-stakes, lightning-fast decision to make: After more than ten years at Google, did she, or did she not, want to take the helm at YouTube?

"What happened was Larry just asked me," Susan said. "I remember he said, 'What do you think of YouTube?' He didn't say 'Oh, I'm offering you the job.' I hadn't prepared anything. I didn't know that's what we were going to talk about that day. But I just gave him my off-the-cuff thoughts about YouTube and said I was really interested. A couple weeks later I became CEO of YouTube."

You can hear it in Eric's and Susan's stories—and you can see it in business history. Many of Google's most strategic decisions come down to moving fast. This may be the aspect of Google's strategy that's least understood. It's why Google buys smaller companies instead of competing for dominance. "We have plenty of engineers," explains Eric, "but let's imagine that we have engineers that can build an equivalent product in one year, versus an acquisition that's expensive. And let's say that we can monetize this fairly quickly. So, choice A is, 'We're going to build it ourselves, do it right.' And choice B is, 'Buy that company and do it now.' You always should choose 'do it now.'"

The morning after the overnight success

Selina Tobaccowala has an impressive history of disrupting industries. Among the innovative companies she's led are category disruptors like Ticketmaster, SurveyMonkey, and the fitness app Gixo. Follow that history back even further in time and you'll find Selina crouched

REID'S ANALYSIS | A formula for expansion

Startups that succeed and scale are, by definition, in a constant state of expansion. While they begin with a laser-like focus on a single product, sooner or later they have to manage the transition into multiple products, product lines, or even business units. This is what I described as the "Single Focus to Multithreading" transition in *Blitzscaling*.

So a critical question for any startup is figuring out how to apportion their resources between their existing, successful products and the new verticals or markets they want to expand into—and also, in which areas they want to focus that expansion.

It can be helpful to adopt a simple 70/20/10 formula—in which you allocate 70 percent of your resources toward core efforts, 20 percent to expansion adjacent to the core, and 10 percent to venture bets with substantial risks.

The way you apply that formula, and even the degree to which it's a reliable rule or heuristic, varies depending upon the nature of the business you're in. And there are different ways to approach it.

One way is to say: "We have six people. We're going to have one or two people spend 10 to 20 percent of their time devoted to experiments on top of our baseline product."

When you're choosing the specific areas of expansion, there are a few critical questions you can ask: *What are the things I'd want to experiment with?* To go deeper on that question: *What are the things that I see as adjacent to what I'm doing or as potential venture bets that could greatly expand where my product and service get to?* Alternatively, a key question can be: *What would I want to do before my competitors do?*

There are a lot of different ways you can ask these questions. You can even ask: *If another company was going to try to compete with us, how would they compete with us?*

Here's a different variation on these questions that goes to the potential 20 and the potential 10. Ask: *What else is happening in the industry?* For example, *Are there technological platform changes?* This could be a move to the cloud, AI, ubiquity of sensors, Internet of Things, drones—these things then might give you an idea of what should be in the 20 and what should be in the 10.

> There's no one way to drive strategic growth. But by asking these questions and applying this formula, it becomes easier to direct your growth in a productive way.

over her computer in a Stanford dorm room in the early 1990s writing code for **Evite**, an electronic invitation website that would upend the business of social planning.

Selina and her co-founder, Al Lieb, had only a vague sense of the site's reception—they never imagined it would soon become the dominant platform for online invitations. One happy accident clued her in to its potential and changed online life forever.

"I am very clumsy, and I tripped over the cord of the computer that was beneath my desk," she recalls. That would have been quite forgettable, except for what happened next. "Almost immediately, the phone rang and somebody said, 'What happened to Evite?'"

She'd not only disconnected her computer, she'd unknowingly cut off customers who were actually using the site—which is how she discovered just how many of them there were. "We immediately plugged it back in, looked at the database, and we were surprised at how naturally the product had grown." It turns out Evite had a built-in viral coefficient—when people send online invitations, the person receiving that invitation may turn around and send invitations to others, and so on. Unbeknownst to Selina (until she kicked the cord), Evite had been growing of its own volition.

When customers complain about a loss of service, it can be a good sign for a startup—because it means you actually *have* customers, and they care enough to complain. But there's a flip side: Those passionate early users can turn on you just as swiftly as they grew to love you. When she got that angry call, Selina was being held accountable, like any other executive (never mind that she was barely of drinking age). As soon as your users can't live without your service, you're a mature business—and that's a heady responsibility.

"We had not, at that time, been thinking about whether this business could scale," Selina says. That means she hadn't thought about nitty-gritty issues such as *How do you create hardware redundancy or database backup?* "And so we had multiple times where the site would just go down, and we had to learn very quickly, on the job."

Founders often dream of "overnight success," but they don't think enough about what happens the following morning. Often, you wake up to find some fires blazing. Take Hadi Partovi, co-founder of the educational nonprofit Code.org. When he launched a music discovery app called iLike back in 2007, he underestimated the power of going live as an early application on Facebook, which at the time had just over twenty million monthly active users.

"We'd planned to have two servers running this, to judge interest," Hadi says. "And in the first hour, we realized that wasn't going to be enough. So we immediately doubled it, and then we doubled it again. And then we doubled it again." Before long, Hadi's entire farm of about thirty servers was needed to handle the load.

"We could see that by the end of the weekend we would run out of servers," he says. So he and his partner rented a U-Haul truck and then started calling people to ask, *Can we come to your data center and borrow machines?* The two partners spent that weekend unpacking and racking those machines to make sure iLike stayed up and running.

It's a recurring story: A new tech product goes viral and the team is caught flat-footed, sending them into a wildly inefficient scrum. It raises the question: *Hasn't anyone in Silicon Valley heard of a contingency plan?*

The answer to that question is: *Who has time for contingency plans?* To be not only the first mover but also the first blitzscaler in a new market, you have to seize every opportunity for growth—even if it means getting in over your head sometimes.

Let fires burn

When you're growing quickly, there will always be fires—inventory shortfalls, servers crashing, customers whose calls aren't answered. You won't always know which fire to stamp out first. And **if you try to put out every fire at once, you'll only burn yourself out.** That's why entrepreneurs have to learn to let fires burn—and sometimes even very large fires.

When you have a fast-scaling company, the focus *must* be on moving forward. And you can't do that if time is spent dealing with spontaneous, scattered eruptions. Fighting every fire can cause you to miss critical opportunities to build your business—you'll be all reaction and no action.

The trick is knowing which fires *can't* be ignored—the ones that might spread quickly and engulf your business—and which fires you can afford to let burn, even as the flames climb higher. Letting a fire burn takes nerves, vigilance, and lots of practice.

Luckily for Selina Tobaccowala, she had already put out a lot of fires (starting with that cord-trip at Evite) by the time she arrived at a funky little website called SurveyMonkey. The founder, Ryan Finley, had built an incredibly popular tool for online surveys, and managed to scale despite an extreme shortage of everything a company normally needs to do so. "He built the business without a penny of funding," Selina notes. "There were essentially two developers and ten customer service agents—and that was it."

When the startup's leaders interviewed Selina to come join them, she became aware there were only three people doing all the coding, which was "*amazing* for a company doing that much revenue," she says. But she knew it also meant the company was likely to have big problems as it tried to scale. Perhaps even more worrisome: Their system had no backup. Meaning that if it got corrupted or went down, all of the company's precious survey data—the bread and butter of the business—could vanish without a trace.

With Selina onboard, the SurveyMonkey team sized up the odds of a data loss and determined this was a fire that couldn't be ignored. Selina says solving a problem like that "is always invigorating," in part because you have to balance what's urgent—in this case, creating backup systems—against what isn't.

When someone can look at potential business-ending disasters and find them invigorating, you know you're dealing with an experienced firefighter. Once she had that blaze under control, Selina worked her way down a long list of troubles. SurveyMonkey, like every fast-growing startup, had no marketing plan, no strategy for international users, and a mess of code that made every customization a headache. Selina promptly hired engineers, marketers, UI designers, translators—an army of specialists to take on these impediments to growth.

It would be easy to look at the state of SurveyMonkey when Selina arrived and characterize it as chaotic or mismanaged. But that would show a deep misunderstanding of how companies scale. Every successful startup is in a constant state of triage, and it's common for fast-growing companies to pile up massive vulnerabilities as they prioritize strategic growth over long-term stability.

Sometimes this will mean taking shortcuts to build something fast (a product, a team, an office) that will need to be rebuilt—more solidly—later on. This may be hard for your team to accept. But as Selina says, "You are going to have to throw some resources away in the short term, and as long as you explain that to people as they're doing the work, they also understand." When you're letting a fire burn, it's important that your team realizes that, yes, you see the problem, and yes, your neglect is deliberate. If your team accepts this, it's a good sign that you've hired the right people: people who can recognize and then calmly deal with problems as they arise—and who have a good sense of which fires are critical enough to require immediate attention, and which ones can be allowed to just burn for a while.

Growing fast means burning cash. Plan for it.

In 1998, Silicon Valley was red hot. Dot-coms were launching along every possible vertical, and investment dollars were flying their way. Twenty-eight-year-old **Mariam Naficy** had just co-founded Eve, an online cosmetics company, with her friend and former roommate Varsha Rao. But there was a minor detail they hadn't gotten to yet—they needed to secure the domain name "Eve.com." That meant they had to convince the current owner of that domain name to sell it to them. So Mariam called up the owner to begin the negotiation process.

There was just one problem: The owner of the domain was a five-year-old girl named Eve Rogers.

"A five-year-old girl gets on the phone and I'm thinking, *What on Earth am I going to say to her?*" Mariam recalls. "And I'm sure Eve's mom, on the other line, was laughing her head off. I mean, this is a great joke to play on this silly entrepreneur from California who's call-

REID'S ANALYSIS | How do you know which fires to let burn?

All our lives, we're taught to prevent fires and to stamp them out when they occur. But to succeed as an entrepreneur, you actually must let some fires burn—and sometimes they're very large fires. You will always have more on your To Do list than you can accomplish in a day—more demands from your partners and customers than you can possibly meet. Many things that can kill your company right now. Making the *right* choices about which fires you let burn, and how long to let them burn, can be the difference between success and failure.

For rapidly scaling companies, customer service, in particular, can raise really loud alarms. The rule is: "Provide whatever service you can, as long as it doesn't slow you down"—and there may be times when that means *no customer service at all.*

Back in PayPal's early days, our users started growing exponentially, and those users often had exponentiating complaints. We had a customer service department of only three people, so we quickly started falling behind on emails from customers. It got so bad that at one point, there were ten thousand new emails each week (and growing) that we didn't respond to.

Naturally, customers got very frustrated with this. Soon all the phones were ringing, 24/7. So what did we do? We turned off all the ringers on our desk phones and started using our cellphones for business.

I know that's bad. Because of course we're supposed to be customer focused; we should be listening to our customers. But the problem is that we had to consider the future customers as well as the current ones. Because if all we focused on were the current ones, we might not have any future ones at all. So we let those complaints continue until we were positioned to solve the problems. We flew out to Omaha and set up a call center. Within two months, a two-hundred-person customer service department was up and running. Problem solved—and I wouldn't have solved it a moment sooner.

When facing these kinds of choices, I start by assessing probabilities: *Is the probability of this disaster going up or down?* And also: *What's the actual damage if it hits?* And: *Is it correctable after it hits?*

If the answer to that middle question is "fatal damage"—meaning there is a strong possibility that the business is just going to be over if the meltdown happens—don't panic. Because lots of startups have faced that risk early on. LinkedIn was in business years before it had a backup database. So here's where probability comes into play: *Is it a 0.1 percent chance of this happening, or maybe even just .01 percent?* Well then, you can probably wait to solve it in three months or six months.

But if it's more like a 1 percent chance per day—well, add those days together and pretty quickly you will be at 15 percent. That means there's a decent chance your venture might actually be dead within thirty days. So if I see a disaster probability reaching those levels, my reaction is: "Okay, let's solve it now." That's a fire you shouldn't ignore.

ing. *I'm just going to watch her be tortured by my five-year-old for a while.*"

Mariam ended up turning this rather unusual negotiation over to her lead investor, Bill Gross.

"Bill gets on the phone with Eve's mom, and he negotiates the purchase," says Mariam. "The deal consisted of equity in the company, a board seat for Eve, and trips to California several times a year."

That's correct: a five-year-old on the company's board.

"She didn't actually show up for the board meetings," Mariam clarifies, "but she did come and visit." When she did, the company sent her on all-expense-paid trips to Disneyland. In the end, it cost Mariam over $50,000 to acquire a domain name from a five-year-old. (In hindsight, Mariam says, she probably should have led the negotiations with those free Disneyland trips.)

With startups, surprises are a way of life—and many of them come with a price tag attached. You'll find yourself facing all kinds of expenses that weren't contemplated in your budget. Sometimes, the surprises are happy ones—but even those can end up costing you more money, as Mariam learned.

Once she had secured the domain name and opened for business, orders came in quicker than expected. So she did exactly what any sensible entrepreneur would have done: In what was then a heated market, she raised as much money as she could—$26 million in the first year.

"We did a very fast scaling of the company, from zero to 120 people in six months," Mariam says. "It was good that we raised that much, and got out ahead of everyone, because we ended up in the number one spot," Mariam says. "Five venture-backed beauty companies launched in after us."

As the category leader with a pack of new competitors in pursuit, Mariam worked furiously—"until ten o'clock every night, seven days a week"—and spent a lot of money. "We started running TV ads," she says. And radio ads. And billboards. "It was a complete land grab."

Mariam was flush with capital, having raised more than she thought she needed at the time. And then . . . the dot-com bubble burst. The stock market crashed; the mood in the business community changed overnight. And this was a very dramatic moment for those of us who lived through it in Silicon Valley. Companies were going under every day.

"There was this website devoted to covering businesses that are failing. Everybody is looking at it every day. And *The Wall Street Journal*'s reporting, and *The New York Times*. So it looks like the world—from a young twenty-nine-year-old's perspective—your whole world is basically imploding, and the internet is over, basically."

"The internet is over" may sound like a punchline. But, back then, people really believed it. The prevailing idea was: Get out fast. And Mariam did. She maneuvered quickly and sold her company just in the nick of time. "I get my investors whole. They've all made money. I've made money. I, at this point, am feeling a sense of relief-slash-exhaustion at the whole roller coaster I've been on."

Because Mariam had outpaced competitors so quickly, she was able to attract strong offers from buyers, even in a challenging financial climate. The moral of the story: Raising more money than she thought she needed, then using that to scale quickly, probably saved Mariam from going bust like so many other startups did at the time.

As Mariam and so many before her learned—everything associated with scaling up costs money. Hiring. Marketing. Product development. To grow quickly, you need a war chest—not just of cash but also expertise and support. And it's almost impossible to know how much money you will need. But it's safe to assume you will need a lot—especially if you're trying to grow quickly.

Which is why "Reid's rule" for raising money is: Raise more than you think you need. (It's right there in his last book, *Blitzscaling*. Rule #8, "Raise Too Much Money.") Because if there's one thing you can be sure of as an entrepreneur, you are *guaranteed* to run into unexpected problems and expenses.

Though she'd emerged relatively unscathed from the dot-com crash, Mariam hadn't forgotten the lessons she learned from those entrepreneurs who'd raised money impressively, spent it lavishly, and failed spectacularly. "When the whole thing came crashing down, there was so much resentment that had been, understandably, built up around these young entrepreneurs who had so much money to spend, that there was a huge backlash from everyone. They were like, 'Thank goodness these people have been shown a lesson.' And so you basically went from being someone to being absolutely no one, and shunned, and it was really humbling.

"I saw a banker after this, who was much older than I was, and he told me, 'Your biggest problem in life from now on is that you are going to be too conservative. I anoint you, therefore, your curse is that you will be forever too conservative.'"

True to the curse, when it came time for Mariam to launch her second company, she didn't want to take a lot of risk. She wanted what's known as a lifestyle business. The kind of business that's predictable and fairly safe, with a steady stream of revenue that supports a comfortable lifestyle for its owners. No big risks. No crazy drama. At least that's what she thought.

"I said to myself, 'Let's not bring in all the VCs at the beginning, I know what I'm doing this time.' So I chose no co-founder this time, no VC this time. Let's figure out how to build perhaps a sustainable lifestyle business—a cash-flow business—this is what I was thinking at the beginning."

And so Mariam turned to a circle of close acquaintances—"my angel friends"—who believed in her enough to back her with a couple of million dollars. And she used that capital to launch **Minted**, an online stationery store.

Minted was initially conceived as a line of bespoke cards, stationery, and artwork for the home, all of which Mariam had commissioned. But it also included a daring little side experiment. Mariam invited unknown artists to submit designs to an online competition. Anyone could participate, anyone could vote. The winners would then become part of Minted's product offering, competing alongside top brand names of the stationery industry.

In 2008, Mariam was ready to release her slightly offbeat selection of stationery to the world. "I opened the doors," she says, "and there's not a sale for an entire month." To her dismay, it seemed that "nobody wants the branded stationery products that we'd spent most of our $2.5 million launching."

Meanwhile, however, the designs that were emerging from her competition slowly started to sell, and pretty soon she'd "sourced sixty original designs that way." Suddenly, Mariam's "little side thing" became *the thing*.

Mariam had stumbled onto the power of crowdsourcing—the idea that ordinary people, coming together in large numbers, can do work once reserved for experts. The implications were clear: Because of new opportunities created by technology, almost anyone could become a stationery designer. And if their designs were good enough, they could rise up—and gain exposure and a following. "It was a true meritocracy that you could actually build and unleash," Mariam says.

There was just one problem: Out of the $2.5 million originally raised, Mariam had only about $100,000 left to promote these crowdsourced designs. Mariam's plan to start a lifestyle business hadn't panned out, and now she didn't have enough funding left to adequately support her Plan B. In startup mode, unexpected opportunities (the happy flip side of unexpected problems, but just as costly) may arise later than you hope or plan, and you need to have the capital to seize them.

So Mariam reluctantly considered going back to the VCs—spurred on not just by opportunity but by a sense of obligation. It was important to her that she ultimately refund the money her angel friends had staked her. She pitched her crowdsourced designs concept and secured another round of funding. And once again her timing was fortuitous. An investor friend warned her that the markets were getting unstable, so she raised the money as quickly as she could, in August 2008.

Two weeks later, Lehman Brothers failed, and the market went into free fall. If she had waited a few more months—even weeks—to raise that money, no one would have given cash to a bold little experiment in crowdsourcing. Which is yet one more reason to take the money whenever and wherever you can get it—because you never know when it will dry up.

Mariam eventually raised $89 million in venture capital for Minted, which is now a nine-figure-revenue company with 350 employees that has shipped products to seventy million households around the world.

Looking back, Mariam says that if she could do it all over, she would have raised even *more* capital, and done it sooner. "Things are always more expensive than you think they are," she says, "and they will always take more time to prove out."

Her rule of thumb: However much money you have, "act like you've got half that much—because you've got to factor in all the failures and all the optimizations that kill great entrepreneurs all the time. I know so many people who had good ideas, were on the right track—and they just ran out of runway."

Know who you are—and who your funders want you to be

There's no question that a war chest can fuel rapid growth. But it's also important to note: **Not all money is equal.** Just as investors should know when to say "No" to a startup that's not a good growth prospect, entrepreneurs should also know when to say "No" to an investor who's not a good fit.

And it's best to decide where to draw the line before you need the money. **Rana el Kaliouby** is the co-founder of Affectiva, a leader in emotional AI, whose software can read your facial expressions and indicate what you're feeling. As Rana explains, facial recognition technology has many potential applications in the areas of healthcare, education, driver safety, and more. "But I'm not naïve," she says. "In the wrong hands, this technology can be quite abusive." For instance, it could end up being used to discriminate against people or to invade their privacy.

So early on, the founders of Affectiva decided they only wanted to play in industries where consent was explicit and where people understood how this data was going to be collected and used. "When we spun out of MIT, my co-founder, Professor Rosalind Picard, and I, we sat around her kitchen table in her house and we said, 'Okay, we recognize that this technology can be used in many, many places. Where are we gonna draw the line?'"

They imagined a lot of dark possibilities. "As an example, security and surveillance is a big area where we could, as a company, make a ton of money. But we decided that that was a space we weren't going to play in," Rana recalls.

"And we got tested on it."

Entrepreneurs get tested by challenges of every shape and size. But they especially get tested when money gets tight. Which is what happened to Rana and her team.

"In 2011, we were literally a couple of months away from shutting down. We were running out of money. And we got approached by the venture arm of an intelligence agency. They said, 'We're going to give you $40 million of funding'—which for us was a lot of money at the time—'on the condition that you pivot the company to security, surveillance, and lie detection.'"

It wasn't easy to decide what to do, Rana admits. "On the one hand, we could take this money and we would continue to exist," she says. On the other hand, the company would be violating its core principles—its very reason for being. "We had to take a stance."

They turned the money down.

And while it took them longer, Affectiva did eventually raise other funding from investors—ones that believed in the company's vision and supported its core values.

"I do feel like it's important that you be very clear around what your core values are. It's also our responsibility as leaders in this space to educate the public about all of the different use cases. Because what I like to say is: Technology is neutral, right? Any technology in human history is neutral, it's how we decide to use it."

"This really became a foundational story for us," Rana says, "a story of strategic patience—of knowing who we are and what we stand for."

I generally favor blitzscaling, or superfast growth. It's a proven method of getting explosive momentum behind your idea. I believe that blitzscaling, or the pursuit of rapid growth by prioritizing speed over efficiency, even in the face of uncertainty, is the way that the great technology companies of the future will be built. When you're trying to win a winner-take-most market, the right strategy is to reach critical scale first, generating long-term competitive advantages that make it nearly impossible for any competitor to overtake you.

In order to blitzscale, you need a war chest—and you need it fast, so you can outpace your competition. This need for speed is why I almost always encourage entrepreneurs to raise money—and raise more than they think they need.

I do realize that not everyone feels comfortable with blitzscaling. Prioritizing speed over efficiency feels risky—and it is! However, it's easy to err too far on the side of caution, and there's a risk in being conservative about how much you raise and spend. You might think you're best serving your investors by being as efficient with capital as possible, but that's actually not the truth. You reward your investors by creating a successful company, which can be hard to do if your competitors outspend you.

Some startups prefer to bootstrap their way forward—and some, like Mailchimp, do it well. But I would argue that even a successful startup like Mailchimp could have grown faster with investment. And if they were uncomfortable taking funds at the outset, they could have taken it later—in VC terms, this would be the Series B, Series C, Series D rounds. Bringing higher and higher levels of investment into an already successful startup could enable you not just to dominate one market but expand into others.

Mailchimp captured their market through a rare combination of luck, tenacity, and skill. However, if they had found *the right VC partner,* I believe they could have done it sooner, and scaled far more rapidly.

Notice I emphasized "the right partner"—because that's a big part of the equation. And the right partner isn't always easy to come by. When I give entrepreneurs advice, I always tell them the vast majority of venture capitalists (up to three-quarters of them) provide negative value and money, while a much smaller percentage are neutral, and only about 10 percent provide positive value and money. Sometimes you just need the money. But still, you should really pick your VC partner carefully.

Look at an investor as a later-stage financial co-founder—a partner for strategy and financing. It's a different role, of course—you're still a founder, you're still CEO, you still run the business. But your relationship with your investors should be a partnership, and a partner who doesn't understand you is one of the biggest impediments you can have. So you have to find investors who are the right match—for your product and your work style. It's one of the reasons I advise founders seeking investment to take on multiple investors over time.

REID'S THEORIES ON GROWING YOUR BUSINESS

Lean in while sitting back

When you embark on the entrepreneurial journey, you have to recognize that the conditions around you are always changing. If you want to go the distance, you sometimes have to be strategically patient. But that doesn't mean just sitting back and waiting. It means leaning in and watching for the moment to break out and move fast. Sometimes it even means building the capabilities in advance to take advantage of a future opportunity.

Start fast but don't burn yourself out

Explosive starts only work if you can sustain the momentum you generate. It's all about figuring out how explosive you can make those opening steps—without getting fried in the process. Startups are a marathon of sprints.

Decide, decide, decide

Rapid decision-making is a key to explosive growth. When you're moving fast, you may make mistakes. But the biggest mistake is not making decisions fast enough, because the only thing that matters is time.

Let fires burn

When you have a fast-scaling company, the focus must be on moving forward. And it's hard to do that if you're spending much of your time putting out fires. Some fires may be too serious to ignore. But others are better left burning.

You can never raise enough money

Opportunities may arise when you least expect them, and you need to have the capital to carry you in new directions. Make sure to have enough funding left to adequately support a Plan B. Make sure you have enough funding to experiment.

Pick your VC partners carefully

Look at an investor essentially as a later-stage co-founder—a partner who understands you and your vision for the company.

6

Learn to Unlearn

I t started with a pair of homemade shoes. As a student at the University of Oregon, Phil Knight ran track, under Bill Bowerman, the Hall of Fame coach. And running with Bill meant field-testing his hand-sewn, Frankensteined sneakers. "He was always experimenting with shoes," Phil recalls. "He felt that getting lighter shoes was important."

"Everybody in those days—all the really great runners—were wearing either Adidas or Puma shoes, and it was a real eye-opener for me when Otis Davis won the Pacific Coast Conference Championship in the 400 meters wearing a pair of Bowerman homemade shoes—which I had been experimenting with before he wore them." Phil was struck by the way this lightweight, handmade shoe powered a high-profile win. But he was equally struck by the influence that win had on amateur athletes. Everyone wanted that shoe. "And that planted a seed."

Phil Knight co-founded Nike (under the name Blue Ribbon Sports) in 1964—with an investment of $500 each from Bill and Phil. Their laser focus: making ultra-high-performance sneakers. "The

world needs a better running shoe. That was the thought behind it."
Branding? Advertising? None of that mattered to Phil. "I never thought
I was a 'sales personality.'" His winning formula: Build sneakers that
drive winning performances—and the rest will follow.

And it did. Thanks to endorsements from Steve Prefontaine and
other elite runners, the nation's track coaches and joggers latched on
to Nike's lightweight shoes—built for speed, not style. "We hadn't
really focused on the appearance of the shoes," says Phil. "We said: If
a shoe performs, and a great athlete wears it, it'll sell."

And that worked, until it didn't. **Nike as we know it today—the
culture-driving, style-setting Nike—exists only because Nike lost
its footing.**

The craze for high-performance athletic gear was overtaken by another craze—high-*fashion* athletic gear. Nike was losing this race—
badly. As Phil puts it: "In the '80s, we got our brains beat out by an
upstart company called Reebok."

Reebok's Velcro-powered high-tops were built for the new exercise
trend: aerobics. And stylish women started wearing their aerobics
shoes with business suits on their way to work. All of a sudden, athletic wear was streetwear.

Phil had spent almost two decades building a dominant business
doing what he knew how to do: designing, testing, and selling high-
performance sports gear to athletes. But the game had changed around
him, and he'd have to unlearn everything he thought he knew about
how to win.

After a particularly dismal quarterly sales report came in, "We
said, 'Well, maybe we should try some advertising after all,'" Phil remembers. "So we walked into an office that had four guys and a card
table. Their names were David Kennedy and Dan Wieden."

They were the founders of Wieden+Kennedy, of course. And
they've since become a legendary name in the advertising world, with
thousands of employees and offices worldwide. But at the time, they
were small and hungry. And they were willing to challenge Phil as
much as he planned to challenge them.

As Phil tells it, "I walked into Dan's office and I said: 'I just want
you to know: I hate advertising.' And Dan says, 'Well, that's an interesting way to start.'"

So they began with first principles. The Wieden+Kennedy team's approach: "We have to know the client. We have to know the product. We have to know who and what they are. We have to represent what they really are." Through this mutual learning process, they realized: It wasn't advertising that Phil hated, it was *boring* advertising.

And through his work with W+K, Phil came to understand how the things that mattered to Nike—the company's scrappy, underdog spirit; the high-caliber athletes they partnered with; their persistence and insistence on quality—could create not just a line of products but a brand. And this brand, Phil believes, eventually gave them sales three- or fourfold what they'd have had without it.

Phil stepped out of his comfort zone when he stepped into that small office with a card table, but he kept his laser focus on what Nike was. Building on Nike's chip-on-the-shoulder attitude, W+K developed their first, now-legendary ad campaign, "Revolution," to the music of the Beatles, featuring iconic athletes and simple, memorable slogans—and extremely stylish shoes. This was of course followed by the iconic, culture-shaping slogan "Just Do It."

Nike also doubled down on design in those years—another new space for Phil. Designer Mark Parker took on a growing role (he eventually became CEO) as they rolled out a broader range of shoes, including the new category of cross-training shoes, the Air Force 1 basketball sneaker in 1982, and the iconic Air Jordan in 1985, which is as much a design platform as a shoe.

"We became a brand in those couple years, when we put all that together," Phil says. "And that's what really sent us on our way."

Phil was willing to set aside two-plus decades of his own hard-won expertise to help Nike shift gears from a shoe company to a brand. He understood that the market for shoes underwent a step-change in the early 1980s—and if he and Nike didn't adapt, they wouldn't survive. It's a transition every leader of an innovative, fast-growing organization will face, often multiple times. It's not enough to learn the ropes. To truly scale an organization, you have to learn to unlearn.

And this is challenging, because humans have a tendency—especially as we get older and more established—to hold on to the strategies that helped them succeed last time, whether or not they still work. So you have to continually question (and often cast off) the assumptions from your last product, your last job, your last year. Especially in a fast-growing organization or industry, the old adage applies: "What got you here, won't get you there." Learning to unlearn is the hidden mindset for scale.

Venture into unfamiliar territory

It's an old Hollywood story: Ambitious kid gets a job in the mailroom, works hard, schmoozes his way up and down the halls, catches the eye of a bigwig, and begins his ascent. . . .

But that's not exactly how it played out for **Barry Diller**. He *did* start in the mailroom—at the William Morris Agency. But while everyone else in the mailroom was, in Barry's words, "sucking up to the agents," Barry snuck off to the file room to study. Within those file cabinets was the entire history of the entertainment business. "And so," Barry says, "I spent three years reading about the business, from A to Z. . . . It was my school."

When Barry emerged, he was ready to apply what he had learned—and to move on from the agency. A friend introduced him to a rising TV executive at ABC, who asked Barry to be his assistant. Barry wasn't particularly interested in making photocopies and answering phones, but he took the job, because, as he puts it, "I've always believed whatever you're interested in, get on the widest road. And television was a pretty wide road."

The network was struggling, and that was actually good news for Barry. "ABC was the third network, the hip-shooting network. It would try almost anything," Barry recalls. "It was also like a candy store. If you wanted responsibility, you just took it."

Barry seized the opportunity to pitch a big idea.

"All television at that time was series, either comedies or dramas," Barry says. "And in both forms, everything was present-day. Those series would go on for seven years, Lucy still lived in her same apartment. She never moved. There was all middle—no beginning, no end. And I thought, *Why don't we tell stories on TV that have a beginning, middle, and end, like they do in movies?*"

So Barry pitched the then-radical idea of a "Movie of the Week"—a movie made specifically for TV. His colleagues balked. *It just wasn't television*, the naysayers said. *That's not what we do.* But having studied seventy-five years of entertainment history back in the William Morris file room, Barry knew there was a precedent for movie-like storytelling, with decades-ago series like *Playhouse 90* and *Studio One*.

Barry fought and prevailed—or, to put it another way, the ABC execs gave him just enough rope to hang himself. "If anybody thought it would work, why would they give responsibility to a twenty-three-year-old?" he says. "Everyone thought it would fail, and they'd get rid of this aggressive kid in the process."

And so the TV movie was born, and became such a permanent fixture in the television landscape that it even earned an Emmy category of its own. Among ABC's more memorable productions: *Duel*, directed by a young Steven Spielberg, and the classic tearjerker *Brian's Song*.

But Barry soon ran up against the limitations of his own format. When he tried to adapt novels for the small screen, he wasn't able to do the storylines justice. "You can't do it in two hours, much less ninety minutes. It needs to breathe more." So Barry found a creative solution—*and* a new format: what he then called "a novel for television" and we now know as the miniseries. These limited-run series would run over the course of eight or ten nights, telling an epic story that couldn't be contained in a single evening. They drew huge audiences, night after night, bringing huge wins for ABC with titles like *Shogun*; *Rich Man, Poor Man*; and an eight-part story about slavery that smashed every American TV viewership record: *Roots*.

Barry's early success at ABC mirrors many of the most successful launches in Silicon Valley. His idea, to create movies for television, went against conventional wisdom—and everyone predicted disaster. But he was right; he saw something others missed. **The reason they missed it was an unwillingness to unlearn what they knew.**

But this came naturally to Barry. He had just reinvented the TV formula, *twice*. And he would do it again. After an astonishing decade at Paramount in Hollywood, where he greenlit a succession of iconic, era-defining films for the flailing studio (*The Bad News Bears, Saturday Night Fever, Grease, Raiders of the Lost Ark, Flashdance, Footloose,*

Trading Places, Top Gun), Barry got itchy for a new challenge and came home to TV.

So now it's 1988, and Barry finds himself in a screening room, presenting an edgy new sitcom to a group of stone-faced executives.

"When you're watching something with a group of people," Barry says, "and you are involved in making it, and they're seeing it for the first time, you laugh a lot—partly out of pride, and partly because you're almost daring everybody else not to laugh."

In this case, not a single person—except Barry—laughed.

Barry had already ordered thirteen episodes of the show. And now here he was, with everyone in the room letting him know, in no uncertain terms, they had a disaster on their hands. Comments ranged from "We can't put this on the air," to "Is there any way to get out of this?"

Barry was CEO of the newly founded Fox Television Network— the "fourth network" in an industry long dominated by three. If his upstart network was to have any chance, Barry knew he had to offer viewers a distinct alternative: prime-time programming that broke the rules. The show he was pitching was about as different from a classic network sitcom as you could get. The son was a holy terror. Mom had blue hair. Dad was a lazy, doughnut-obsessed slob.

Oh, and it was a cartoon.

Barry Diller's "disaster," of course, turned out to be the most successful series in the history of television, *The Simpsons*. Nowadays, an animated, adult-themed TV series seems pretty normal. But at the time there was nothing even remotely like it—which is part of what attracted him.

"All my life, the only things that interested me were things that hadn't been done."

It's a refrain you often hear from entrepreneurs who have to do things *their* way. Barry wasn't drawn to *The Simpsons* simply because he thought it would help his new network stand out from the competition, but because he gets excited by projects that break fresh ground. Put Barry into unfamiliar territory and he is forced to learn, adapt, and experiment—which also happens to be when he does his best work. "I learned really early," he says, "that you are best when you know nothing."

Barry is the paradigm of what we call an infinite learner. He's actually on the extreme end of the curve. But this mindset—of casting off your assumptions from your last product, your last job, your last year—is essential for anyone aiming to make their mark.

Using the framework from Reid's first book, *The Startup of You*, Barry might best exemplify the concept of "being in permanent beta." Approach everything with a new mind; seek out new challenges and new learning opportunities; and never presume that you know this new game already.

Abandon what you know

From TV to movies and back again, Barry had established himself firmly in the upper echelon of media titans. But now, he was . . . bored.

"I'd been running movie and television companies for eighteen years, and I felt that if I never saw another script, I'd be a happy person," he says.

While he was pondering what to do next, Barry's wife, the fashion designer Diane von Furstenberg, told him about the new QVC shopping network. "I saw something that I had never seen before," Barry says. "It was this early convergence of telephones, televisions, and computers. The screen was interactive, used for purposes other than narrative. That whacked me," he says.

So . . . he bought it. Even back in 1992, when the internet barely existed, he was mesmerized by the idea of an interactive screen. He saw how it could shake up the media industry—to say nothing of retail. And what allowed him to make the leap was that he was ready to *unlearn* everything he'd previously learned about the art of making TV. Forget about telling stories—it was time to put the audience in charge.

QVC became a testing ground for a much grander ambition. Barry set up an operation that became InterActiveCorp, or IAC. Then he began a series of acquisitions that ranged across genres, snapping up companies at a dizzying pace.

The first of those companies was Ticketmaster, which soon became the leading online hub for tickets to concerts and shows. Then he moved into online travel by acquiring Expedia.com. Then dating, with Match.com, Tinder, OKCupid. Then Vimeo, Ask.com, The Daily Beast, College Humor, Dictionary.com, Angie's List. Search for almost anything and you're likely to land on a Diller property. IAC quickly became the rare internet conglomerate.

With many of these businesses, Barry had limited knowledge of the subject matter and even more limited experience in the industry involved. He views such ignorance as an asset. "The more you know, the worse it is." Instead of relying on what he thinks he knows, Barry takes the time and effort to deconstruct complex issues. Similar to Netflix's Reed Hastings and the team he built, Barry is a quintessential "first-principle" thinker.

In truth, he has no choice but to approach each new challenge this way—it's just the way his brain works. "My brain is slower and more literal," he says. When Barry encounters something he doesn't understand, "I have to break it down to its tiniest particle and only then can I understand it. But that is joyous work to me—getting through those layers, down to the very base of something."

As soon as he'd figured each new business out, he'd be ready to spin off that property and move on. In one year alone, IAC spun off the Home Shopping Network, Ticketmaster, and LendingTree.com. Though IAC is considered a media conglomerate, in some ways it functions more like an incubator—one that hatches ideas in just about the time it takes for Barry to lose interest. It's a portfolio constantly poised between Barry's desire to learn and unlearn.

What allows Barry to leap from one field to another so successfully is not just his ability to learn and unlearn, but his instinct to move away from the things he knows, and to bring an outsider's fresh perspective to each new business he enters.

In the early years of Microsoft, **Bill Gates** was pretty sure he could solve anything. "I'd completely dive into a problem"—regardless of whether it involved engineering, human resources, or sales. "I thought all IQ was fungible, and rightly or wrongly, I viewed myself as self-taught across all these domain areas."

Bill has always viewed himself as an infinite learner who could easily move across disciplines. And it worked for him—for years—as he took on challenges in software, engineering, management at scale. But when he launched the Bill & Melinda Gates Foundation, there were challenges he hadn't anticipated.

Inspired by a shocking article he and his wife, Melinda, read about children dying—by the millions—of preventable diseases, Bill set out to focus his foundation on diseases that needed cures. "So we'd go in and solve that," Bill recalls. It wasn't arrogance. It's more a testament to Bill's optimistic belief that technology (with enough money behind it) can overcome almost any problem. He knew that science was making great advances on many diseases, and now it was time to scale those advances to reach the most people in need. "And I thought, *Okay, that plays to my strengths—let's build a team to go do that.*"

Bill had the entrepreneur's bias toward action. But he quickly realized that before he could act, there was *a lot* he had to learn—about the science involved, about the role of government, about cultural differences between countries, even—or rather, especially—about the practical logistics of delivering supplies.

"I thought that the breakthrough—the new vaccine or the innovative drug—was the only missing piece," Bill says. "Sadly, the delivery mechanism in many of these countries—the primary healthcare system—was also very, very poor."

This was a hard lesson about the need to focus on mundane details, like delivery, that support grand innovations. "I admit for a year or two, I thought, *Gosh, isn't someone else going to solve this delivery problem?*" he says. "And eventually I became convinced that, no, it wouldn't be solved by someone else—and it would be almost pyrrhic to invent more new vaccines that wouldn't actually get delivered."

The learning curve was steep for Bill and the foundation. "Understanding how to work in poor countries, and get things delivered—that hadn't been an area of specialization at Microsoft. Hiring smart engineers was."

Bill also had to immerse himself in the products and workings of the pharmaceutical business. "I tried to figure out who was doing it best, in terms of both design and going in and drawing some of the best people out of pharma—because in a virtual way, we needed to become a pharmaceutical company and actually create more successful products than any pharmaceutical company was."

And he had to study the existing models: which countries were doing good work combating diseases, and how. "I really dove into the historical exemplars, like Costa Rica, Sri Lanka, and the contemporary ones, including some African countries," he says. "Telling the stories of the heroes individually and the system's approach, that was key to us."

Of all the issues, "the delivery problem," as Bill calls it, was perhaps the most perplexing. Why was it that vaccines and drugs could be effectively delivered in some regions and not others?

He learned that it often comes down to government. "Governments in rich countries, even now in middle-income countries, are pretty amazing," he says. "We kind of take for granted that the water system, electricity system, education system, justice system, these things work pretty darn well.

"But as you get into very poor countries, salaries don't get paid—and even for vaccines that are lifesaving, sometimes the funds don't get allocated, or they could even be stolen. It's pretty shocking how bad government can get."

To deal with this huge problem, Bill needed to learn—or rather, *unlearn*—how to work with government. In Bill's years at Microsoft, the government had been more of an adversary than an ally.

But now, Bill knew he and the foundation would have to figure out how to get these lifesaving drugs delivered: "Are you going to get the government to step up to its role, or are you going to try to go around it?" Eventually, he says, "we realized we have to get governments to step up. It's the only long-term solution."

Getting various governments to step up "involved a huge learning curve," Bill says. Every country had a different set of problems, and different attitudes about how to solve them. Some welcomed help more than others. For example, the prime minister of Ethiopia wanted to improve the country's health services, "so building up their health system, and even improving their agricultural system, we got to do that in partnership," Bill says. "That became an exemplar for us."

But it was a very different scenario in Nigeria, which once accounted for half of the world's polio cases—largely because vaccines weren't reliably delivered, especially in the troubled north of the country. In that instance, the foundation backed an effort that routed around the government, and supported two hundred thousand volunteers—who together immunized forty-five million children. It made a tremendous dent on the disease. Nigeria hasn't recorded a new case of polio for three years. But it's an ongoing effort to maintain the partnerships that ensure vaccines get to those who need them.

Still, even the toughest challenges have long-term payoffs.

"The biological sciences that give us new ways of inventing vaccines; that's gone super well," Bill reports. "Even though there's some miracles that haven't emerged yet—an HIV vaccine, a TB vaccine—over the next ten to fifteen years we are going to have those. So it's well worth making sure that the delivery system is going to be there, not only for what we have today but for those things that are coming down the pipeline."

Bill has the long view in mind now, knowing how long it takes to set up the right systems and relationships. But the work has borne out his ambitious vision: In the past two decades, childhood deaths declined by 50 percent, from ten million to just over five million annually. Four and a half *million* children who would have died before the age of five of something completely preventable are still alive as a result of the foundation's efforts. It's an achievement that ranks among humanity's best work.

Waive all the rules

It's 1943, the height of World War II. Any scientific breakthrough or technical innovation could turn the tide of the war—in either direction. The German army had recently created the Messerschmitt Me 262, the first jet fighter meant to be deployed in combat, which gave them a tactical edge. The U.S. military had to come up with a response—fast.

But the Americans were lagging behind the Germans on jet engine technology. Then, an opportunity arose: The British government offered the U.S. Army the design for the de Havilland H-1B Goblin engine, free of charge. The only catch—the Americans had to build a plane around it.

The Air Force handed this task to the aerospace company Lockheed Martin. But Lockheed was already cranking at full capacity. They had no spare factory space and no spare engineers. They were tapped

REID'S ANALYSIS | Be a "learn-it-all," not a "know-it-all"

We chose to name this book—and our podcast—*Masters of Scale,* in honor of the iconic leaders who have taken their company or idea from zero to a gazillion. But this name might be misleading. Mastery suggests we've reached a pinnacle—that we've figured out how to do something about as well as it can possibly be done. But the reality is, none of us actually reaches an end state of mastery. We're all constantly learning. Or should be. We're in permanent beta.

One of my mantras is: Success imprints more strongly than failure. That's because as you've succeeded, you take pride and comfort in having learned something that actually works. And the assumption is, this thing I've learned, this tool, will keep on working—so I can just keep applying it. Which is exactly what can lead you to keep doing the same thing over and over—even as the train comes off the tracks.

Because, of course, the same tool, the same knowledge, the same tactics *don't* keep on working—not when the problems you're trying to solve change, and not when markets change, competitors change, industries change, and you change.

And so, frequently, an entrepreneur has to wonder, *Which of the old lessons have to be thrown out? And which things do I have to unlearn or learn anew?* To unlearn, you have to let go of what you thought was true. And to purge the very knowledge or expertise that made you successful is very hard to do.

For example, if I tried to go start a new consumer internet company, and I tried to do it in the exact same way that I started LinkedIn, I'd fail. Mobile technology is different. Virality is different. The job search ecosystem is different. The platforms that people are using are different. They're all different.

And the same is true for your next venture, whatever it is. So if you want to succeed, you have to use a different playbook. Basically, you should be thinking, "Look, I know the game will be changing. Of the things I've learned before—only some of them will still apply when the game changes." For all entrepreneurs, my advice is to have a learning mindset. You have to figure out the new rules of the game before you can devise a winning strategy. Be a "learn-it-all," not a "know-it-all."

out. Nevertheless, Lockheed's chief engineer, Kelly Johnson, volunteered to head up the project. "He had been asking for an experimental aircraft division," says Nick Means, director of engineering at GitHub and a passionate student of aviation history. "The Lockheed board largely gave him the project to shut him up, because they thought it would be too difficult to pull off."

Johnson had a very specific plan for building the plane, and it started with throwing out every single assumption they had about how planes were built.

Johnson set up a circus tent on some unused Lockheed grounds—right next to a rotten-smelling plastics factory (hence, the name given to the project: Skunk Works). Inside that tent, a small group of hand-picked engineers, draftsmen, and fabricators began constructing a mock-up of a plane around a mock-up of the engine. "They didn't even have the engine in house yet," Nick Means says, "but they wanted to start building anyway."

This was an entirely new way of working. "Normally when you build a plane," says Nick, "you do lots of drawings, lots of test fitting—but in this case, Kelly essentially waived all the rules and said his engineers and fabricators were free to fabricate parts on the spot that would fit on the plane."

The tight feedback loops between designer, engineer, and fabricator allowed ideas to move from pencil sketch to tangible part in a matter of hours. This meant less time was spent drafting blueprints—and more time was spent building, collecting data, and iterating based on results. Because of that flexibility, and how quickly it allowed them to move, they were able to get the prototype built in 143 days—a remarkably short amount of time to build a jet aircraft.

In aviation, all of the planning and building obviously means nothing if the plane doesn't fly. But this plane flew—and it flew fast. The P-80 Shooting Star that Johnson's Skunk Works produced was the first American plane to fly five hundred miles an hour in level flight. While the P-80 never saw combat in World War II, as the F-80 it fought in the Korean War, and as the T-33 it saw extensive use as a training aircraft. Over eight thousand of the planes were produced, and the U.S. Air Force kept the T-33 in service until 1997. The design that Johnson's team developed in 143 days ended up serving for fifty-four years.

There are so many reasons why this *shouldn't* have worked—perhaps starting with the part where Kelly Johnson "waived all the rules." That's not something you would expect from an aerospace engineer, but the Skunk Works team didn't have time for a multiyear plan. And they couldn't afford to make any assumptions. They had an urgent question that needed answering. So they experimented.

Today, every business should do likewise. Because even if you have the most solid, well-thought-out business plan, that plan is likely based on assumptions—and those assumptions could prove wrong once your product or service is released into the marketplace. In a way, your business itself could be thought of as an experiment. And **for the experiment to succeed, you have to be willing to throw out—or at least challenge—what you originally believed to be true.**

Learning to experiment (and experimenting to learn)

Eric Ries is the founder of the Long-Term Stock Exchange and author of the iconic book *The Lean Startup*. But at twenty-five, Eric was co-founder of an unknown, unproven startup, IMVU, which built 3D avatars for social networking platforms. IMVU had a terrific business plan from the outset—Eric knows, because he wrote it. "It was fifty pages of just the most eloquent prose," Eric says, "with data sourced from the U.S. census, and all of this analysis. It was just like, you would weep to read it."

But there was one small problem. The *customers* Eric needed to actually buy his product didn't read his business plan. And they didn't behave the way his plan predicted they would, either.

Before the product launched, Eric had spent many long nights coding, trying to get everything just right. Even so, just before it went live, he worried that something would go wrong: like maybe crowds of people would download the software and crash their servers.

Eric's software didn't crash a single computer. Because nobody downloaded it.

"We didn't sell a single copy," Eric admits. "Nobody even tried it for free!" This failure, while catastrophic in the moment, gave Eric the critical insight to develop what would become his signature theory. His company had built a product based on an assumption so far off the mark that six months of coding was wasted.

The question this experience sparked for Eric was: *How could we have found out our assumption was wrong sooner?*

As Eric and his team, still reeling from the failure, sifted through usability tests, they came to understand the mistakes they'd made, and they pivoted their strategy. Eventually they got it right, their avatars caught on, and the company started to scale.

But those lost six months really stuck with Eric. What bothered him most wasn't that they got the product wrong. It was how much time and effort had been wasted building it.

Many of us tend to believe that in order to do something well, you must do it slowly, carefully, and privately. That means taking time to refine it, and not unveiling it to the world until it is perfect. As the aphorism goes, you only get one chance to make a first impression.

That may have its place in the arts—the suffering poet, alone in her garret, laboring over the placement of commas. But for startups?

It's a bad strategy.

The problem is that what you *think* you know—about what customers want, about what will work and won't work in the real world—is often based on untested assumptions. The solution: Test those assumptions as quickly as possible.

To do that, you must **be willing to share your imperfect work-in-progress with the outside world—very early on and continuously thereafter—to get fast feedback**. This is what Eric dubbed the "Minimum Viable Product," or MVP: the most bare-bones, least-polished version of a product that can be used to test a hypothesis.

This catchy terminology was new at the time, but as Eric readily acknowledges, his test-and-learn theory is derived from the scientific method, which developed over centuries. "We're not breaking any really new ground here," he says, "but just applying those lessons to business."

It's worth noting that Eric's approach is not just about learning—it's also about how you *respond* to what you've learned, achieving "perfection through iteration." As with the scientific method, it involves assessing the results of your experiment and asking: *Did it bear out my hypothesis? Or do I need to make adjustments?* In the business world, those adjustments might be as small as adding a feature or as big as pivoting your entire strategy. (By the way, Eric is the person who popularized this now-ubiquitous term—pivot—which we'll cover in Chapter 8, "The Art of the Pivot.")

Eric quickly put his theory into practice at IMVU, where his engineers started shipping code more frequently—sometimes multiple times a day—to get product updates into users' hands. His team would then study the data on how those users responded. Pretty soon, the distance from hypothesis to experiment to results got shorter and shorter. His company started to scale. But one thing nagged at Eric.

"As we're starting to do things in this very unusual way, it clearly works—but no one can understand *why*," Eric recalls. "It drove our employees crazy and our investors crazy." Eric knew he had to be able to codify and fully explain the "why" behind this new approach. So he then did something that took him from "startup founder" to "movement leader." He took these ideas about adapting a scientific, experiment-based method to launching new products and businesses, and began to dig deeply into the research.

Eric pulled from a wide variety of sources: from management theorists and military strategists to Toyota's "lean manufacturing" system, which identifies and eliminates waste at every step of the process. Then he applied these concepts to software development, the way a scientist might observe a drug's effect on one species and apply that learning to another.

In the midst of his research, Eric left IMVU and became an advisor to other startups. He also began writing blog posts, anonymously. And eventually, these posts became the basis for his book. It arrived at exactly the right time. In the wake of the 2008 financial crisis, entrepreneurs needed to achieve liftoff without huge amounts of capital or years of development time. *The Lean Startup* has since sold more than a million copies. But more importantly, it became a handbook for a new way of doing business.

One of the biggest champions of experimentation in Silicon Valley has been Mark Zuckerberg, whose early mantra—"Move fast and break things"—was a foundation for Facebook's success. And the company continues to experiment constantly today, even at its current size—though its mantra now is "Move fast with stable infrastructure." As

REID'S ANALYSIS | **Get·ready to be embarrassed!**

I often say, "If you aren't embarrassed by your first product release, you've released it too late." Why? Because you need to test a real product with real customers as soon as possible—basically the moment you have a *bare-bones* version. But the point of releasing ASAP isn't speed for speed's sake. It's to get data from your customers—while you still have enough time to *use* that data to make improvements. Then you build again, and test again, creating a feedback loop that allows you to continuously improve. And not just a handful of times.

Don't fear imperfections in software products. They won't make or break your company. What will make or break you is speed—how quickly you're able to build things that users actually love. So learn to live with the small embarrassments that come with releasing something that isn't perfect.

Over the years, some people have interpreted my theory as permission to cut corners, act recklessly, or proceed without a clear plan. But notice: I said, "If you're not embarrassed by your product." I didn't say, "If you're not deeply ashamed of your product," or "If you're not indicted for your product."

If your product generates lawsuits, alienates users, or burns through capital without any apparent gain, you likely did in fact launch too soon. Without doubt, there are risks that come with experimenting at scale—but you also gain invaluable opportunities to learn and improve.

So show your work early. Show it often. And above all, don't hole up in your garage and try to perfect your product on your own. You'll be wasting not only your time; you'll also be wasting your window of opportunity. You can read more about this topic in *Blitzscaling*, where "Launch a Product That Embarrasses You" is #4 on my list of Counterintuitive Rules of Blitzscaling.

Mark says, "At any given point in time, there isn't just one version of Facebook running—there are probably ten thousand. Any engineer at the company can basically decide that they want to test something."

That means an engineer can launch a customized, experimental version of Facebook—not to the whole community, but to perhaps ten thousand people, or however many are needed to get a good test of an experience. Then, the engineer can get a virtually immediate readout of the results: *How were people connecting with this version? What were they sharing, and how?* Armed with this data, Mark says, "the engineer can come to a manager, and say, 'Hey, here's what I built, and these are the results. Do we want to explore this further?' Which means you don't have to argue with managers about whether your idea is any good; you've got evidence."

And even if the experiment *doesn't* produce good test results, it still yields a valuable piece of learning; it becomes a part of their "documentation of all the lessons we've learned over time," Mark says.

The test-and-learn approach isn't right for every company or product. There are instances where releasing an imperfect version of a product, even to a limited audience, may be unwise—or even unsafe. Some entrepreneurs simply aren't comfortable with the idea of putting something flawed out into the world. Sara Blakely of Spanx, for example, believes that "you only get one shot" for your product to make a first impression on customers—and you'd better not squander it with a subpar version of that product. And where you have only one impression through a retail channel versus multiple chances through the internet: She is right!

Many of us struggle with the notion of imperfection. But becoming an experimenter requires us to unlearn earlier lessons from school, where we're taught not to hand in that term paper until it's perfect.

When Kara Goldin, the founder of Hint, made the bold decision not to add sugar or preservatives to her bottled fruit-flavored water, she knew it would mean that the drinks would have too short a shelf life. But she still wanted to know if people liked the flavor. So she started selling this imperfect version of Hint even as she was searching for natural ingredients that might extend its shelf life.

"A number of entrepreneurs I've talked to are in this holding pattern because they think that something needs to be perfect before bringing it to market," Kara says. "If you're not okay with flying the plane as you're building it, if that really makes you uncomfortable, then you're in trouble."

Of course, that's not to say that you should release a shoddy or nonfunctioning product. "I tell entrepreneurs, 'If you don't think that your product is perfect, but you think it's *pretty good*—and you want to figure out if it's going to get some sort of reception—then get it into some stores,'" Kara says. "Just get it out there and you can always improve it along the way."

Just-in-time learning

Remember **Melanie Perkins**'s first experience as an entrepreneur, selling handmade scarves to small boutiques around her hometown of Perth, Australia, at age fifteen? As she says in Chapter 2, she learned that she could take on something that was really scary and then succeed. And it also meant that she could make a business herself rather than having to work for someone else. "Both of those learnings at such a young age really helped to shape where I was going," she says.

The path from selling chunky scarves to building and running Canva, a global design platform with fifty million users, came with a lot more of what she calls "just-in-time learning." When she and her partner, Cliff Obrecht, first decided to launch a design tool, they started small in order to learn: "We intentionally tackled the niche market of school yearbooks, because we didn't have the resources or experience to tackle the entire market at the start," she says. They learned a lot about user testing, gathering feedback, customer service. And as their first company, Fusion Books, found passionate users, they started learning something new: how to scale a startup.

As she looks back on this period, Melanie says: "I feel like every single lesson that you learn in a startup is just in time—or sometimes just after you needed to know it."

She knew that to deliver the new product she wanted—a global design platform that was dependable, rock-solid, and extremely high quality—she needed VC funding to scale it globally and hire tech talent. Which was not in her wheelhouse. "I went in with a learning mindset. I had no other option, to be frank."

"Even though we'd been a startup, we didn't know anything much about startups or venture capital. I didn't understand, when someone says, 'I will fund you,' that didn't mean that they were going to fund your entire company for the rest of its lifetime. What it actually meant was, 'I would be interested to participate as an angel in a larger round that you need to put together.'"

Melanie went looking for VCs to talk to. She'd met a Silicon Valley funder, Bill Tai, when he was over in Australia for a conference, and they hit it off; he invited her to come visit him in the Bay Area next time she was there. Every year, Bill holds his own rather unusual annual conference in the Bay Area, where he gathers a crew of entrepreneurs and VCs and they all go kite surfing. "So, of course, I had to learn kite surfing," Melanie says. "I'd never had any experience kite surfing whatsoever. It was horrible. I was wearing this full body suit, it was cold, apparently there are sharks around.

"But it worked. I got an invite to this kite-surfing entrepreneurship conference. I got to do a talk one morning—the scariest talk of my life. I ended up meeting a bunch of great people through that process. It was terrifying, speaking to the most accomplished room of investors and entrepreneurs I'd ever met. And our first pitch ever was terrifying, but it was really helpful because we got a lot of feedback."

Here was another just-in-time learning. Melanie did not hit her first pitch out of the park. In fact, finding the investors Canva needed took quite a while. She learned to frame each pitch as an opportunity to learn and to refine the next pitch: "Every time we did a pitch, at the end of the pitch, investors would have a certain number of questions. And so, if we could just alleviate all those questions by pre-answering them, by the time we got to the end of the pitch, they wouldn't have any questions, and all they could do was say that they'd invest. That was our theory. And eventually it worked."

This is what just-in-time learning looks like: putting your idea out there and truly listening to what you get back, good or bad—then acting on it, iterating, and trying again. Every new objection they heard to their pitch got added to their knowledge store. As they refined their deck, they also learned which investors were most likely to hear them out, and what types of advisors would give investors more confidence. Most importantly, they learned more about who they were as a company. In some pitches, "there was quite a disconnect between our mission- and goals-driven style of thinking and a more iterative Lean Startup approach." These investors, she realized, "were not going to ever get on board with the way we were thinking, because we've always been and continue to be very much long-term thinkers."

Melanie and her partners did not start their entrepreneurial journey knowing everything they needed to know. Nor should they have. When you have an idea that you want to make the foundation of your company, you can't afford to spend twenty years prepping for the job you want one day. By the time you're ready to start, someone else has long since taken your idea and run with it.

Instead, you need to learn as you go, solving more and more complex problems. And with luck, learning the answers to your questions just in time.

Suddenly, CEO

Tobi Lütke had two passions: snowboarding and programming. And he launched his online snowboard store, Snowdevil, to combine the two. But then something unexpected happened. There were more takers for his e-commerce software than for his snowboards.

After a series of twists and turns (which you can read about in Chapter 8), Tobi and his co-founder saw the bigger opportunity at play. They shed their roots in sporting goods and refashioned themselves as the e-commerce platform **Shopify**. But as they started to grow, Tobi's co-founder, who managed business affairs, jumped ship. It just wasn't what he signed up for.

Tobi wasn't sure what to do. He didn't see himself as the business guy. In fact, the business side of his company was a black box for him—something separate from his role as the tech guy. "To me, business people were all kind of weird people," he says. "Like, I didn't know what they did. The real people who carried the show were the engineers, right? At least that's the way I was thinking back in those days."

Tobi spent the next two years searching for a CEO for his fledgling company. Eventually, an angel investor took him aside and told him he'd probably never find anyone who would care as much about Shopify as Tobi did.

So Tobi, the engineer, became Tobi, the CEO. And now all he needed was to learn how to do that job.

"I started the same way I start everything," he says. "I thought, *Okay, I have no idea what this is like, I don't know the components of it or the shape of it all. So let's read some books on it.*" The first book he read was Andy Grove's *High Output Management*. "Andy taught me that building a business sounds a whole lot like an engineering challenge. And that gave me a lot of hope. I tried to divide everything about every problem I had into smaller problems—the way I do it when I design software—and took it one step at a time."

This crash course on leadership isn't uncommon for engineers-turned-CEO. Dropbox founder Drew Houston has a similar story. When Drew was twenty-one, on leave from MIT and starting up an online SAT prep course venture, he decided he needed his own prep course on the fundamentals of running a company—which he taught to himself, primarily by reading.

Off the top of his head, Drew can rattle off the names of the books that comprised his course of study: *Competing Against Luck* by Clay Christensen and Karen Dillon; *The Effective Executive* by Peter Drucker; Ben Horowitz's *The Hard Thing about Hard Things*; *Becoming* by Steve Jobs; *The Hard Drive*, the story of Microsoft; *Founders at Work* by Jessica Livingston; and the aforementioned Andy Grove book ("probably my single favorite book on management," says Drew).

Drew isn't just listing impressive-sounding titles. Name a book, and he can tell you what insights he took away, and how he has applied those learnings again and again as his companies—and his experience—have scaled.

"I've always found it incredibly helpful to be systematic about training yourself," he says, "because no one's going to do it for you." While Drew felt very secure in his knowledge of engineering and getting a product out to market, "I did not know anything about sales or marketing or financing a company or managing people. And there's not a lot of time to learn it."

It's a feeling every founder knows. And Drew attacked the challenge of learning how to run a company like a student cramming for the SATs the night before the exam. "I'd go on Amazon and type in, say, 'sales marketing strategy,'" he says, "and buy the top-rated books—and just crank through them." When he came across a book he thought could be particularly useful, he'd jot down notes in the margin and study it like a textbook—a habit that continues to this day, and one that he makes sure to instill in other leaders in his company as well. He and his team pick a book to read for their leadership-team offsites every quarter, and for a larger offsite that takes place twice a year.

REID'S THEORIES ON LEARNING

Be a learn-it-all, not a know-it-all

When you're trying to do something that hasn't been done before, you often find yourself in a state of supreme ignorance. What enables entrepreneurs to thrive in those conditions is the speed at which they zip up a learning curve.

Keep moving away from what you know

Success imprints even more strongly than failure. So when you've figured out something that works or you've found success in a particular area, there's a natural tendency to stay put. But infinite learners know that if you stand still or keep doing the same things that worked in the past, the world will leave you behind.

Collect wisdom along the way

Business leaders and entrepreneurs often take a zigzag route to get to their destination. At each stop they should absorb useful bits of learning and add them to their greater understanding of the world.

Teach yourself to lead

Entrepreneurs who know how to launch a new company often have no idea how to actually *run* a new company. But there are many ways to learn—by reading, consulting with mentors, and partnering with investors who have worked with other CEOs who've gone through the startup process.

Experiment to learn, and learn to experiment

Your assumptions about what your users or customers want will never be exactly right. Testing a real product with real people as soon as possible is the fastest way to build something that can scale.

7

Watch What They Do, Not What They Say

I t was early days at Google, long before Google Docs or Google Maps or Gmail made their way onto the world's screens. The company's founding team had just launched their fledgling search engine, and they were singularly, obsessively focused on what they called "excellence in search." The problem was, they didn't know what "excellence in search" actually looked like.

Their home page was brilliantly simple—just a search box and two buttons, one of which said, "I'm feeling lucky." It was a radical departure from cluttered portals like Yahoo! that were popular at the time. The search results page was just as contrarian. No ads. No news headlines. Just really good search results. But how many should they have? And what should they look like?

Co-founder Larry Page wanted Google's design to be based on objective data, rather than subjective design sensibilities. So he had his engineers build something they called the "experiment framework." **Marissa Mayer**, a key engineer on the Google Search team, implemented the first of these experiments, designed to determine the ideal number of search results to display after a user typed in a query.

As a first step, Marissa surveyed users, asking how many search results they wanted to see per page. Was it twenty? Twenty-five? The answer was thirty. Users' feedback was clear: The more results you showed people per page the better. Based on what people *said*, at least.

But something unexpected happened during the next test, when they watched how users actually behaved. Google deployed different versions of the search results page, each identical except showing a different number of results, and counted: How many searches did a user perform? How many pages deep did they go? And how many users abandoned the site altogether?

It became clear that in reality, less was actually more.

The magic number was ten results per page, rather than the thirty the survey data had indicated. "When we looked at first-page search results requested per user," Marissa says, "it fell off dramatically between ten and twenty; twenty-five was even worse; thirty was worst of all."

What accounted for this dramatic gap between users' perceptions and their actions? It turned out more results per page came at a cost—one that was extremely important to users, even if they didn't realize it consciously: *speed*. A page with twenty or thirty results loaded more slowly than a page with ten. The difference in load time was barely perceptible, but the impact was undeniable.

"Time matters a lot more to people than they usually articulate," Marissa said. "Waiting that split second longer for more results was something people didn't want to do—especially since the first ten results were generally good enough."

This discovery had a huge impact on Google—it was a formative lesson not only on the specific question "How many search results per page do users want?" and on the primacy of speed, but also on the process of truly understanding user feedback. Surveys are great when you need to understand nuanced sentiment and feelings. But if you want to understand what your users will actually do, you need to watch them do things.

· · ·

This chapter is about developing a product or company in tandem with your customers—deeply understanding what they want and fine-tuning your product to serve them.

Many leaders have been taught that the way to understand their users is to listen to them: Survey them. Hold focus groups with them. Read their reviews, their social posts, and their incoming emails. And all of those techniques *will* get you closer to your users—helping you understand what your product means to people and spot opportunities for growth.

But listening to users can also lead you astray.

In her search result experiment, Marissa discovered what all great product managers and entrepreneurs know: There's often a vast divide between what customers say they want—and what they actually do. If you follow their suggestions too literally, you can find yourself without followers. An essential skill for anyone bringing a new product or service into the world is to balance those two forms of user feedback—and when in doubt, watch what they do, not what they say.

The problem with predicting the future

Something similar happened at Facebook, which famously began as a service for Harvard students before spreading to other universities and then the wider world. But if founder **Mark Zuckerberg** had listened to what those early users told him, it would've been a different story.

It seemed clear that the one thing Harvard students loved most about Facebook was its exclusivity. So when Facebook first launched at Yale, Mark says, "All the people at Harvard were like, 'Oh, come on. *Them?*' Then you go from Yale to launch at Columbia, and the people at Yale say, 'Aw really? Those guys?'" Each time Facebook expanded to a new campus, existing users complained. But no one deleted their profiles or abandoned the site; in fact, they used it more than ever. "As the network grew and became stronger, they actually *liked* being part of that," Mark says.

The same thing happened when Facebook added its photo-tagging feature, which meant friends in your network might see you in pictures you weren't even aware of. When Mark described this new feature, "most people would say, 'I don't want that product! No, no, no! I don't want that.'" But again, their behavior told a different story. Mark's takeaway: "People are very poor at predicting their own reactions to new things."

Mark's observation has been borne out time and time again for companies across industries. Customers don't always do what they say. And there are a lot of reasons for that. Sometimes, they self-report in a way that's more aspirational than practical. For example, most city dwellers will tell you they care about their city having an opera house, but few actually buy opera tickets. Other times, their behavior is influenced by factors they don't fully grasp, like how quickly they get search results.

So if you want **to truly learn from your customers, you have to be willing to follow them wherever they lead you, and even let them hijack your product** and use it in ways you hadn't intended. Of course you can always ask for feedback. But sometimes it's valuable to ignore what they say, and just watch what they do.

To be a leader, first be a follower

Julia Hartz was a fourteen-year-old barista at the Ugly Mug coffee shop in Santa Cruz when she had her first painful brush with an angry customer. Actually, there were several brushes.

"I learned how to make a great latte there," Julia recalls. "But this woman would show up at the door at 5:55 A.M. and walk in and yell at me for a good fifteen minutes about how bad the coffee was." This went on for weeks. "Then, I just realized one day: She didn't have anyone to talk to. It wasn't about me. It's not about the latte."

It's not about the latte. Almost everything you need to know about customer service is contained in that sentence. Because often, your most passionate customers are also the crankiest. And cranky customer feedback turns the flywheel of your company.

"That was one of the most important lessons I've ever learned in my life," Julia says. She learned how to listen, and also how to hear what was underneath the words. **Eventbrite**, the event-management website Julia co-founded, has thrived in part because she knows how to figure out what's *really* driving her users.

By 2006, the online ticketing space was already crowded. But Julia and her soon-to-be husband, Kevin Hartz, along with a third partner, saw an opportunity to serve a neglected segment: small-event organizers. These customers had little, if any, money to spend on their events. But there were *a lot* of them.

Julia decided early on that Eventbrite would "build the product hand in hand with our earliest users." And those early users were mainly tech bloggers, who began using the platform to host meetups.

Here's the thing about tech bloggers—they are a very vocal bunch. "We created a very tight feedback loop with literally the most critical people you could possibly have using your product," Julia says. "We all tend to be gluttons for punishment around here."

Among these vocal early customers was the tech blog TechCrunch. It's hard to imagine a more finicky audience for your new technology than actual tech critics. But in Julia's eyes, their sharp tongues—and even sharper observations—made the TechCrunch team an ideal partner.

"There's no better way to get great feedback than to build a product for people who build them themselves or write about them all the time," she says.

In those early days, Julia went to extremes to keep Eventbrite's feedback loop spinning. Both she and Kevin gave out their cellphone numbers where they could be reached to handle their customers' real-time issues and complaints. By reacting to all this feedback fast, Eventbrite was able to create a revenue stream from the long tail of small-event organizers that their competitors had left on the table.

Pretty soon, those TechCrunch meetups Eventbrite helped ticket grew into the TechCrunch Disrupt Conference—a dominant feature on the tech industry calendar. Year after year, Eventbrite found a larger, equally vocal customer base, helping them further refine their product, setting them up to service bigger and more complex events. Eventbrite was evolving in sync with its customers.

But as much as Julia and her team paid attention to what customers were saying, the real learnings came from closely monitoring what customers were *doing* with Eventbrite, even as they moved into unexpected new areas. Which was how they first learned that their platform had become a part of the East Coast speed-dating scene, for example, and later a brisk business developed among purveyors of some unusual fads—like goat yoga.

"When we started to see the platform be organically adopted by event creators in different categories and in different locations—that's when the lightbulb went on for us," Julia says. She began to see how Eventbrite might scale. But first she needed a way to identify and understand the distinct needs and priorities of each group.

The key to observing your customer is *not* to do it with a bias toward what you're trying to confirm, or a hypothesis you're trying to prove. Instead, keep an open mind and let the behavior speak for itself.

"At the beginning, organizers were asking us to help them sell tickets and to be reliable in transacting tickets," Julia says. "When we really observed who the organizers were and what their needs were, though, we realized that building an enablement platform—with marketplace dynamics on top—would be one of the most important things that we could do for them."

As Eventbrite delved into the psyches of event planners, they found it wasn't always a happy place. "Event planning is an anxiety-ridden process," says Julia. There's a reason "event organizer" is routinely listed among the top five most stressful jobs in the United States. The worries are endless: *Are people going to show up? Am I going to sell this out? Is the talent going to show up? Is the venue going to come through? Are the vendors going to deliver? What will go wrong?*

But Julia also realized that event planners can be some of the most inventive, entrepreneurially minded people she'd worked with. Case in point: a man named Chad Collins. Chad and his daughter had started making videos of their LEGO creations and posting them on a YouTube channel, and within a year they'd amassed hundreds of videos and millions of followers. One day, Chad's daughter casually remarked, "It'd be fun to do this with other people who love LEGO." Chad ended up going on Eventbrite and setting up a LEGO enthusiast event called Brick Fest Live—and sold five thousand tickets right out of the gate.

But Chad didn't stop there—he started thinking about other types of events he could organize, including festivals for gamers, inventors, and more. "Now he's a full-time event entrepreneur," Julia says. "I'm slightly obsessed with Chad, to the point that I'm sure he's now got a restraining order out on me, but it's because he embodies that entrepreneur we so desperately want to support."

Over time, EventBrite's original customers grew larger, and that in turn attracted new and larger events—conferences, summits, festivals. And they continued their practice of watching customers closely—not just digitally but in real life as well. Julia's team started to notice that at larger events and festivals, there were often bottlenecks getting people through the doors. So Eventbrite invested in RFID technology to allow festival planners to scan tickets electronically as people passed by a chip reader.

But rather than investing in tech and declaring the problem solved, Julia's team went out to observe this new technology in action. It turns out that the RFID chip readers were themselves embedded in huge immovable gates that created more bottlenecks. So Eventbrite made a bold move for a company that had, until that point, been an entirely digital platform. They went hardware and actually *made something*: a small, specially designed RFID reader that could be clamped to any existing gate.

After they built a prototype, they went out *yet again* to observe it in use. The new chip-reading device worked well—except it required a wrench to be moved from one gate to another. Who walks around with a wrench in their back pocket? So Eventbrite created yet *another* version with an easy-to-use clamp. Problem, finally, solved.

If it sounds like digging this deep into everyday customer problems creates headaches, well, that's true. But Julia is convinced that these efforts have an upside: Each time Eventbrite gets a jump on helping one customer solve a challenge, they can turn around and offer the same solution to other event organizers—pre-solving for problems the organizers may not even know they have. The key is to look for those universal challenges: ones for which you can provide a scalable solution.

That kind of proactive problem solving has enabled Eventbrite to grow from a scrappy startup to a company with a thousand employees at fourteen offices in eleven countries. Being a follower made them a market leader.

REID'S ANALYSIS | Treat your customers as your scouts

As a company founder, you are like a field general. As such, you're presented with many tempting targets for your efforts, as well as severely limited time and resources. You need a way to identify the most strategic targets and then quickly bring your arsenal to bear.

But if you pay attention only to what your customers say and not to what they do, you may end up with bullets flying in the wrong direction. If you're too reactive to what your customers say, you risk losing focus on your core product. If you listen to what too many customers say, you risk spreading yourself too thin, trying to be all things to all people.

One of the best ways to take your cue from what customers *do* (rather than what they say) is to treat your customers as your scouts, pushing the frontiers of your early product, and bringing back important insights that you can use. Then you have to hone your ability to interpret that information and make sure you're primed to act on this feedback as quickly as you can.

The best entrepreneurs devote themselves to understanding and serving a tiny cohort of customers that serve as an accurate proxy for their future customer base. And that's so important because meeting the needs of these early customers may be precisely what enables them to evolve their product for the mass market. That's one reason I encourage entrepreneurs to release a product earlier than they'd like. Release, observe, react—over and over again.

It isn't just about speed, and it certainly isn't about sloppiness, but rather a precise dance between a tiny team and its growing user base. The users normally take the lead—but not always. Sometimes the founder has to break the choreography and give the users a twirl.

The most visionary founders can picture in vivid detail what their customers want. But these founders also recognize that that picture has been painted by their overly active imaginations, and they need to be ready to revise this imagined future, based on the reality of customer feedback. You can't get that feedback simply by describing the future to your customers, because most people are not good at accurately visualizing the future.

Watch what they do—and what they don't do

In the early days of Dropbox, **Drew Houston** was worried—really worried. And he had good reason. His customers were disappearing in droves, and he didn't understand why. A full 60 percent of all people who signed up to Dropbox via referral abandoned the service and never came back.

"This was stressing us out," Drew says. "So we went on Craigslist and offered forty bucks to anyone who'd come in for a half hour— a poor man's usability test."

They sat respondents in front of a computer and gave them basic instructions: "This is an invitation to Dropbox in your email. Go from here to sharing a file with this email address."

Drew's team planned to watch each user complete the task and look for clues on what could be improved. They found a lot more than they bargained for.

"Zero of the five people succeeded, zero of the five even came close," he said. "Most couldn't even figure out how to download it. This was just stunning, because we're like, 'Oh my god, this is the worst product ever created. This is the hardest thing. What kind of rocket scientist could figure this out?'"

This "poor man's usability test" was what we'd simply call "a usability test"—and an effective one at that. Drew's team discovered there was a lot they needed to learn about how their product was being used in the wild. They went on to watch their paid users more intently and found that this wasn't the only stumbling block.

"Someone would start the download, but the download would take too long, so they'd begin browsing something else. But then they would click back on the browser and couldn't figure out where it downloaded. Little things like that." But these "little things" were having a big impact on whether or not a customer would actually use the product.

Drew and his team leapt into triage mode, moving between user tests and product improvements. Eventually, they sanded down all the rough edges in user experience. And it became a lesson that Drew has kept top-of-mind over the years: Never assume that what's intuitive to your team is easy for users. The only way to be sure is to watch them.

See how they . . . cheat

Jenn Hyman's entire company was inspired by watching what women do. First (as we read in Chapter 3), she watched her sister stare mournfully into an overflowing closet and declare she had nothing to wear to a party that night. She had already been captured on social media in every outfit she owned. It was all repeats! Then Jenn learned from the president of a major department store that some of their best customers found a way to "rent" their designer dresses. They'd leave the tags on when they wore them to a single event, and return them the following week.

When she launched Rent the Runway, a service that rents designer dresses and gowns, Jenn assumed that her customers would wear their rented gear to a single special event: a prom, a gala, a cocktail party. But her customers found a clever way to get more bang for their buck, Jenn says: "They would keep the cocktail dress they had rented for a party they had on a Saturday night, and they'd wear it in to work on Monday with a black blazer over it."

Jenn could have wrung her hands over the additional wear and tear on the dresses (dry-cleaning and shipping are the secret engines behind the business; in fact, Rent the Runway operates the world's largest dry-cleaning operation). She could have made the one-use expectation more explicit or tightened the rules around additional rental days. But instead, she saw an opportunity hidden inside this "cheat." An invitation to play a much bigger role in her customer's lives.

Jenn realized something that made immediate, intuitive sense: Special events weren't the only times her customers wanted to feel more confident in the way they looked. It was happening five days a week. Rent the Runway had an opportunity to become part of their customers' everyday wardrobe—and that was a much bigger business. Jenn pivoted from an à la carte business model, renting one dress at a time, to a subscription service that let users rent several pieces at a time and rotate them out. This "closet in the cloud" became the new foundation for the business.

• • •

Payal Kadakia spent her childhood performing traditional Indian dance. As an adult, she still feels happiest and most herself in a dance class. "I've danced my entire life. It's such a big core part of who I am. I danced through MIT, I danced through Bain. It was something I just never let go of." As we read in Chapter 4, her deep connection to dance created a profound belief that the most reliable fitness routine should feel less like a chore and more like a calling—or an escape. You shouldn't have to force yourself to go to class; your class should be a source of inspiration.

In 2012, driven by this conviction, Payal launched a company that was first called Classtivity, an online hub where users could sign up for all types of classes—not just fitness, but painting classes, pottery classes, and just about any activity you could hope to master. Her business model was to take a cut of each class that was booked through the site.

But customers were using the site more for search than for booking. "We had thousands of classes listed, a beautiful design," Payal remembers. "And we did about ten reservations a month. It was terrible."

Payal wasn't the first entrepreneur to have an empty stadium on opening day. And she won't be the last. It almost always means you got a key assumption wrong. "That's when I realized this was not the way to approach this behavioral change we wanted to create."

Noticing that lots of fitness studios were incentivizing people to join by offering a certain number of free classes, Payal wondered, *What if we could offer a thirty-day period where people could try ten different kinds of classes?* She figured that once they found their "fitness calling," it would be far easier to get them to return. So she packaged the fitness classes together into one product called a Passport, which allowed a user to hop from class to class.

The Passport was an immediate success—so much so that when their thirty-day grand tour expired, some users began "forging" passports, cheating the system by signing up for a new passport from a different email address.

Payal could have responded by cracking down on the users who were double-dipping. But instead she asked herself: *Why are they doing this?* By bending her product, the forgers had pointed the way to a new opportunity. Customers weren't discovering *one* true "fitness calling"—they were finding inspiration through variety. "They wanted to do a spin class on Monday, a dance class on Thursday, a yoga class on Saturday," she says. Out of this realization emerged an idea for a subscription model that would essentially allow customers to renew their passport any time they wanted (instead of forging new ones). "So, we did a survey, and 95 percent of our users said they would buy the product again if they could go back to their favorite studios."

One pass that granted fitness dabblers entry into a wide range of classes at a confederation of gyms—that was a truly scalable idea. In 2013, Classtivity reinvented itself as ClassPass. For a $99 monthly fee, users get ten classes a month, and they can dabble away. ClassPass was an instant hit, and it is now in more than forty cities worldwide.

Once Payal realized that her core customer was the fitness lover who loved variety, ClassPass started to grow—and fast.

Every customer-facing business deals with "churn"—the users who join and then leave—and it's a leader's job to understand why people churn. A significant source of churn at early ClassPass? Members who signed up for ten classes but only made it out to six or eight. They didn't renew, because they didn't get what they paid for. To gather some data on how many classes people actually wanted to attend when they set their own pace, the company rolled out an unlimited membership as a summer test promotion. They found that many users wanted only five classes, not ten, so they started a new lower-priced pass. But users also loved the unlimited pass—and in fact, it was so popular, it inspired copycat competition. Payal knew they had to keep the unlimited pass to compete, without letting it bleed the business dry.

She had little choice—she had to raise the price of the popular unlimited pass. Price hikes are always risky for a startup, but Payal felt it was the only way for the unlimited option to stay on the menu.

Her customers didn't agree. The chatter around it online got loud, and not very nice.

When the unlimited subscription price went up a second time, one user tweeted, "Raise your hand if you've been personally victim-ized by ClassPass."

Another chimed in, "No no. Canceling my membership NOW."

Ouch.

But here's the thing: For all the threats to defect, very few custom-ers did. If she'd listened to the squawkers, Payal might have scaled back the offering to keep prices down. But the sheer variety of classes is precisely what made ClassPass a hit. Payal kept her eye on customer behavior—what they *did*, not what they tweeted. When the dust set-tled, "we lost very few of our members."

Some amount of backlash on price hikes is inevitable—it's just human nature. No one *wants* to pay more for anything. But if your vi-sion and your business model are truly aligned and you've created something people love, your users will likely drop their pitchforks. As Payal reflects on it, she maintains that ClassPass was never "just about the prices. It's a feeling of being limitless. We're still on that journey of making sure that the product feels that way. And I think that's on us to figure out, because that is what our core mission is."

Welcome the hijackers

What do you do after you launch a world-changing dating app? Well, first, you might vow never to launch another one, ever again. As trans-formative as Tinder's "swipe right" was, its co-founder, **Whitney Wolfe Herd,** knew it also empowered some seriously bad behavior, even ha-rassment. And despite her never-again vow, she continued to think about how an app could help people connect more authentically and meaningfully. That became her goal in founding **Bumble,** a dating app that empowers women to make the first move. (At launch, the service was focused on heterosexual couples.) The idea immediately reso-nated with test users, but the product team worried that women might be reluctant to start a dialogue. To provide a nudge, when the app matched women with potential partners, it gave women just twenty-four hours to send the first message. If they didn't send the message, the match was gone. Whitney and her team didn't think men needed that same incentive to respond, so men were allowed to take as long as they wanted.

REID'S ANALYSIS | How to avoid a mob reaction

ClassPass was not the first company to experience customer outrage over pricing. And they definitely won't be the last. When Netflix raised its subscription prices, for example, customers were outraged—not about the new price tag per se, but about how it made them feel. "I can definitely afford it," one angry ex-customer said, "but I dropped them on principle."

Like it or not, raising prices can be unavoidable for fast-growing companies. What often happens is that you start with a pricing structure that's unsustainable because it's the only way to hook that vital set of early users. But if you stay with that business model for too long, your company won't survive.

This was true of PayPal. Our early promise to pay customers $10 for adding a friend to the platform was an easy, effective way to build out our early user base. But our burn rate was tens of millions of dollars each month as a result. Eventually, it got so expensive that co-founder Peter Thiel wanted to scrap the entire incentive (even though it was his idea in the first place) in order to keep costs down.

But eventually we found a way to keep that sparkly, eye-catching promise intact. We just had to dim the sparkles a bit. We still gave users and their friends that gift of $10 each, but to get it, they had to give us a little more: They would have to enter their credit card, validate their bank account, and load fifty bucks into their new PayPal account. No one could accuse us of not keeping our promise. But once we made people work a little harder for it, the number of customers we actually had to pay immediately went down.

When you're making the critical transition from bleeding your business to saving your business, you have to be hyperaware of your messaging if you want to avoid a mob reaction. Mobs rally behind very simple statements. They're going to get fired up if they read "PayPal stops giving new users the money that they promised them!" But they're probably not going to linger for too long on "PayPal asks for slightly more information from new users but continues to give them the money they promised them."

You also have to know what it is about your product that customers find invaluable, and then protect that above all else. That's the only promise that really matters. Pricing riots die down, and if you are selling something customers really love, they are eventually going to let you out of the doghouse.

"So we launch the product," says Whitney, "and we have the best intentions in mind, genuinely." And then women users spoke up, saying, in effect, "We get why you're giving us a twenty-four-hour time constraint. That's fine. But it's not fair that *he* doesn't have to respond to *me*."

"We heard the feedback once, totally recognized it," Whitney says. "Heard it twice, it was in development. We moved fast." Bumble added a requirement for men to respond within twenty-four hours, apologized for the unintentional double standard, and thanked their users for helping them make a positive tweak to the app.

"Like any obsessive founder or CEO," says Whitney, "for the first two or three years I spent the better part of my waking hours on the product. Tinkering with it. Playing with it. Experimenting, talking to people: *Why are you here? How did you hear about this—exactly when and where?* I wanted to go into the mind of the user."

As she did, Whitney noticed something. "We saw young women and men alike saying, 'Not here for dating. Husband just got a new job somewhere.' Or 'Looking for this new life thing.' It had nothing to do with dating."

It turned out the Bumble rule of interaction—that a woman could make the first move with the help of the app—had appeal not just for finding dates but for finding friends, too.

"We realized our users were basically hijacking our product to use it in a different way," Whitney says. "For instance, we would meet customers and they would say, 'I just found my roommate on Bumble.'"

Her users had forged a new path, and Whitney had to race to keep up. Her team quickly built Bumble BFF for finding platonic friendships.

"Lo and behold, inside BFF, they start networking with each other," says Whitney. "They don't want roommates. They don't want friends. They don't want to go to yoga. They want to build a business. They want to meet someone that works in HR recruiting."

So in 2017, a new app mode designed for professional networking and mentoring was born: Bumble Bizz.

Each of these ideas was inspired by customers who were using the app in ways Whitney and her team hadn't imagined. By listening and watching, they found unexpected opportunities for growth.

"Our expansion was really just letting the users operate as they wanted and going with them," Whitney says. "Humans just want to connect. You can't define what they're looking for. You've got to let them define that. And so we're just trying to build a platform where people can connect."

As Bumble expands internationally, Whitney remains vigilant about spotting customer-driven tweaks that will allow Bumble to scale in different cultures. User norms will be especially tested as Bumble expands further into India.

"While women now are more empowered than they've ever been and their voices are being heard," says Whitney, "some women in the Indian culture aren't even allowed to talk to men there, let alone be on a dating app—let alone *make the first move*."

But that's changing quickly. In its first few weeks in India, a million women made "first moves." As Whitney says, "It will be interesting to see how it works—and where our customers in India lead us."

The Culture Code

It started as a conversation among startup CEOs. Brian Halligan, co-founder and CEO of HubSpot, had joined a group of fellow founders, who would convene to swap stories and advice. As his co-founder and CTO Dharmesh Shah describes it, "There were a group of CEOs that got together once a quarter. They would sit around in a circle— I always pictured it like group therapy for CEOs."

This particular meeting took place early in HubSpot's history. The CRM (customer relationship management) platform was in its fourth year, and tightly focused on serving other fast-scaling startups. The theme for the meeting was culture, and Brian didn't have a lot to add. "When it was Brian's turn, he was like, 'Well, that's not something we're really spending time on. We're busy building product, and we're busy selling product, and culture is something we'll deal with some other day.'"

This didn't sit well with the circle of CEOs. "They came down on him hard. They were like, 'Brian, we don't think you understand. There's nothing more important you can work on than culture. That's the thing that will define the company's destiny over the long term. If you don't get that right, nothing else will matter.'"

Brian took that in and thought it sounded like a job for Dharmesh—a conclusion Dharmesh found . . . puzzling. His initial reaction: resistance. He still remembers his reaction: "Of all people to even look at culture, I'm the least qualified. I know nothing about it. I'm an introvert and antisocial. This doesn't make any sense."

He was a bit baffled by the assignment. "But being the good cofounder that I am, I'm like, 'Okay, I'll dig into it.'"

Dharmesh found himself far outside his comfort zone as he tackled the question of culture. A computer scientist by training and disposition, he took a data-driven approach. He started asking questions and analyzing results.

Dharmesh sent a survey to all HubSpot employees, asking two questions: (1) "On a scale of zero to 10, how likely are you to recommend HubSpot as a place to work?" (2) "Why did you provide that answer?"

Note: If you have experience with customer satisfaction surveys, you'll recognize that first question as the one used to measure a brand's Net Promoter Score. It's widely agreed that a person's willingness to recommend a product is a reliable indicator of happiness and loyalty. Dharmesh figured: Why not ask the same about a company? And the result told him a lot.

"We learned two things: One: People were exceptionally happy working at HubSpot. And that was good news. Two: The reason they were happy were the other people at HubSpot. Which was good, but somewhat circular." He wondered: "How do I translate that into something that's kind of actionable?"

Dharmesh's position resonates with many startup founders and team leaders. An employee's happiness is always at least partially dependent on their co-workers. If you like them, your day usually goes pretty well. The question becomes: What is it about those people, specifically, that you like?

To answer that question for HubSpot, Dharmesh—in true technologist form—wrote a formula. He asked himself: "If I were to write a function that was going to calculate the probability of success of any given member of the team, what would the coefficients of that function be? What are the inputs going into that function?"

To gather his inputs, Dharmesh had to answer the question: "What are the attributes of the people that tend to do well at HubSpot?"

He surveyed the staff again, and people identified, among other things, *humility*. "People like the fact that the other people at HubSpot didn't have ego, didn't have an arrogance about them."

As he identified the different traits and inputs, he put his findings into a short slide deck, which he called the Culture Code. He chose that name "not because it's code of ethics or a code of morals. It's literally code"—the computer code that determined the results.

This deck allowed Dharmesh and Brian to share and codify their lens on culture. It started as 16 slides, for internal use only. But it grew into a public-facing deck with 128 slides, viewed more than 5 million times by both prospective employees and partner companies, looking to define their own culture. (You can see it at CultureCode.com.)

And however you arrive at your culture's key attributes, this step—writing it down, communicating it out—is key. Why? Partly because it's generative. An engaging, up-to-date culture deck reinforces culture for existing employees and draws the right people toward you—including those who might otherwise not have realized they're for you. A culture deck creates a flywheel in which great culture begets more great culture. And great culture in turn creates great work.

But equally important, the act of defining your culture works to combat cultural blind spots. "Every entrepreneur that I know is like, 'Oh yeah, we hire for a culture,'" Dharmesh says. "But my feeling is: 'You are not allowed to say that if you have not expressly written down what your culture is. Otherwise, what you're really saying is we hire people like ourselves.'"

When you define your culture by attributes (humility, curiosity, collaboration . . .), you create a lens for determining cultural fit beyond someone "feeling" right. You allow candidates who don't *look* or *sound* like you to identify with your culture and feel a sense of belonging; and you help your hiring managers to identify those candidates with a lens that circumvents their implicit bias. And that actively prevents a monoculture from taking hold.

Dharmesh's only regret: that they didn't start sooner. "If we were more intentional earlier in the process, we would have recognized earlier the value of diversity. Companies take on all sorts of debt, and we're used to talking about technical debt. But culture debt is also a very real thing. When you have a monoculture—where everyone looks like everyone else—that's some of the highest interest-rate debt you can have in an organization. So if I could do it all over again, I would, on week one, talk about culture."

"There's nothing more important that you can work on more than culture," Dharmesh says—and we agree. "That's the thing that will define the company's destiny over a long term. If you don't get that right, nothing else will matter."

To watch what they do—watch the data

There comes a point in every founder's journey where they need to take a terrifying step: giving someone else the login details for the company inbox. To get to scale, founders need to find systematic ways to understand customer data, beyond their own direct observations and gut reactions. As the event platform Eventbrite grew, co-founder Julia Hartz had to move on from reading every single piece of customer mail herself. She now had teams of engineers and customer support staff to scour the usage data and search-engine traffic, while customer support staff reported back on the emails they received. Julia's new role here? Constantly finding new ways to process all that feedback.

One of her techniques is a standing meeting called Hearts to Hartz, bringing together a cross-section of Eventbrite staff, including both data analysts and the support team who actually talk to customers. "To watch them connect, and to watch how their experiences could converge, was pretty fascinating," Julia says. "It was like this manifestation of vision and true empathy for the customer, coupled with what the data is telling us."

You can think of this pairing like one of the vital relationships in *Star Trek*: The data is your Mr. Spock, detached and logical. And customer empathy is your Dr. McCoy, passionate and all too human. To get the best out of each, you need to bring them together.

"I actually think the data insights team we have has in a way benefited from *not* talking to customers all day," says Julia, "because they are actually looking at just the data." The data team could see what people do—rather than what they say they'll do. But the data picture is incomplete until you understand *why*. "Which is where the customer support team comes in," Julia says. "And then looping that together with folks who are really creating that human connection—bringing all of that together creates this matrix picture of where we're seeing heat and light."

This matrix is an essential—and available—tool for any company. When you combine data and empathy, you can see the bigger picture of what your customers want and need. Not just in the present, but in the future.

It's no surprise that a digital platform like Eventbrite relies heavily on data—as well as emotional connection—to inform the fuller picture of their customer. But you might be surprised to learn that Jenn Hyman's clothing rental biz, Rent the Runway, is also deep into data, and always has been.

"Actually, 80 percent of our corporate employees are engineers, data scientists, and product managers," says Jenn. "We have very few people in merchandising and marketing. The first C-level hire that I made was a chief data officer, and he was in my first ten employees. From the very beginning of the company, we were thinking about data.

"We are getting data from our customer over a hundred times a year," says Jenn. "And she's letting us know: *Did she wear it? How many times did she wear it? Did she love it? Was it just okay? What occasion did she wear it to?* All of that data that we receive, we're able to port back both into what we buy or manufacture in the first place to how do we clean it, how do we increase the ROI on that unit, and how do we now fill in the gaps of demand that we see."

It's true that when it comes to clothing, consumer choices are driven largely by emotion. But that doesn't mean that data doesn't have a role to play in helping entrepreneurs better understand those choices. "We understand a huge amount about our customers," says Jenn, "because our customers are telling us not only about their style or their fit preferences, but they're telling us about their lives: They're telling us that they're pregnant before they tell anyone else in their life; they're telling us that they have a business meeting this week or they're going to Miami next weekend. So we understand a whole lot about the users and a lot about the inventory and we're able to match those two datasets together."

As a result, Jenn and her team "know more about what women want to wear than most retailers on Earth," she says. "And that has given us power now to not only buy from brands, but also to take that data to brands and to co-manufacture new collections together."

That's what happened with Jason Wu, a young designer who rocketed to fame after Michelle Obama fell in love with his designs. Based on their data insights, Rent the Runway knew that their customers were very interested in his brand. But they'd also learned that the styles he was producing didn't exactly match up with their customers' needs. Jenn's team took these insights to Wu, and together they created a new line initially called Jason Wu Grey, which proved a huge success.

As Rent the Runway grows, Jenn and her team will be keeping a close eye on the data, watching what their customers do, learning from it, and porting those insights back into both their client-facing and behind-the-scenes businesses, in a reinforcing, healthy loop with their customers.

The counterpoint: When you should listen—closely

You'll always learn more from watching what customers actually do, rather than just listening to what they say. But it's also important to listen. You just have to know what to listen for. And no one listens better than **Mariam Naficy**, founder and CEO of the online design marketplace Minted, a private company with nine-figure revenue.

Whenever Mariam has questions about product or company direction, she invites customers in for focus groups or user tests. But she doesn't delegate this to product developers or marketers—she asks questions herself. "I do a lot of my own focus groups myself," Mariam says. "I moderate them, and I write the scripts. People are shocked when they come in for a focus group, and the CEO is moderating."

Mariam knows the power of hearing *firsthand* what customers are thinking. Their direct, candid responses—in their own words—give

REID'S ANALYSIS | When to ignore your users

Scaling can happen in one of two ways—the easy way and the hard way. And you may not know you're doing it the hard way until it's too late.

The easy kind of scaling is when you got the product right on the first try. When you've created something users love and instinctively want to share.

This kind of scaling happens organically, as users bring in other users.

The hard kind of scaling is when you only get the product half-right. When you've created something users kind of like, and that they'll use, but not something so good that they'll stick with it or share it with others.

Successful products usually happen the first way, but I can think of at least one exception: LinkedIn.

Our early users loved us. They called themselves "open networkers," and even put "LIONs"—"LinkedIn Open Networkers"—in their headline. The problem was, they loved us for something different than what we actually were. They wanted us to be a social network where "everyone should be able to connect to Bill Gates and have him connect back."

But of course that isn't realistic, which is part of the reason why our passionate set of early users were not the users that helped us get to scale. We were grateful, we appreciated their support, but what they ultimately wanted from us wasn't something that we could deliver.

We had a chicken-and-egg dilemma. The truly magical features we envisioned for LinkedIn simply couldn't come to fruition until we had a vast network of users, so that a recruiter could say, "I'm looking for an accountant based in Biloxi, Mississippi, who has a humanities degree plus ten years of work experience," and then find that candidate in one click.

And, unlike the LIONs, those valuable users just weren't going to love us straight out of the gate. So how do you get there? You work in batches, adding one narrow group of users at a time. You've got to find some set of people that are going to use you a lot in the early days. And that may be a small, narrow-but-deep wedge, and then you expand it later.

It's great to have your core users love you, but we got to scale when *other* people started loving us—the kind of people that we were targeting.

her aha moments that third-party reports almost never deliver. So even as Minted scaled, Mariam held on to this direct connection. She finds it fascinating to get inside people's heads—because invariably, what you find there will surprise you. For instance, Mariam learned that charging the same price for different kinds of designer stationery led to a kind of "analysis paralysis." Counterintuitively, she had to change the prices simply to give customers a reason to make a buying decision.

Observing her customers closely also surfaced surprising differences in needs and priorities, just as it had for Julia and her team at Eventbrite. When Gen Xers buy beautifully designed stationery, it turns out they don't care much who created the design. But millennials care deeply, Mariam says. "They told us, 'Why aren't you telling the story of these artists? I need to hear about these people.'"

This is also how Mariam realized that modern weddings are no longer driven by the woman alone; it turns out, millennial men are very involved in the decisions. "They're more involved dads," she says, "and they're more involved husbands. Through a focus group, we learned that our wedding designs were too feminine."

Had she not attended that focus group, Mariam wouldn't have picked up on that nuance. It may not have even made it into the findings, because it was outside the stated purpose of the study. "You wouldn't even think to ask that question," Mariam says. But when you're motivated to pay attention to each response in its entirety—even the details that go beyond the scope of the questions being asked—you may learn something eye-opening.

In the late 1990s, **Robert Pasin** became CEO of **Radio Flyer**, the iconic American brand synonymous with its bright red toy wagons. But the company, founded by his Italian immigrant grandfather in 1918, was at a crossroads. They were losing market share to other, more nimble competitors, who built their wagons and toys out of plastic. He found himself asking some existential questions: *What are we? Are we a manufacturer or a design company? What can we be the best in the world at?*

For guidance, Robert wanted to understand what Radio Flyer *meant* to people. He began to do customer research, asking people to describe the Radio Flyer they had as a kid. Many people talked nostalgically about the wagon, of course. And others had fond memories of the Radio Flyer tricycle.

"We'd ask them to describe the tricycle," Robert remembers, "and they'd say, 'Well, it was shiny and red, and it had chrome handlebars, and a big bell on it. . . .'"

There was only one problem: "We never made a tricycle."

Robert had discovered a hidden nostalgia *for a product they never made*. In response, he could have laughed off this imaginary tricycle his customers had conjured up. Or he could have dismissed the entire research report as invalid. Instead he brought that figment of his customers' imagination to life.

He made the tricycle.

The shiny red Radio Flyer tricycle quickly became one of the company's top products—and the number one brand in tricycles. But more important, Robert realized that customer perception of the brand isn't just about wagons—it's about childhood nostalgia, wholesome outdoor play, and shiny little red *vehicles*. And Radio Flyer has since gone on to make everything from little red scooters to little red Teslas.

REID'S THEORIES ON LEARNING ABOUT—AND FROM—YOUR CUSTOMERS

Watch what they do, not what they say

Watching what your customers are doing—or *trying* to do—with your product can light the way forward. But you have to be careful to pay attention to what they do and not just what they say.

Expect to have your theories of human behavior tested

Your theory about how individuals and groups behave should underlie your strategy, your product design, your incentive program—every decision you make. But be open and alert to when your customers show you a different theory or direction. That could become your product's point of differentiation.

Follow the leaders: Your customers

To grow your business, you may have to give up control. Look for instances when your customers hack or hijack your product, and then go along for the ride.

Get Mr. Spock and Dr. McCoy working together

Customer data is your Mr. Spock, detached and logical. Customer emotion is your Dr. McCoy, passionate and all too human. Think of yourself as Captain Kirk, responsible for making the two work together to get the best out of each.

8

The Art of the Pivot

I n 2004, a new word was invented, for a new kind of media with a special interest for anyone who then owned an Apple iPod. The word was *podcast*. And it gave new momentum to the format that changed the rules of audio forever—allowing anyone to record and distribute their own content, unbeholden to radio's broadcast rules or gatekeepers. The shows weren't *just* for iPods; you could listen to them on any computer. But the catchy new name for the relatively new medium created a swell of interest among early adopters and audiophiles. Ev Williams had a plan to ride that wave.

Ev had already made a name for himself in Silicon Valley with a startup called Blogger, a trailblazing service that enabled users to easily set up their own blogs. Blogger captured the cultural zeitgeist but had a bumpy run as a business; in Blogger's last year as an independent company, Ev worked on the site alone, without staff or salary. He eventually sold to Google. Success! But now Ev was ready to try a different form of communication.

His underlying passion was connecting people—or rather, con-

necting their ideas—through technology. He had grown up on a farm
in Nebraska, and he always felt like a bit of an outsider—a school-
oriented kid in a football-oriented town. He got interested in computer programming, and then online bulletin boards, as a way to
connect with people far from his small town. But what really set his
imagination ablaze was an article he read in the first issue of *Wired*
magazine. "The article talked about connecting all the brains on the
planet," Ev recalls. This vision led him to move to Silicon Valley and
start Blogger, and now it had piqued his curiosity about podcasting.

And Ev figured if people had been so eager to express themselves
in writing, they might be even more likely to share ideas online by talking. He secured $5 million in funding and built a platform that made
it easy for podcasters to publish their work and listeners to discover
content. He founded a new company, Odeo, and envisioned it as the
premier platform for podcasting.

Then, just as Ev was getting Odeo off the ground, he discovered
that a competitor was entering the field.

And not just any competitor. Apple.

In 2005, Apple announced that it would integrate podcasts into its
iTunes software, already popular for music, making it infinitely easier
for iPod users to access podcasts. Of course, Apple's installed base of
iPod owners represented the vast majority of Odeo's potential audience. It was a devastating blow.

"It kind of blew our minds," Ev says.

Ev wasn't sure what his next move would be. He went to his board
of directors and said, "Should we shut down? Should we give the
money back?"

But to Ev's surprise, the board members asked if he had any other
ideas to pursue. "And I thought, 'Sure, I've got ideas. I always have
ideas.'" And Ev knew how to get even more ideas to supplement his
own. "I went to the Odeo team and said, 'I don't know if podcasting is
still our thing. Who's got ideas?'"

Ev and his team turned to a tried-and-true method of generating
ideas: the hackathon. The process is simple: You bring together all
your employees and challenge them to come up with an idea they can
build in one marathon work session. Often, a hackathon is intended to
solve for a narrow, specific problem—but in this case, it was an at-

tempt to answer a more fundamental question: *What should we do next?*

This hackathon proved not just fruitful but historically so. Odeo's co-founder Biz Stone and web designer Jack Dorsey came up with the winning idea—a group texting product that grew out of some side tinkering Biz and Jack had been doing with text messaging. Ev quickly warmed to the idea because it reminded him of something he'd done back in his Blogger days.

"I built a blog for status updates, and shared it with my Blogger team," says Ev. "Then I went on a family trip and during the trip, I was sending status updates to a blog. It felt like something interesting—sharing this thing that you didn't normally share."

Those "status updates" would later be known as tweets, and the product, of course, would become **Twitter**.

Ev and his team sensed very quickly that Twitter had great potential. Which raised a difficult question: Was it time to pivot away from Odeo entirely and toward this new thing called Twitter?

It wasn't an easy call. At board meetings, Ev presented the latest developments on Twitter and updates on Odeo—which, it seemed, was not quite ready to die. It wasn't growing, but it did have engaged users. And this is often the most painful kind of decision for a leader. **It's easy to kill a product that's failing; it's much harder—and more strategic—to kill one that lacks the potential to truly scale.**

"I remember thinking at the time that sometimes it's better to just fail so you can move on," Ev says, "but Odeo wasn't a total failure. So we kept iterating on it, and thinking, well, maybe there's something here."

Meanwhile, the team was using Twitter internally and with friends and family. "There was enough of a network that we felt a connection in a new way," Ev says.

In April of 2007, Twitter spun off from Odeo. Odeo was gradually wound down, and Twitter took its place in history.

In this chapter, we'll explore the art of the pivot. To pivot literally means to turn in a new direction; in a business sense, it's about deviating from the original plan to try something related but different. The pivot is often a response to changing circumstances or market conditions; it may be triggered by the rise of a new opportunity or an unexpected roadblock, or a deepened understanding of a product's potential. It can take a variety of forms, ranging from a step shift in strategy to a complete reboot of a company.

The truth is, most entrepreneurs pivot many times before they find their footing. And often, even *after* they find their footing. And it can feel perilous. You have to steer toward a new opportunity, often before it comes into clear focus. And, equally challenging, you have to turn *away* from something—specifically, an idea that previously inspired hopes, dreams, and investment of time and money. Human beings don't let go of old ideas easily. In pivoting, you risk blowback from your co-founders, your staff, your investors, and your users. For those reasons, it can be the single greatest test of your leadership skills.

But as hard as it is to abandon a beloved idea or a once-brilliant strategy, there often comes a time when an entrepreneur must do it. The key lies in recognizing *when* it's time to pivot and then being able to rally people to move in a new direction—even if it means you must slash and burn the rest of your business.

The closer you look at successful startups, the more you realize that many began as something *completely* different—then pivoted to become the thing that actually scaled and succeeded. But even when they involve a radical change to the product or the business strategy, most successful pivots stay somewhat close to the company's original mission. That has been the case with Ev Williams, a serial pivoter whose four startups might seem unrelated—but actually all sprang from a singular mission that Ev has been pursuing his entire adult life.

The reboot

In 2010, **Stewart Butterfield** felt the entrepreneurial urge for the second time in his life. His first company had taken dramatic turns. He had co-founded with Caterina Fake the pioneering photo-sharing service Flickr—which grew unexpectedly out of a single feature of their failing online videogame called Game Neverending. It was a classic pivot—and also a foreshadow of his next company, **Slack**.

Several years had passed since Stewart and Caterina sold Flickr.

And Stewart wanted a second shot at launching an online game. This new game was called Glitch, and he told himself it would be different this time. He wouldn't have to face the same challenges he had with Game Neverending. "From our perspective, now we have some money. We have better connections. Also, computer hardware had gotten better the past few years. And we were more experienced and capable as engineers and designers. So the thought was, *Oh, we can't fail this time.*"

The stakes were certainly higher. Stewart and his team of forty-five employees invested four years of development, engaged with tens of thousands of players, and raised $17 million, and Glitch ultimately won a small, committed fan base.

But it was failing.

The game "was incredibly powerful for the small minority of people for whom it worked—they spent twenty hours a week playing," Stewart says. "But most people—like 97 percent who signed up—would be out of there within five minutes."

Stewart and his team kept trying to keep their new users through a series of *"what if we try this?"* experiments. "It did always seem like the next thing was going to be what saved it," Stewart says.

When Stewart tells the story you can still hear the emotion in his voice: He still asks himself what more he could have done. And these questions form the inner dialogue of most entrepreneurs in the thick of a transition.

Finally Stewart realized it was game-over: "I had tried the fifteen stack-ranked best ideas we could possibly come up with to turn this around—and I didn't think the sixteenth was going to work if the first fifteen didn't."

Stewart faced one of the hardest moments in any entrepreneurial journey—the day you admit to yourself and your team that you're not going to achieve your dreams together, *this time.* So for the second time in Stewart's life, he'd have to close up shop on a product and team he loved.

On the day he told employees that Glitch was closing, he held an emotional all-hands meeting. "And I stand up and start to talk—and I didn't even get to the first sentence and I was starting to cry," Stewart recalls.

"Man, it is so hard, because the job of a CEO is often just to come up with a story that enough people believe that you can make something happen in the world. You have to convince investors, and you have to convince the press, and you have to convince potential employees, and you have to convince customers. And I had done a lot of convincing of people—to come work on this project, to leave whatever thing they were working on before, quit their job, get paid poorly in exchange for equity in something that just didn't work."

Once he regained his composure, Stewart told his team how bad he felt about having to let them go—so bad, in fact, that he was going to do everything he could to make it right. "Stewart and some of the web developers decided to build a page on Glitch.com," recalls Tim Lefler, one of the Glitch engineers. It was called "Hire A Genius," and it featured LinkedIn profiles, photos, and portfolios for everyone on the Glitch team. As soon as the press release went out on Glitch closing, there was information on the site saying, "These people are looking for work."

Stewart and his partners also wrote reference letters and offered résumé coaching for the laid-off team. As Tim Lefler recounts: "Stewart and the group decided, 'We're gonna keep working until everyone else has another job.'"

But company employees weren't the only ones saddened by the news of the game shutting down. Remember those loyal fans who spent twenty hours a week playing the game? Stewart decided to give their customers a choice of their money back, or a charitable donation made in their name. "So we were able to do all of this in a way that built a lot of goodwill," Stewart says.

That would soon pay off.

While they were essentially shutting down the game company, Stewart and his team started looking for the Hail Mary pass. They still had about $5 million in the bank, and a mandate to make something, anything, that could scale. Stewart had offered to return the money to investors, but they had challenged him to find a new direction.

Stewart and his team took a long look at all the software they'd developed in and around the game and asked themselves: *Is there anything here?*

It took a couple of weeks, but eventually they identified something:

an internal communication system the team had developed while working on the game. It was a chat-based communication tool that allowed asynchronous conversations and preserved them over time. It offered different channels for different teams and topics; it had potential, Stewart thought.

Now, a chat-based communications tool may have been a far cry from the online game that Stewart set out to build, but then again, it was a tool they already used and loved themselves. Over a period of three years, they had fine-tuned this product to meet their own needs—to communicate quickly and transparently in a way that made for smoother, more efficient collaboration. They figured other companies would have a need for this tool, too—the tool that eventually became Slack.

This pivot was a reboot in more ways than one; when Stewart started Flickr all those years ago, his online game had still been alive (if just barely), which meant he was able to transition his team from one project to the other. But in this case, the game was already shut down, and people had been laid off. Which meant that not only was Stewart starting fresh with a completely unrelated product, he also had to relaunch the whole operation, with a new office, new staff, new everything.

And because they had closed shop gracefully, Stewart was able to go back to some of the same people from Glitch and ask for their help. One of those people was Tim Lefler. "He gave me the rundown of what was going on, and just said, 'Hey, we'd like to have you back and working on this product with us,'" Tim recalls.

At this point Tim had another job already, so why would he go back to working for the guy that laid him off? Partly because that same guy had taken the trouble to help him after laying him off, but mostly because that guy had a new idea that sounded pretty good.

When he arrived at Slack's offices, he was surprised to find that he wasn't the only Glitch employee to rejoin the team. In fact, Tim says, "it felt like a bit of a reunion." Stewart's commitments to Tim demonstrate the principles from my book *The Alliance*: Maintain a mutual commitment within the organization that leads to a lifetime alliance.

This time, Tim didn't have to worry about another shutdown—the reboot known as Slack went on to become an immense hit, going public in 2019, and being acquired by Salesforce.com for $27.7 billion in late 2020.

The platform play

Some leaders move deliberately through their careers as they build toward a long-term vision. Others stumble or slide into the role that becomes their calling. **Tobi Lütke** is firmly in the second camp, having made one of the least likely pivots we've come across—from selling snowboards to scaling the e-commerce platform powerhouse known as Shopify.

As a kid growing up in a small town in Germany, Tobi "fell in love" with computers and with a pastime he later learned was called "programming." He had a coder's mind and disposition: "I love sinking myself into something that's really interesting, and tuning out everything else in my life," Tobi says.

What he didn't love was school. "School was hard for me. I just liked computers better." But—thanks to what Tobi dubs "the wisdom of the German education system"—he was able to leave school early to begin an apprenticeship as a computer programmer. Tobi eventually emigrated from Germany to Ottawa, in Canada, where his youthful love affair began to lose its luster. He worked as a coder but found that once it became his day job, the joy went out of it. So he pivoted toward a new career, to "recover programming as a hobby." Likewise, a hobby became his new career.

In Canada, Tobi had become an ardent snowboarder, and it occurred to him that he could combine his love of snowboarding with his technical skills. "I had just done the deep research of what the best boards were for myself, so I had a good overview. I thought, *Hey, I can sell snowboards online, and that would be a good starting point for a business.*"

So in 2004, Tobi began work on an online snowboard store called SnowDevil, expecting it would take just a few days to get the online store up and running. But he immediately hit a snag.

"The first thing that happened is that I tried to find the right software to use for this business," says Tobi, "and I was stunned that I couldn't find anything. It's not that there wasn't e-commerce software, but it was just all basically user-hostile database editors, at best. It was so clear that no one who's ever run a retail business had had any part in building these pieces of software."

Tobi decided that the best option was to just build his own software from scratch.

"I found Ruby on Rails, a new technology which I really liked, and did the day-and-night thing, probably working sixteen hours a day for a couple months," he says. Tobi coded the entire website from the ground up, and finally launched his snowboard store. "It ended up working really, really well. I started selling all across the United States and Canada, and some to Europe as well," he recalls.

Coding the website's back end—the bit that would take payments, process orders, and update listings—had been just a means to an end for Tobi, but soon his customers across the world showed they were interested in more than snowboards and padded jackets. People started asking Tobi if he'd build the back-end software for their online stores, too.

This is a crossroads many entrepreneurs will recognize. Entrepreneurs always have to solve side problems along the way to realizing their original vision. And **every so often, you solve a problem that's so vexing and so prevalent that your side solution becomes more valuable than your original idea.**

The notion of a possible shift began to take hold, and Tobi found himself building an e-commerce platform for retailers around the world. The goal was to make it easy for anyone to set up an online store—so that other retailers wouldn't need to wrestle with hostile systems as he'd had to do. They could just go to one place, register, and set themselves up in a matter of minutes. "Shopify was the perfect piece of software that I wish I would've found when I started my snowboard store," Tobi says.

But when Tobi decided to officially pivot from snowboards to digital shopping carts, his co-founder pivoted out of the picture. He had signed on to build a snowboard shop and just wasn't, well, on board for what SnowDevil was evolving into. "He said, 'This is getting big. This is becoming a different kind of thing,'" Tobi recalls.

And so he lost his co-founder and CEO. And this is often the painful but necessary consequence of a pivot. The team that was drawn to the original mission may not be inspired by the new turn.

But Tobi himself found the new mission exhilarating. "We realized that what the company was always about, and that we are in love with, is the concept of internet entrepreneurship," says Tobi. "The internet is supposed to be participatory and democratized by opportunity. So we've pursued this idea, or this question of, 'Well, what would the world be like if entrepreneurship could really be easy?'"

And just like that, programmer Tobi became CEO of the platform eventually called Shopify, today a multinational e-commerce company based in Ottawa, Ontario. The idea that started as a better digital shopping cart for a snowboard shop morphed into a worldwide platform for online shops everywhere. If you bought something online in the last year—and it wasn't on Amazon—then Shopify's platform probably powered the purchase.

One of the keys to Tobi's success: He turned Shopify into a platform that not only allowed merchants to easily set up online stores but also enabled app developers to build specialty stores for merchants.

By opening up Shopify in this way, Tobi made a conscious decision to let developers make money off his platform, rather than trying to keep it closed so he could capture all of that app revenue himself. "What we did to get the platform off the ground is to basically leave all the economics for Shopify on the table and give it to the third-party app developers," Tobi says.

This helped him to rapidly attract more and more users to Shopify. And in retrospect, these decisions paved the way for their widespread success. But they were tough calls at the time. "It's hard to do, because you are leaving a lot of economics that you could easily take for yourself on the table—or actually, you are investing it into your own future by giving it to other people," Tobi explains. "And that's very hard to do for most businesses."

The combination of a strong platform, a well-populated app store, and a community of developers helped protect Shopify against competition and built a positive feedback loop that ratcheted up innovation, attracting more users *and* more developers.

But, as Tobi is quick to point out, that takes time. "We built a lot of the technology underlying it in 2009. And only in 2018, almost a

REID'S ANALYSIS | Make a pivot feel like a joint decision

There's more to a pivot than a sharp left turn. First, there's the opportunity you're pivoting toward. Can you see it clearly enough to navigate toward it? Can you convince others to come along?

Then you have to pivot away from your old idea. This can be incredibly difficult, because it involves humans. And humans don't tend to let go of old ideas easily. You risk blowback from your co-founders, your staff, your investors, and your users. This will likely be the single greatest test of your leadership skills, because your credibility will come under scrutiny. Are you even believable anymore?

Working for a startup is kind of like going to war together. When you're crouched in the bunker with the rest of your platoon, you form massive trust. If I've seen you look out for me, I'm going to look out for you.

Here's the key to managing through a pivot: Those employees, if they feel taken care of, will keep taking care of you.

I believe that, as CEO, you always have to bring the core team along during a pivot. You have to make them feel like it was a joint decision. It doesn't have to be democratic; in fact, it *shouldn't* be democratic. But it has to feel *participatory*. People have to feel they have a voice. They have to feel like their vote counts; that the company has their interests at heart.

When your team is split on whether to stay with an old strategy or pivot to a new one, for example, it might seem smart to hedge your bets and pursue both ideas at once. That's the most democratic way to keep the peace, right? But as a founder, you never want to say, "We're working on X, and we're also working on Y because my team likes both ideas." That may be the expedient solution. But I can tell you how that story ends: like Thelma and Louise, holding hands and driving over a cliff together.

You actually owe it to your team to force a decision: X or Y, choose one. It's ultimately the founder's responsibility to make that call. But as you do, be sure to bring your team along.

decade later, did we cross the 'Gates line.' I think Bill Gates said this: 'You are not a platform until the people who are building on you make more money than you do.'"

In 2018, more than one million businesses made over $40 billion in sales using Shopify, and app developers for the platform made over $90 million. All thanks to that initial pivot—when Tobi decided to shift from selling his own product to helping others sell theirs.

The straight and narrow

Sometimes, extraordinary circumstances drive a leader to pivot in their careers. But this isn't how it happened for **Stacy Brown-Philpot**. After growing up on Detroit's west side and getting her MBA at Stanford, Stacy joined Google and spent eight years there. It was 2013. She was just back from a tour of duty in India, and everything was . . . good. "I looked around and I was in an office, two floor-to-ceiling windows. My dog at the time was there, had his own bed. I had a table. I had a couch. I had an assistant. I had everything that most people dream of in a corporate job, and I felt like my work wasn't done," Stacy recalls. "I said, 'I've got to go do something else that grabs at my heart, in a way that's going to allow me to accomplish more.'"

As luck would have it, Stacy soon met Leah Busque, the founder of **TaskRabbit**, a popular app connecting users looking to hire someone— or be hired—to do miscellaneous jobs. Stacy tried the service out and loved what it stood for. "I'm a mission-minded person," Stacy says. "We talk a lot in Silicon Valley about missionaries and mercenaries, and I'm definitely in the missionary bucket. TaskRabbit's mission around revolutionizing everyday work really grabbed me, and it brought me back home to Detroit. It brought me back to the people who were good, hardworking people who lost their jobs because of the failure of an entire industry, who couldn't find work but had strong work ethics."

In 2013, Stacy joined TaskRabbit as COO and soon realized it faced deep underlying challenges if it was going to scale. She dug into the numbers and concluded: "We've got to do some things differently in this business in order to get to where we want to go."

There was one particular area Stacy zeroed in on: the freewheeling bidding system that connected the two sides in the marketplace of taskers (those bidding for the jobs) and clients (those looking to hire) that drove TaskRabbit. Under the current system, taskers had to go through a bidding process for every task, which meant that many found themselves in a race-to-the-bottom to offer their services for the cheapest price. Meanwhile, for clients it often took too much time to sort through all those bids and choose a winner.

This open-ended "anything goes" framework seemed to work about half the time; some taskers and clients thrived in the bidding wars. But the other 50 percent of the people had a bad experience, either being overwhelmed by confusing choices or undercut by too many competitive bids. Stacy understood the dynamics at play. Unhappy customers "mentioned that bad experience to ten times more people than the ones who had a good experience," Stacy says. "That just wasn't going to work for the long term. We had to change it."

This would require a significant pivot for TaskRabbit—a shift toward more structure and reliability, less choice and chaos. Stacy and her team had a strong instinct for this better system, but it required them to reimagine the whole way they conducted the business. They came up with a plan to jettison the open-ended job offerings—like "celebrity impersonator" or "birthday party clown"—and streamline the types of tasks people could offer to just four popular and easy-to-understand categories: handyman work, home cleaning, moving help, and personal assistant.

At the same time, TaskRabbit opted to give the taskers more agency—including an opportunity to decide when they wanted to work, how they wanted to work, and what hourly rates they wanted to charge, rather than have their rates effectively set by the auction process.

No longer would taskers have to anxiously check their phones in case they were outbid on a potential task. Meanwhile, clients would be able to book a tasker in a single visit to the site or app—no more scrolling through long lists of bids. Instead, clients would be presented with a shortlist of recommended taskers based on their rates, reviews, and skills.

When you're considering a major pivot like this one, you always want to test the idea first. And Stacy wanted to test among *new* users—customers who could start fresh with the platform, without any in-grained assumptions about what it was *supposed* to be. They chose London for their test market, because there was some awareness of the TaskRabbit brand there, but the service had never been available locally.

To Stacy's delight, the streamlined iteration of TaskRabbit tested well: The assignment rate went up, and the close rate rose from 50 to 80 percent. "We knew that we were on to something, and then we brought it back to the United States," Stacy says.

If the Brits loved it, then the Americans would, too, right? Well, not exactly. Changing an existing system is never as simple as introducing a new one. And in this case, the problem wasn't necessarily the change itself, but how the taskers, in particular, heard about it. For the taskers, this was their community, their livelihood. Stacy knew this, of course, but assumed the news would just be a clear win. "We thought, 'They're going to be so excited because this is going to be great for them.'

"We told them about the changes the same day that we told *TechCrunch* and *USA Today* and everybody," says Stacy. That was a mistake—and the taskers revolted. "They were upset, mostly because we didn't tell them that we were going to do this, and partly because they were going to have to work in a different way."

Stacy had implemented an objectively positive program at TaskRabbit—one that she knew would ensure taskers were more fairly compensated and also made the process more streamlined and easier to use for customers. But changing the rules governing an entire platform is not trivial, especially if you forget to tell the users of the platform about it. Worse yet, TaskRabbit wasn't just a platform, it was a community, where people felt a sense of ownership. And when people feel ownership, they expect to have input . . . or at least learn about the news before they read it online. In failing to involve the community early, Stacy had unwittingly undermined their sense of investment.

In hindsight, it's clear to Stacy what TaskRabbit *should have* done. "At that point, we had over twenty thousand taskers who were working and earning on the platform," she says. "We should have treated the taskers as part of the communication chain. Instead, we said, 'You know what? They're just users and they're going to find out when everyone else finds out.'" But the TaskRabbit management should have tested that assumption by checking in with users to make sure everyone was ready to make this pivot with them.

Even with the blowback, Stacy and her team stuck to their guns.

At first, they lost revenue and users. But over time, the new system yielded higher customer satisfaction, happier users on both ends, and more profitability. The pivot had worked.

It also led to improvements in TaskRabbit's culture. Having learned—albeit the hard way—the importance of engaging the community in major decisions, "we created a Tasker Council," says Stacy. "On the council, we have some people who are really excited about TaskRabbit and others who are always skeptical. We tell them, 'We really want your input, and once we get you on board, we also want you to help us talk to the rest of the community.'" Stacy believes that if she'd had the council during the pivot, the change would have gone down easier.

And there was another unintended consequence—an extraordinary one: Once TaskRabbit got rid of the competitive bidding between taskers, a supportive, sharing community of taskers began to emerge. They started holding classes and posting videos to teach each other skills and increase each other's earning power—creating a dynamic, self-reinforcing loop that benefited everyone.

Now TaskRabbit is harnessing the power of that growing community to do training and development. "Some of the taskers create courses, and we pay them to do it," Stacy says. It's a way not only to boost skills but to give some taskers a sense of meaning and purpose— and revenue—that extends beyond just completing their everyday tasks.

But the true power of this community didn't fully hit home for Stacy until it quite literally showed up at her front door. A tasker had come over to fix a light switch, and Stacy realized that this same person had previously delivered a birthday cake for her. So Stacy asked how he went from delivering cakes to doing electrical work. "Because of the TaskRabbit community," he told her. "I took some classes, I learned, and now I'm making like twice as much as I was making before on the platform."

The rebound: Pivoting in a crisis

As the COVID-19 crisis began to take hold in early 2020, **Nextdoor CEO Sarah Friar** noticed some interesting things happening on the

---

REID'S ANALYSIS | **How to know when it's time to pivot**

Everyone loves to think they were more or less born with their big, scalable idea. People tell stories like, "When I was two, I knew what I was going to do when I was forty." But it's usually fiction. Plans change. People pivot. So, you should think, "When the time comes, let me pivot intelligently and early."

That doesn't mean you don't have persistence with your original plan or idea. It doesn't mean you panic and bail as soon as the going gets tough. It just means knowing that pivoting is part of the game.

I advise people to think about major pivots in terms of your confidence in your investment thesis. You say, "Well, in order to make this intuition work I've got idea one, I've got idea two, I've got idea three, I've got idea four." Once you've tried five ideas, you have to ask yourself, "Is my sixth idea as good as or better than the other five ideas?"

As you begin to realize that you're scraping the bottom of the barrel for ideas to try to make that original plan work, that's when you want to pivot—immediately. People mistakenly think, "When the company is shutting down, *that's* when I will pivot to something else." But by then it is almost certainly too late. You want to make your move *before* the market hits you in the face with a two-by-four.

Nextdoor platform, originally designed to make it easier for neighbors to get to know one another. First off, engagement levels were up about 80 percent. But beyond that, the *nature* of the interactions was changing. People weren't just saying hi and asking for handyman recommendations. They were using the platform to try to determine if anyone out there in the neighborhood needed help during the crisis—and they seemed ready, even eager, to step in and provide it.

"We saw that conversations about 'help' were up 262 percent on the platform in the first month of the crisis," Sarah says. Stay-at-home orders had gone into effect throughout most of the communities Nextdoor serviced, and people who were particularly at risk of infection were staying home. "Everyone suddenly was offering, 'I can go get groceries for you, I can pick up a prescription for you. . . .'" And some of the helpers even began to self-organize: In her own neighborhood, Sarah saw a Nextdoor help group form that grew to more than five hundred people.

The leader of that group took the time to actually match neighbors who needed help with those offering it. Sarah jumped into the fray on her own local platform and was matched to an older woman named Elizabeth. "She felt really bad about asking for help," recalls Sarah. "I could tell she was on the defensive when I first spoke to her because she spent a long time telling me how fit she is." Elizabeth's preexisting conditions made her particularly vulnerable to the virus, and she couldn't risk leaving the house—so Sarah picked up prescriptions and bagels for her.

All of this inspired Sarah to create some new offerings and features on Nextdoor—and the platform quickly pivoted from mere neighborly networking to more of an active outreach and informational clearinghouse.

Sarah began by creating the COVID-19 Help Center, a central resource for accurate pandemic information and ways to support local businesses. She followed that up by launching the Neighborhood Help Map, which made it easy for neighbors to find and offer help based on proximity to where they lived. Later in 2020, that map showed it had staying power as it morphed into a Voter Help Map, which matched up people who needed help printing out their voter registration materials with neighbors who could print at home.

When the pandemic hit, Nextdoor had been in the process of alpha testing a new Groups product. Sarah decided to stop testing and just launch it. "It had been trapped in the slog of iteration and we just said, 'Okay, enough, rip the Band-Aid off.'" Nextdoor Groups became virtual meetups that helped to ease the psychological impact of social distancing, an idea with lasting value for elderly neighbors beyond the pandemic era.

You could say the crisis lit a fire under Nextdoor, forcing them to come up with new ideas and act on ones that weren't quite ready to launch. "I think in times of crisis your customers give you a little bit more latitude for things that might not be perfect," Sarah says. "If they know it's coming from a good heart, they'll be more forgiving of products that might be a little raggedy on the edge."

As Nextdoor continued to adapt the platform to developments unfolding around it, Sarah also found herself thinking ahead to the future. She asked her Nextdoor team to consider questions like *What are the new emergent themes? How will things be different in the future? How might they be the same? What are the newer, creative ways that we can think about how communities pull together?*

"I think the great thing, if there's something great to say about a pandemic, was that I no longer felt like I was evangelizing Nextdoor to people," says Sarah. "People just got it—the power of proximity, the need for our neighbors to be our front line of support. It's no longer something that we have to shy away from. Now if we hear those snarky comments like, 'But aren't some of your neighbors kind of kooks?' I'm like, 'Maybe, but they might go get you that thing that will save your life.'"

If a pivot is defined as making a swift turn in response to unexpected developments or obstacles, then it's fair to call 2020 the Year of the Pivot. Startups that already had to deal with the usual challenges of scaling—raising money, hiring, fine-tuning the offering, developing the company culture—have had to add on a whole additional layer of complications, ranging from mass panic, to a sudden drop-off in business, to huge drops in consumers' disposable income, to social distancing requirements, and much, much more.

In some ways, entrepreneurs are built to thrive in challenging times and conditions, says BuzzFeed founder **Jonah Peretti.** "I've noticed that **times of crisis favor founder-led companies, because they're headed by people who like improvising.** They think about things through first principles and are okay adapting and changing their business."

"During times like this," he adds, "you have to be totally open to changing everything that you've been doing and pursuing opportunities you didn't know existed." That plays to the strengths of founders. As does the fact that entrepreneurs are just used to struggling—they often *relish* the struggle.

In Jonah's case, the pandemic turned what was anticipated to be a banner year for BuzzFeed into one in which the company had to struggle to break even. The biggest impact came from loss of advertisers on the site. "We saw tens of millions of dollars just evaporate," says Jonah. As a result, BuzzFeed had to eliminate about $40 million in costs by cutting back on international expansion and reorganizing the business, with an increased focus on e-commerce, transactional platform revenue, and programmatic revenue (which has benefited from BuzzFeed's increased traffic in the past year). Meanwhile, because of the crisis, BuzzFeed may end up strengthening its relationships with client companies—some of whom have turned to BuzzFeed for help in shifting to e-commerce.

A crisis ratchets up the pressure to make smart, fast decisions—while also narrowing the margin for error. It forces you to use limited resources—including your own energy—more efficiently and wisely. And it demands that a leader really step into that role and rally the battered troops.

Neil Blumenthal, co-founder of Warby Parker, rose to the challenge in a number of ways. When the COVID crisis hit, Warby Parker had to shut down its stores, as well as much of its headquarters. But Neil had to make sure the online business kept delivering on customer orders. "People need their glasses to function day to day," he says. So Neil's first step was to make sure the supply chain was secure and the fulfillment centers were up to speed. "Then it was trying to figure out unemployment benefits if we furlough folks. Then it was trying to figure out, what do we do with 120 retail leases when your stores are closed?" As the stores reopened, Warby Parker instituted tight controls over store traffic and "guided shopping experiences" wherein a retail associate would actually disinfect every glasses frame before and after a customer tried it on.

Neil says he learned that one of the most critical skills during a crisis is communication. "You need to communicate two to three times more than you did beforehand," he says, "and you need to simplify that communication." Neil and co-founder Dave Gilboa normally had a weekly all-hands meeting that was recorded and shared with everyone. "During the pandemic we moved to two all-hands videos a week and shortened them, so they're a little more digestible. They would come out Tuesdays and Thursdays, so the team had the information they need to make informed decisions and so they know what's going on—because, especially not being in the office, you lose all the hallway chatter. You lose all of these informal modes of communication, and you need to supplement that with a lot more structured and formal communication."

Ellen Kullman, former CEO of DuPont (which has navigated its share of crises through the years) and now CEO of the 3D printing startup Carbon, points to the need to "create your own trajectory" during a crisis. Most leaders already have a planned trajectory for their business—but the problem is, a crisis will overturn the old plan, forcing you to pivot to Plan B, then perhaps Plan C or D. As that happens, "you really have to write your own story. Don't play the hand you've been dealt, play the hand you want." That means the leader must lay out a new trajectory that acknowledges things have changed—and makes it clear that the company is adapting to that change, has a clear outlook on what it will mean in the future, and has a solid plan for how to win in this new environment. "If you don't have a specific hypothesis on what the outcome is going to be," Ellen says, "then you're not going to know—and your employees won't know—whether you're winning or losing."

Airbnb co-founder **Brian Chesky** felt this uncertainty rather acutely when his company took a huge hit during the COVID-19 crisis. Leading up to the spring of 2020, "we were preparing to go public," he says. "I was working on our S-1 document, and I was also working on a really big launch. We had a plan, and I felt great about it. And all of a sudden, it felt like I was a ship captain and a torpedo hit the side of the ship."

Airbnb saw its business almost come to a standstill as many people stopped traveling, virtually overnight. "First, there was this feeling of panic—and I reminded myself that I had to breathe." It's true for any leader in a crisis: Take the time to slow down, regain your bearings, and keep an eye on your stress levels.

But Brian didn't slow down for long. He undertook a series of pivots to help Airbnb respond to the crisis. The company increased its focus on long-term rentals and monthly stays, to meet the demands of people looking to temporarily relocate during the crisis. And it also began providing more local and virtual experiences—from concerts in living rooms to a virtual tour of a New Zealand sheep farm and even virtual salsa dance parties. Brian sees these new offerings as a long-term addition to the Airbnb offering, and he expects they'll remain popular even as people return to their old travel habits.

Brian's main piece of advice for those adapting to a crisis: Focus on your core principles. Think about what you're trying to achieve and stand for as an organization—and what's most important to you as a leader. "When things are really bad," Brian says, "it's hard to make business decisions because you cannot predict how it's all going to play out. But you can ask yourself: *How do I want to be remembered in this crisis?*"

Stacy Brown-Philpot of TaskRabbit and **Danny Meyer** of Union Square Hospitality Group shared a similar thought: A crisis is a time to think big and look beyond your own company. Stacy says: "I would like to see the companies that are here in Silicon Valley come together and be more coordinated about our relief efforts. We have greater access to technology, we have a deeper understanding of how technology can and should work, even when horrible things happen, and we know how to communicate really fast and efficiently."

Stacy's goal is that TaskRabbit be "there and ready right when we are needed, but also that we are coordinating with other tech companies—we all have millions of people that we can contact at a single point in time to deploy against a single effort to help people recover in a crisis situation."

Danny, for his part, is already looking beyond his restaurants and thinking about how the COVID crisis could be a spark that brings about long-needed change in the restaurant industry. "As one of my colleagues said, 'The restaurant industry is like a COVID patient in their nineties with preexisting conditions. It didn't actually take COVID to bring us down. Almost anything would have. But this has really, really done it.'" Danny has already spent a lot of time talking to his industry colleagues, asking, "What is the opportunity that this crisis is providing to deal with things that none of us as individuals have succeeded at dealing with in the past?" They're now looking at ways to improve how restaurant people are paid, the tipping system, the problems restaurants face with payroll taxes and liquor laws, and relationships with landlords.

Wences Casares, CEO of the Bitcoin wallet platform Xapo, and **Matt Mullenweg**, founder of Automattic, both believe that a crisis can be a good time to make your company more adaptable and flexible—specifically, by changing the way the company is structured. More specifically, by pivoting to a remote office structure. If there's one positive change wrought by the pandemic, it's that companies large and small have witnessed firsthand the benefits of shifting to an all-remote work-force. But Wences and Matt have been proponents of the distributed office model for years, before it became a necessity. Wences says that by having his hundreds of employees spread out in smaller regional offices or at-home offices (in fifty-plus different countries), it has en-abled him to more easily recruit the best talent from anywhere in the world. But you have to do it right, he says. "The difference between going to work at an office and working remotely is like the difference between living with your parents and moving out and living alone. If you're not very conscious about this, it can easily lead to feeling discon-nected and disengaged from the world." New Xapo hires are advised to put a lot more effort into their routine than they would if they were going to an office, and to create a work space that is separate and dis-tinct from where they conduct the rest of their lives.

Matt, whose fully distributed company Automattic runs the WordPress blogging platform, notes that "what makes a great distrib-uted company are almost exactly the same things that make a great in-person company. It's trust, communication, transparency, open-mindedness, and iteration." If you're in a distributed situation unex-pectedly because of an office closure, or deliberately, such as working from home one day a week, Matt suggests using this as an opportunity to do a personal pivot, by rethinking the way you work. "So much of our lives, we live by default," he says. "Any chance you have to zoom out, reimagine, look at it with a beginner's mind or fresh eyes, I think could have a huge impact on any person's life regardless of the work situation."

When a change like remote working is forced upon a company, Matt advises asking the positive question, "Okay, what is actually *en-abled* by us being distributed?" You may decide a remote meeting over videoconference is a lot better than conducting the meeting over the phone, so you invest in headsets and maybe even better cameras, so people look and sound professional wherever they might be. Or you may find that even if you have invested in state-of-the art videoconfer-encing technology, certain objectives simply are better accomplished over email. The change in work routines becomes a good opportunity to revisit—and improve upon—norms and processes.

A crisis can necessitate not just a pivot but a massive one—and there's no doubt that it can be painful and, in some cases, devastating. But as these examples show, there are upsides to hard times. A crisis can push you to sharpen your focus and act more swiftly. There's no limit to the ingenuity that can be unleashed when the chaos around us forces us to recalibrate our assumptions and look at the world in a new light. As we have seen throughout the book, some of the greatest startup companies in existence today were born out of desperate circumstances.

REID'S ANALYSIS | In a crisis, be human first

How do you help your business to navigate a crisis? By thinking not just of the business but of all the *people* involved in the business—inside the company and out.

In times of crisis, it's more important than ever to pause to say, "Okay, let me be a human first. Let me make sure that I'm being responsible to my employees, to my community, to my society. What are the things I need to do?"

Start from a place of compassion and caring—not just about what is good for the company and its employees but also what's good for the community, good for families, and good for society as a whole.

As entrepreneurs, we're so focused on building these businesses and getting to scale. It's such a hard thing to do. There is fear. And failure. There is the sheer challenge of creating something new, something from nothing. And you get very focused in order to do that—so focused that it's easy to forget *why* you do it.

It's important to remind yourself that you do it because it's the thing that allows us to create these new businesses, these new jobs, these new products, these new services. It's the thing that creates the future. It's super important. But you always have to pause to say, "Okay, let me be a human first. Let me make sure that I'm being responsible to my employees, to my community, to my society. What are the things I need to do?"

REID'S THEORIES ON EMBRACING PLAN B

The shift

Even the most focused entrepreneurs who are pursuing a particular vision must constantly shift and adjust to changes in technology, the market, or the world in general. Pivoting in this way doesn't mean giving up on the vision; in fact, they're often more successful at pivoting *because* they're guided by a vision.

The switch

Pivots often occur within an existing business: for example, when the company switches from one strategy to a different one. It's important to get early feedback on changes like this—or at least communicate those changes to as many of your stakeholders as you can *before* you flip the switch.

The swerve

Some pivots are reactions to an unexpected development: a new problem or opportunity that suddenly manifests itself. It might be blocking the path forward, requiring a deft sideways maneuver to avoid a crash, or it could be something compelling that has cropped up on the side of the road. You may find it's worth swerving to investigate and perhaps pursue this new possibility.

The reboot

A pivot can sometimes—not often, but sometimes—be a complete departure from the original mission of the company. A total reboot like that can work, but it rarely goes off without some bumps.

The rebound: Pivoting in a crisis

Crises can cause some unwelcome pivots. But they also can offer opportunities to learn, experiment, and make improvements to your current business. So, even while navigating a crisis, look toward the future and ask questions like "Within these constraints, what are the newer creative possibilities? How can we make our business more flexible, and stronger, over the long run?"

9

Lead, Lead Again

S he wasn't expecting the call.

Angela Ahrendts had hit her stride as the CEO of Burberry. In just eight years, she had led the British heritage brand through a high-profile turnaround. The stock price had risen 200 percent. Revenues and operating income had both doubled. The change was so dramatic, Angela herself was declared by the British press to be the highest-paid executive in the United Kingdom.

She and her family had settled happily into their life in the United Kingdom, and she had just shared a plan with her board—to double revenue again, over the next five years.

And then Apple called.

Or the search firm anyway. Apple CEO Tim Cook felt she should become Apple's next Head of Retail. "And I said, 'I'm honored, absolutely honored to be considered, but I have the greatest job in the world and I'm on a mission. So, no, thank you.'"

Six months later, they called again. "And I said, 'Look, it's only been six months and nothing has changed. There is no reason for me to have a conversation. And oh, by the way, I had two kids in university in London, right? And a husband who thinks we're living there the rest of our life. So, leave me alone. Thank you, but no thank you.'"

Any leader who's recruiting talent, take note: Persistence pays off. Apple came back again. "'Would you just have a cup of coffee with Tim?' I'm like, *Ugh, really?* And so I thought: *You don't want to be disrespectful and you don't want to be arrogant. He's the biggest CEO in the world.* And so I said, 'Fine, I'll have a cup of coffee.'"

But as persuasive as Tim Cook was face-to-face, she turned him down. A bunch of times.

"I told Tim, I said, 'Trust me, I'm not the right person. You don't know me. I'm instinctive. I'm creative. I'm not a store operator.' He said, 'We run the most productive stores in the world. I think we've got a lot of good operators.' And I said, 'But I'm not a techie, either. I don't code.'

"Very calmly, he said, 'We have enough of those.' And so only after a while did I realize that it was really leadership that he was looking for, that he wanted the teams to be very united again."

Angela agonized over the decision. She asked herself, "Why is it when your life is perfect that somebody wants to flip it upside down?"

But ultimately she decided: It's *Apple.* She had to say yes. And she left her high-flying role as CEO of an ascendant London fashion label to helm the retail division of Silicon Valley's mother ship. Apple was itself dominating in retail. Over ten years, they had quadrupled the number of stores worldwide. But with growth come growing pains.

Angela's challenge: Maintain the iconic magic of Apple while managing crowds that now include technological late bloomers as well as obsessive early adopters. To pull that off would require a big vision. But it also required a change agent who could unite the global team. Angela was ready for the challenge.

And how did it work out when she arrived?

"I hated it."

Angela's candor is surprising, but her response—not so much. Any time you're making the leap from one organization to another—and especially when you're scaling between two mountains as different as

Apple and Burberry—you're going to discover it's hard. It's hard because it's *different*. The rules, the goals, the assumptions, the communication.

"It was actually like going to Mars," Angela says. "It's like it's a different language.

"I got so insecure the first three or four months," Angela remembers. "But then you have a talk with yourself, right? There's no way in the world I could possibly learn everything. And they didn't bring me in to learn all of that. They brought me in because I have gifts and I'm supposed to focus on applying those. The first six months everywhere are difficult. But then I realized that I had to do it my way and they brought me in to do it my way."

Before Angela could rally the troops, she had to rally herself. And every leader of a fast-scaling organization can recognize themselves in her story. Because the shock Angela faced as she moved from Burberry to Apple isn't so different from the disorientation leaders feel *within their own companies* as they scale.

Leadership at scale—and leadership *as* you scale—means you're constantly adapting and evolving. You can't follow a single style or approach. You're always leading through transitions. Your company is always changing around you. And this means you're naturally going to have a very resilient kind of leadership, producing a resilient team and company.

It was about three months into Angela's new job as Apple's head of retail and online sales when somebody suggested she send an introductory email to the company's seventy thousand employees. Angela had other ideas.

As a mother of three teenagers, Angela knew that a wordy email wasn't the best way to communicate with Apple's younger employees. "I picture my three teens in these Apple Stores and they don't read email," she says. "So I said, 'I'm going to do a video instead.'"

"We don't do videos," she was told.

"I said, 'I'm going to do a video, and I don't want a studio and I don't want hair and makeup. We'll use an iPhone. It's going to be three thoughts in three minutes or less, no editing, nothing.'"

So Angela recorded her first video memo to Apple employees from her desk, using an iPhone. "I just said, 'Hi, sorry I haven't reached out before, but we're going to do these videos. I'm going to talk to you once a week, because I want you to be aware of what our plan is, where we're going. I want us to connect.'"

About a minute into recording the video, her phone rang. It was her daughter. With the phone camera still rolling, Angela excused herself, took the incoming call and said, "Angelina, Mommy will call you back in two minutes." Then she resumed her video message to Apple employees.

When she was done recording the video, someone suggested that she edit out the phone call, "because Apple's got to be perfect," she explains. "And I said, 'No, it does not have to be perfect. They have to see that I am authentic. They also should see that I put my kids first.' The next day, I must have gotten five hundred messages from people thanking me for taking my daughter's call."

And just like that, Angela had begun to forge a connection with her new team at Apple—something she knew she'd need as she set out to bring change to a business whose success hinges on remaining innovative and nimble. Whether your staff is seventy thousand or only seven, a leader needs two things to create a strong unified team: an elevated mission and everyday human contact. Angela managed to squeeze a little of both into that three-minute video.

Previously, as CEO of Burberry, Angela had led an astounding turnaround after years of flat sales. She arrived at Burberry after a highly successful stint as a top executive at Liz Claiborne, and found herself in charge of eleven thousand people who were not completely thrilled with their employer. Burberry's once-sophisticated brand name had gone plebeian.

Angela and lead designer Christopher Bailey agreed: They would do everything in their power to reinforce the "Britishness" of the company. Angela had deftly identified the one defining factor from which all else flowed. Every subsequent decision would be tied back to this one: From the models to the music playing in Burberry's stores, Britannia ruled.

But Angela knew the company also needed something aspirational—something to elevate the work of each employee from the transactional to the purposeful. She added a critical new element to Burberry's brand: social impact. The Burberry Foundation took proceeds from every sale to support social causes.

As Angela began to implement these changes, she decided about six months in that it was time to issue a direct call to action to the company's leaders. Two hundred of the top executives from around the world were flown in for an offsite meeting. Plans and strategies for Burberry's turnaround were laid out. And then Angela got real with the group.

She stood up and said, "Look, this is what we're doing. And I know some of you are skeptical. You've been here a long time and you may think the way you're now doing things is the best, but it's not working." Then, the kicker: "I am happy to meet with you after this meeting and give you the greatest retirement package. Otherwise, you need to walk out of here 100 percent believing in everything we're doing."

It was a tough speech in a difficult moment. Too many leaders avoid those kinds of hard conversations—but the truth is, especially in a turnaround, people want directness and clarity around adopting a new mission. And Angela knew that if you don't get people united and all-in on that mission, you won't achieve liftoff.

That meeting opened the door for Angela to begin fostering a stronger connection with her global team. Back at Liz Claiborne, she'd learned an important lesson about connecting from the company's CEO, Paul Charron, who was known for regularly stopping by employees' offices to see how things were going. Angela did the same at Burberry, and she focused on celebrating employee successes, too. She set up awards programs for managers and employees around the world, often traveling to those celebrations, which were documented and shared online so the whole company could see them. She made videos to honor departmental achievements—and played them at board meetings.

But the best morale booster of all was the results that started coming in. When Burberry stores started seeing double-digit growth in sales, it became clear that Angela's leadership style was equal parts vision and substance.

• • •

Her success at Burberry was what got Tim Cook's attention. Angela may have been hesitant to sign on to Apple at first, but she couldn't resist the challenge Tim laid out for her. From its inception, the Apple Store had almost mythic status as a mecca for Apple superfans. But as the brand grew more and more popular, Apple's customer base had grown and changed, too. The challenge now was to maintain the stores' allure for techies while also appealing to more mainstream crowds.

To pull that off would require a big vision. But it would also require everyday hands-on coordination among retail teams separated by language barriers, time zones, and geography. Angela's iPhone video memos, which by then had become a regular practice, were a big part of forging and strengthening that connection. Angela recorded those videos every week for four years, from wherever she was in the world. And she'd regularly rotate in appearances by different senior execs from Apple's offices across the globe, to build that sense of one cohesive team.

Angela also worked to create more human-to-human contact across Apple's network of retail stores: for example, through apps designed to make it easier for people working in different stores to connect and solve problems together.

The mission she brought to the Apple Stores started with a question inspired by a quote from Tim Cook. Says Angela, "Tim used to always say, 'Apple Retail has always been about so much more than just selling.' So if it's not just about selling, then what is it about?"

The answer she landed on? Community and connection. Angela helped launch Today at Apple, a program of free daily lessons and activities offered in all Apple Stores worldwide. The mission was to encourage connection and face-to-face interaction with people in local communities—while also potentially onboarding new Apple customers by teaching them how to use the products.

Today at Apple wasn't just good for customers and good for business; it also gave people working at the stores a greater sense of purpose: something they could feel invested in and put their own stamp on. "We told the retail teams, 'You are the beating heart in your community,'" says Angela.

In that role, store managers had a big say in what kind of offerings might work best. That included in-store programs like Teachers Tuesdays, where educators could come in and learn about apps for the classroom. Some stores had "boardrooms" where entrepreneurs could meet and learn from business leaders. And on Saturday mornings—as an alternative to watching cartoons on TV—kids could come in and do an "Hour of Code."

There were other changes Angela brought to the Apple Stores, too, like replacing the traditional checkout counter with roving customer service agents who could ring up your purchase from anywhere in the store. Also gone: the Genius Bar with its inscrutable wait times and implacable wizards at the back of the store. Instead, customers can now schedule a service repair request remotely and bring devices in at the appointed time.

Angela thinks of Today at Apple as her signature achievement (she left Apple in early 2019 and now sits on the boards of directors for Ralph Lauren and Airbnb). It tapped into her greatest strengths as a leader and a connector.

And like any signature achievement, the program continues to evolve and improve even after Angela's departure. That's how a leader unites a global team: Inspire them with a guiding mission, then connect them with each other. And then watch them take ownership of that mission and become leaders themselves.

Setting the drumbeat

"To build a drumbeat 101, the most basic pulse of a lot of popular Western music would be the four-on-the-floor on the kick drum—and you kind of build from there. Then you'd bring that snare backbeat in, and you're probably going to add some high-hat stuff."

That's **Chris Tomson,** drummer for the indie rock band Vampire Weekend. That four-on-the-floor beat is one that all drummers know well. It's the gateway rhythm to more complex beats. Chris has relied on the four-on-the-floor since the very first days of Vampire Weekend in 2006. Well, almost the very first days.

"The first couple of rehearsals that Vampire Weekend ever had, which were in some dorm rooms at Columbia, I was supposed to be the guitarist," he remembers. "That ended up not happening, mainly because we couldn't find a drummer."

So he said he'd give it a shot, and just like that, Chris the guitarist became Chris the drummer.

Because Chris hadn't spent the years that most professional drummers spend honing their craft, he was forced to rely on simple, effective beats. "No frills, no ornamentation—just this backbeat that allows the song to build."

Chris knows that even if he's in the background of the music, he's also the backbone of the band—his beats set the rhythm that the rest of the band follows. He's what keeps them all in sync.

Even all these years later, don't expect Chris to start hijacking Vampire Weekend concerts by launching into twenty-minute drum solos. That's fine for some, but as Chris says: "I always felt if a show went by and I was not particularly noticed, that was a successful show for me. I feel like it's almost cooler and more badass as a drummer to be ego-less about it. It's not about showing off. It's about serving totally the band context and the song."

So what can a business leader learn from the drummer of Vampire Weekend? A lot, it turns out. Because every leader has to create a cultural drumbeat for their company—one that can, in Chris's words, get the whole band in sync. A great leader's drumbeat doesn't force people to follow them; it inspires them to *want* to move in the same direction.

There's no one "correct" drumbeat for a leader or an organization. Your drumbeat depends on your temperament, your experiences, and the people you lead. Your drumbeat might be focused on efficiency, or innovation, or work-life balance. Or perhaps a mix of all these.

The drumbeat for **Jeff Weiner** was compassionate management. But it wasn't always that way. Before becoming the chief executive at **LinkedIn**, Jeff Weiner spent seven years in various leadership roles at Yahoo. One day, about midway through his time there, a flyer for a management seminar landed on his desk. Jeff promptly tossed that flyer into his Someday-Maybe-Never pile.

He had acquired a healthy skepticism toward management consultants—because he'd been one himself, early in his career.

"There's an old adage that sometimes consultants will take your watch and tell you what time it is," Jeff says. He didn't disagree.

But other members of Jeff's leadership team at Yahoo had gone through the program and recommended it strongly. Eventually, Jeff's curiosity wrestled his skepticism to the ground and he signed up for the seminar that focused on the human side of management, run by a consultant named Fred Kofman.

That seminar completely changed the way Jeff thought about leadership.

"I had never heard anyone talk like that on the subject of leadership—about how important it is to remain mindful and conscious," Jeff recalls. Kofman's message was about "getting out of your own head" as a leader—about putting yourself in the shoes of the people that you're working with and trying to understand where they're coming from: their motivations, their strengths, their weaknesses.

Previously, Jeff says, he'd had a more egocentric approach to leadership. "I think I made the mistake of always expecting the people around me to do things the way I did." In this way of thinking, the leader marches out in front, and everyone else is expected to follow. It had always seemed to Jeff like a natural, confident way to lead—but not anymore.

Later, as Jeff was contemplating a move from Yahoo, he arranged to have dinner with Kofman. "I was talking about what I wanted to do next," Jeff says. He didn't have LinkedIn specifically in mind yet, but he did mention to Fred that he was interested in pursuing a goal to "expand the world's collective wisdom."

To which Fred responded: "I can see why you're excited about that. But wisdom without compassion is ruthlessness, and compassion without wisdom is folly."

"Wow, Fred, is that the Dalai Lama?" Jeff asked.

"No," Fred said, "that's me after a couple of Belgian beers."

Whatever inspired those words, they resonated deeply with Jeff. In particular, that word *compassion* became a mantra for him and a central tenet of the new leadership style he would bring with him as he left Yahoo and landed at LinkedIn in 2008.

As LinkedIn's new CEO, Jeff presided over astonishing growth: Over the next ten years, the company surged from 338 employees to more than 10,000; from thirty-two million members to five hundred million; and from $78 million in revenue to $7.9 billion. And he achieved that growth with compassion at the center of his leadership philosophy and style.

As Jeff Weiner succinctly puts it, "Managers tell people what to do. But leaders inspire them to do it." And it doesn't hurt if you've got rhythm and a flair for the snare.

As Jeff set out to spread that rhythm throughout LinkedIn, his first step was to establish direct human contact—with literally every person in the company.

Jeff knew that with three hundred-plus employees, this would be a significant undertaking. But if you're going to think of yourself as a "compassionate leader," he reasoned, you need to care enough about people to make time for them. Moreover, it was the most reliable way for him to get an accurate read on the existing culture. "Before I decided on any plans going forward, I wanted to make sure I understood what was happening—to learn as much as possible from the people who had developed the company up to that point," Jeff says.

While compassion is about understanding other people and being willing and able to see everything through the lens and perspective of the people around you, it also requires some self-examination and reflection—and an effort to resist emotional, gut reactions. As Jeff puts it, you have to try "to be a spectator to your own thoughts, especially when you become emotional. If something triggers you, you have to get out of your own head before you have that knee-jerk anger and say, 'Wait a minute, I wonder what they're experiencing that's making them do that.'"

By taking the time to consider those factors, you can reset conversations, turning potential clashes into more collaborative exchanges. Trading in the occasional blowup for a more productive conversation may sound relatively minor, but those small human interactions add up. When you start to compound that throughout an organization—not just among employees but also customers, shareholders, the press, analysts—"it can really create a lot of value," Jeff points out.

While Jeff leads with compassion, that alone won't necessarily inspire people. If you're trying to create a cohesive culture, there are three specific beats a drum major can lay down. "Number one is to have clarity of vision," Jeff says. "Two is the courage of one's conviction. And three is the ability to effectively communicate those two things."

Clarity of vision is about what you're trying to accomplish as an organization. It's critical that people have a clear sense of where they're trying to go—why they're trying to scale this particular mountain. "The more unique and compelling that vision, the more likely people will be to follow it," Jeff says.

Courage of convictions is about upholding and defending that vision, even (or especially) when there is resistance.

Lastly, you have to be able to effectively communicate both the vision and the conviction—whether through words, actions, or ideally both—to create a compelling narrative that will stick with people.

Jeff is almost obsessive about communicating the vision and values of LinkedIn to its people. He and his team labor over finding precisely the right language. And once the message has been honed, he repeats it, over and over. The drumbeat is incessant.

Some leaders are afraid of repeating themselves, with the assumption being that people will get tired of hearing something they've heard before. They're simply wrong about that, Jeff insists. Citing the work of the renowned political speechwriter David Gergen—who's taught some of the world's most effective communicators—Jeff believes that as a leader, you should repeat key messages even as you get sick of hearing yourself say it. "It's counterintuitive," Jeff acknowledges. Since you're the one saying the words, you're very aware of the repetition. But other people are focused on other things—and need to hear messages repeatedly before they're truly absorbed.

Ensuring that the drumbeat comes through—loud and clear—becomes even more important in a time of crisis. For LinkedIn, one of the biggest tests came in February 2016, when reduced forecasts caused the company's stock value to crash by more than 40 percent in a single day. Rather than trying to shift focus away from the news, Jeff called an all-hands meeting to address it head-on. A video of Jeff making that speech went viral. His main message to his employees: While the stock price might be lower, that was the only thing that had

REID'S ANALYSIS | Keep a consistent drumbeat

One of the most common mistakes companies make as they scale is to drift from their consistent drumbeat. This can happen when new employees join by the hundreds—or by the thousands—and they're so far removed from the leader that they don't really hear the beat. So while they may understand the "what," they may not be clear on the "how." Meaning, they may know what their job is and what the company is trying to do, but they don't appreciate how the company goes about doing what it does. The "how" is all about culture and values of a company, which must be communicated clearly.

At smaller levels of scale, the organization is compact enough that a strong leader can transmit the drumbeat directly to every member of the team. After all, that leader probably interacts with each team member on a regular basis. But as the company scales up, this kind of dialogue becomes impossible. The leader simply doesn't have enough time in the day to engage every employee one-on-one. Instead, the leader needs to switch to one-to-many broadcasting so that every employee hears the drumbeat. Angela Ahrendts used regular videos to broadcast to her team at Apple, while Brian Chesky of Airbnb writes an email to all employees each Sunday to keep them in the loop on what's top of mind for him. You can read more about this transition in my book *Blitzscaling*, where "Dialogue to Broadcasting" is one of the key transitions of scaling.

That dialogue requires more than words. Part of maintaining that consistent drumbeat is for leadership to behave in a consistent way that reinforces the culture and values of the company. For example, often organizations reward people who achieve results without regard for how they achieved them, rather than asking: Did they do it in a way that's consistent with our culture and values?

This tendency to celebrate and reward the "what" instead of the "how" is one of the ways companies lose their character as they grow. You need a clear vision not only of *what* you want to achieve but also *how* you want to achieve it, and you should share that vision, loudly and often—especially if your company has achieved scale and you're cascading those messages to five thousand, ten thousand, or

> fifteen-thousand-plus employees. With more people, there is more distance from the leadership—which means you need to pound the drum harder and more often just to be heard.

changed. "We still have the same mission," Jeff told his people, "and we still have the same culture and values, the same leadership. And the work we're doing is more important than ever."

It's a clear example of how your team's shared beat can be a compassionate, consistent bulwark against despair that everyone can rally around in times of war and times of peace.

The truth-teller (and seeker)

For more than forty years, **Ray Dalio** has made constructive disagreements a bedrock of his company, the legendary hedge fund Bridgewater Associates. As founder, Ray shepherded Bridgewater from a one-man operation run out of his apartment to the largest hedge fund in the world, managing some $160 billion for about 350 institutional clients globally.

But it wasn't a straight path. The story begins back in October 1982, in the halls of the U.S. Congress. Ray was a smart-looking young global macro investor in a dark suit and striped tie, who'd gotten attention for predicting that Mexico was going to default on its foreign debts. He saw a global debt crisis coming—a rolling recession, even total economic collapse—and now Congress had asked him to testify about this.

Ray wasn't the only one calling the future this way. A book called *The Coming Currency Collapse* was soaring up the book charts. Internal White House memos advised President Ronald Reagan on how to manage permanent economic decline. Ray was there to warn the public. He was loud and confident, and he bet his own investment portfolio on the decline of the economy.

But . . .

"I couldn't have been more wrong," Ray says. "It was the exact bottom in the stock market—and we moved into a bull market after that. I lost money for me, my clients. And I only had a small company then, but I had to let everybody in my company go and I was down to me, and I had to borrow $4,000 from my dad to pay for my family expenses."

It was a devastating, humbling loss for Ray and his company. In retrospect, it's easy to see how he made this mistake: He had seen a pattern emerging, and he thought he had the whole picture. But he missed something. He failed to predict that the Fed would loosen monetary policy, which jump-started the markets and led to the '80s economic boom.

His mistake was understandable—but it was also avoidable. Had he consulted anyone, had he built a system for testing his assumptions before betting big, he might have hedged his bets and reduced the company's exposure. In short, what he needed was more opportunity for people to tell him he was wrong.

Ray clawed his way back from the disaster of 1982, and Bridgewater eventually recovered and started to expand. But he was determined not to make the same mistakes again. "I've got a principle that it's okay to make mistakes, but it's not okay to not learn from them," he says.

Asking himself, *How can I find the smartest people I know who disagree with me?*, Ray re-envisioned the way his team interacted with him and with each other. He told them, "I think every organization, or every relationship, requires people to decide how they're going to be with each other. I'm going to be radically truthful with you and radically transparent, and I expect you to be radically truthful and transparent with me."

"Radical transparency" became an organizing principle for Bridgewater, and for Ray personally: a rigorous, formalized method of truth-telling that puts the highest premium on speaking uncompromising truths. The idea behind this method is simple: May the best ideas win.

For radical transparency to work, people in the organization—particularly those in power—had to be clear and open about why they made certain decisions. Ray immediately began to model this behavior himself: With each decision he made, he would reflect on it afterward, documenting the criteria or principles driving the decision. Doing this "creates a clarity in your own mind," Ray explains, "and it allows you to communicate that to other people."

Ray then shared all of his reflecting process with people in the company—tapes, videos, and written documents explaining all of the principles behind what was happening each day. Employees could look at that and decide for themselves, "Do those make sense? Would I do something differently?" That would lead to discussion groups within the company around the principles.

But this didn't mean people could disregard those decisions or simply choose to make their own rules. One of Ray's guiding principles is: *Make sure people don't confuse the right to complain, give advice, and openly debate with the right to make decisions.*

A common reason some organizations resist inviting open debate is because they don't want it to result in chaos or a total lack of boundaries. However, this can be easily avoided as long as it's clearly communicated that the leaders are still the leaders, and they still make the key decisions—but they also are committed to listening and truly considering input that comes from anyone, anywhere in the company.

As Ray continued to document and share his principles at Bridgewater, they began to take on a life of their own. What started as an internal memo became a downloadable PDF that quickly spread beyond the company (it was eventually downloaded about three million times). Then it became a best-selling book, *Principles,* and from there an iPhone app, a children's book, and a popular Instagram account.

It should be noted that when you invite people to speak freely, as Ray did, you may not always like what you hear. At one point, Ray was told by colleagues at Bridgewater that some of the radical candor that he and others at the company were sharing could be harsh at times—and that in some cases, it was hurting morale.

Ironically, the fact that Ray's colleagues were able to tell him this hard truth—and that he listened—makes a good argument for a system of radical candor and constructive disagreement. The criticism showed him that his system worked—but that it might need some tweaking. So the company also developed some protocols and guidelines to try to keep disagreements and criticism constructive and positive. For example, disagreeing parties were urged to follow two-minute rules limiting the duration of a disagreement and to turn to others in the company who would serve as mediators. And guidelines suggested that everyone (Ray included) should endeavor to frame criticism in more positive terms—for instance, recasting failures as learning opportunities.

To get the most out of radical transparency, Ray says, it should be approached with a spirit of mutual respect, curiosity about others' views, and a recognition that everyone's on the same team—even if they're not always on the same page.

Sheryl Sandberg of Facebook also champions this approach. She believes it's incumbent on leaders to invite people in the organization to be completely honest with them, because if people don't feel free to speak up, then they simply won't do it—and you'll miss out on critical information. Sheryl learned this lesson years before arriving at Facebook, way back in Google's early days, when she was hired by Eric Schmidt to build out the advertising revenue that would fuel Google's growth. And to build revenue, she had to build a team.

Sheryl started with a cozy team of four people, who were concerned about how the team's eventual growth would affect their team dynamics. On her first day, she assured them that each person on the team would be involved in interviewing new hires.

Two weeks later, the team had tripled in size, and it proved problematic to have a job candidate interview with twelve people. "So, this promise I had made to make them feel good about scaling, I took away in a week," she says. Sheryl was encountering a classic challenge of leading at scale—when your assumptions one week are overturned the next.

As her team kept growing, Sheryl continued to interview everyone who joined. When they reached one hundred people, she noticed that her interview queue was holding up the hiring process. In a meeting with her direct reports, she said, "I think I should stop interviewing." She fully expected that they would jump right in and say, "Absolutely not. You're a great interviewer. We need your personal recommendation on anyone on your team."

"You know what they did?" Sheryl asks with a smile in her voice. "They applauded. And I thought to myself, 'I've become a bottleneck, and you didn't tell me. And that's on me.'"

Notice that Sheryl wasn't bothered by her team applauding her decision to step aside. She was, however, disturbed by the fact that no one had told her the truth earlier. She knew she needed everyone's honest input to make the frequent, fast decisions Google's business demands. But that kind of openness doesn't happen on its own.

"I realized: I had to make it safe to speak up," says Sheryl.

This is a leadership lesson that entrepreneurs in particular should heed. The skills that make someone a brilliant and visionary founder— someone intensely focused on vision—aren't always married with the skills of being a good communicator.

REID'S ANALYSIS | Harnessing constructive conflict

The ancient Greek philosopher Socrates is famous for championing the power of cooperative argumentative dialogue to stimulate critical thinking. His approach, eventually dubbed the Socratic method, involved one person asking questions, and the other answering, until together only one hypothesis was left. The discussion could get heated, but both parties understood that they were challenging each other in service of a greater truth.

It's probably worth mentioning that Socrates was put to death for his beliefs—and for spreading those beliefs too widely to the youth of Athens. So it's safe to say that challenging established thinking doesn't always sit well with people. But I'd argue it's not only a good idea to harness constructive conflict, it's critical to the decision-making process. You can't effectively set a strategy or decide direction if you're unwilling to grapple with tough questions and have some disagreement over ideas. Thoughtful leaders thrive on disagreement because it gives them the information they need to improve their ideas before they reach the world.

We all have our own personal threshold of comfort around conflict. Some people thrive on lively debate; others find it deeply stressful. But if the boss can't be challenged safely, then no one can. I believe it's your job as a leader to invite good criticism. By constructively harnessing disagreements on your team, you improve ideas and fuel great focused work.

The pirate tamer

It's never easy for a new leader to take the helm at an established company. But when that company is Uber—and it is going through the kind of turmoil and scandal that Uber was experiencing in 2017—what kind of a person would want to wade into that quagmire?

Dara Khosrowshahi is that kind of person. An experienced leader who'd been running fast-growing companies ever since his boss Barry Diller plucked the twenty-something Iranian American out of nowhere and put him in a senior leadership position, Dara knew what it looked like to be thrown into the deep end of the pool and left to sink or swim. Dara's father had been a successful business leader in Iran who had everything taken from him and was forced to flee the country during the Iranian revolution—only to rebuild his career and life from scratch in America. So Dara saw firsthand that it's possible to survive and come back from even the most devastating setback.

But still . . . walking into Uber in 2017? When asked what that must have been like, Dara responds: "I'm sweating because I'm remembering that first week."

A bit of background on just what Dara was walking into: First it should be acknowledged, without a doubt, that Uber was a huge success. Fueled by more than $22 billion in VC funding, Uber had, by 2017, become nearly ubiquitous, operating in six hundred cities around the world.

But its size came with a cost; as Uber scaled rapidly, its culture began to veer out of control, owing to a combination of toxic leadership and questionable business tactics. Soon the company was awash in bad press, tales of political infighting, allegations of corporate espionage, and even criminal investigations. It didn't help that the company's leadership team, headed by founder Travis Kalanick, also displayed a cavalier attitude toward spending.

There were run-ins with regulators, taxi firms, and even Uber's own drivers. Uber saw a backlash in its key markets and withdrew from some, such as China. Back home, Uber's controversial approach to charging higher fares at peak times came to a head with the #DeleteUber campaign.

And then there was Uber's notorious, hyperaggressive "bro" culture. In February 2017—six months before Dara became CEO—a blog post by former Uber engineer Susan Fowler blew the lid off the misogyny and harassment that was rife at the company.

As the only woman on Uber's board of directors, Arianna Huffington had become deeply involved in trying to fix the company's culture. Arianna felt that Uber was an extreme manifestation of a larger problem in the startup world at that time—"the whole culture of worshipping at the altar of hyper-growth. Where if you are a top performer, anything is allowed," as she describes it. As the board began to crack down on Uber, Arianna issued this promise on behalf of her fellow board members: "Going forward, no more 'brilliant jerks' will be allowed at Uber."

Still, the board could only do so much. It was up to the new chief executive to climb aboard this pirate ship and get things under control—ideally, without completely losing the good parts of the bold buccaneer spirit that had helped fuel Uber's early success. After all, many successful startups have pirate-like qualities—scrappiness, inventiveness, a willingness to venture into unknown areas (and sometimes onto others' turf), and a penchant for disregarding or breaking rules.

As Mailchimp founder **Ben Chestnut** puts it: "When you're a startup founder, it's all pirates. Who joins a startup? Crazy people, because startups are so risky. They've got a chip on their shoulder. They've got something to prove. They don't want rules. They want to do everything."

But those pirate founders sometimes have trouble as their startup grows—because at a certain point, that pirate ship has to join the navy. It has to become a more mature, responsible organization. Startup founders often enlist outside help at that point. "The founders build something great, and then they hire other people to maintain it," Ben explains. "And those people are different." Usually, the outsider is an experienced executive who knows how to "run things" and put systems in place.

For Dara, the first surprise upon arriving at Uber was meeting the rest of the leadership at the helm of this notoriously swashbuckling operation. "The public perception of the company was so different from the people that I met when I got there," he says. Dara found a

company filled with smart, capable people who could've easily abandoned ship and gotten good jobs elsewhere—but wanted to stick it out
because they believed in Uber.

Dara saw firsthand that most people working at Uber were not a
bunch of lawless bandits. But the culture there had clearly promoted
a level of reckless behavior. Which meant that Dara faced a challenge
familiar to other leaders in charge of rapidly scaling startups: How do
you tame the pirates just enough, but not *too* much?

A good starting point was to recognize the difference between
ethical pirates and criminal ones. Ethical pirates may overturn conventional rules of business, but they don't break laws or do things that
cause actual harm. They're driven by their own strong moral code.
(Think Captain Jack Sparrow in *Pirates of the Caribbean*.) Criminal
pirates have no such moral compass. They'll do just about anything in
pursuit of success, glory, thrills, and riches.

Dara knew that to right the ship at Uber, he'd need to firmly end
the era of rule-breaking pirates, while encouraging the many ethical
warriors he found among its ranks. From the outset, he took a leadership approach that he'd begun to develop in his years working for Barry
Diller as head of the travel website Expedia. Rather than coming in
and trying to impose a new culture on Uber, Dara wanted to see if he
could encourage the people already there to help shape and guide the
necessary transformation.

So Dara immediately asked the Uber employees: *What do you
think should represent the culture of Uber going forward?*

Before Dara, Uber's cultural guidelines included full-on bro-tastic
maxims like "Superpumped" and "Always be hustlin'." But as Dara
began to hear back from the employees, it became clear that everyone
was ready and eager to leave the bro nonsense behind. In fact, some
of the themes were squarely aimed at overcoming the toxic culture
they had been living with. There were calls to celebrate diversity of
background, race, religion, gender, and sexuality. There was the notion
that "no matter what you bring to the table, you should be able to contribute to what we call Uber."

What also emerged was that the people at Uber were committed
to "doing the right thing." But they also wanted to be trusted to do
that—without being constantly micromanaged.

For Dara, this harked back to a specific lesson he'd learned at Expedia in 2005. As the CEO of the then-struggling travel website, he was "working day and night, making decision after decision after decision." He thought that all the work he was putting in meant he was doing a great job. That is, until a young Expedia manager said to him, "Dara, you keep telling us what to do, instead of telling us where to go." The manager explained that this demotivated people and actually wasn't all that productive—because as people got used to Dara telling them what to do, it meant that when Dara wasn't around, nothing happened. So the manager asked, "Can you just tell us where you want us to go—and then let us figure out how to get there?"

"For me, it was like, boom, eye popping," Dara says now. "I had to really work hard—because I was a bit of a control freak—to let go of what people are doing and really start talking about where we're going and trust my team to get us there."

What Dara's talking about is a challenge for almost any founder, most of whom start out as problem solvers who are used to doing it all themselves. But the job of a leader is not to micromanage and come up with solutions. It's to define both success and the very real constraints of a project for the team, and then let them come up with the solutions.

With this in mind, Dara made a serious effort not to be overly prescriptive with Uber's staff. As he collected input from them, a drumbeat message emerged that was simply: *We do the right thing, period.* "We didn't want to define to the employees what the right thing is," Dara says. Instead, Dara told them, "You already know what the right thing is. And from now on, that's what we're going to do."

Dara also started an employee-led listening program called 180 Days of Change that immediately focused in on the company's strained relationship with drivers (a problem that had been very publicly highlighted in a video of Travis Kalanick yelling at an Uber driver, which had gone viral). Dara, who makes a point to meet with local drivers everywhere he travels, took a markedly different approach to that critical relationship.

"We call our drivers 'driver-partners,'" he says. "And I wanted to treat them like that." Employee input led to some immediate pro-driver changes, like allowing tipping and paying drivers for time spent waiting on late-arriving passengers. Uber also launched a new driver app that was built and tested at every step with driver-partner input.

In general, Dara has tried to mend the company's relationships by moving away from confrontation and more toward collaboration. This attitude applies to his give-and-take negotiations with city transportation authorities like the Transport for London (TfL), which wanted to revoke Uber's license. In the past, the company would have gone straight into corporate battle mode over this. Now, Dara flew over himself to meet with the TfL's commissioner. "Instead of going through lawyers," he says, "the dialogue was now happening through two people sitting across the desk talking, maybe not agreeing on all things, but trying to come up with some compromise."

There's usually a moment in the turnaround of a company when the leader suddenly feels: "We've dug ourselves out—we're on the right path now." When Dara was asked a year and a half into his Uber leadership if he had that feeling yet, he was candid. "I'm still waiting for that moment," he said. "We're in a much better spot now—but cultural transformation is hard and it takes a long time."

So, as we write this, the Uber pirate ship hasn't fully joined the navy just yet—maybe it never will. And maybe that's all right, because under Dara, the fireworks have quieted, the bro culture has been banished, and the "brilliant jerks" no longer need apply.

The star-maker

As we've seen, leaders of scaling companies are called on to do the hard work of defining the mission, setting the tone, connecting the disparate parts and personalities, and bringing at least some order to a chaotic environment. But when **Marissa Mayer**, Google employee number 20, was hired as the company's first female engineer, she faced a different kind of leadership challenge. From the outset, Google needed an army of flexible, versatile top performers who could help the company quickly get to the next level. In other words, Google needed a bunch of stars—yet didn't have time to find and hire them. So Marissa had to make those stars herself.

Google in those early days had many small teams working on different products and features. When it was time for new offerings to go

REID'S ANALYSIS | Why even pirates need to evolve

For decades now, startups have had an affinity for pirates. And it began—like so many things in tech—with Steve Jobs. When Steve was building the first Macintosh, he coined the phrase "It's better to be a pirate than to join the navy." The Mac team got on board, creating a homemade pirate flag with a rainbow Apple logo as an eye patch. In Silicon Valley, the pirate image stuck.

It's easy to be seduced by this image of the entrepreneur as pirate. Who doesn't want to imagine themselves leaping across the rigging, cutlass in hand? And truth be told, early-stage startups are a lot like pirate ships. Pirates don't convene a committee meeting to decide what to do—they strike quickly, break rules, and take risks. And you need this buccaneering spirit to survive when the cannonballs are flying and the odds are against you.

But some startups cross the line from swashbuckling hero to dirty rotten scoundrel, especially as they grow. It's all too easy for a culture to cross the line from one that joyfully flouts orthodoxy to one that truly believes that winning is all that matters, ethics be damned.

And there's a second problem with piracy: It doesn't scale. If you succeed as a pirate, your stockpiles of treasure will grow. The territories you control will widen. But you can't protect and patrol that much territory with only a ragtag fleet of pirate ships.

This is why every startup needs to shed its lawless, anything-goes culture at some point, and evolve into something more akin to a navy—no less heroic, but more disciplined, with rules of engagement, lines of communication, and long-term strategy. You can read more about ethical pirates and commanding admirals in my book *Blitzscaling*, where we discuss the key transition from pirate to navy.

live, they would often turn to Marissa for design or engineering tweaks. This gave her a clear view of every product and every team throughout the organized chaos of the entire company. She was also one of the few people who knew how Google's systems worked.

As the company grew increasingly complex, there was a new imperative: Google needed more product managers—people with minds nimble enough to cover any and every aspect of the company's fast-growing range of products, and who could also quickly achieve the same impressive level of mastery that Marissa and other early employees commanded. But how to find these people?

It was at this point that Marissa entered into a historic wager with her manager, Jonathan Rosenberg. "Jonathan wanted to hire experienced MBAs and more senior people," remembers Marissa. "I bet him that I could hire new people right out of school and train them to be great product managers at Google—and do it faster."

Marissa's first hire was twenty-two-year-old Brian Rakowski, fresh out of college. What project did Marissa choose to ease him in? She gave him . . . the whole of Gmail. She did likewise with other new hires: "We brought them in and gave them all these huge unfilled jobs. They had to have been the most stressed-out bunch of twenty-two- and twenty-three-year-olds in the world."

Marissa named this trial by fire the Associate Product Manager program. From the beginning, Google's APM program was founded on the principle of exposing new product managers not just to one product but to many. At the core of the program was a yearly rotation that moved the new product managers between different departments.

It's human nature that once people learn a job, they tend to want to stick with it for a while—so APM members initially resisted being rotated. But Marissa coached them to embrace this opportunity—and devised a Mad Libs–style exercise as a way to illustrate the benefits.

As they were going through a rotation, APMs were asked to fill in the blanks on the following statement: I used to do X and now I'm going to do Y, and by making this change, I'm going to learn Z: As in, I used to work on AdWords, now I'm moving on to Search. By making this change, I'm going to learn the difference between having advertisers as my users versus consumers as my users.

Google's APM program became a well-oiled machine that churned out the very product managers that Google needed. Meanwhile, this system also encouraged the spread of ideas throughout Google. It brought resources to new projects. And it brought new thinking to existing ones.

"By going across disciplines, it meant you knew someone at YouTube, somebody working in social, or infrastructure," Marissa says.

"This started creating a really wonderful element of glue across the organization."

In the program's first year, 2002, Marissa hired eight APMs. By 2008, she was hiring twenty a year. Now more than five hundred APMs have gone through Google's program. Started on a bet, the APM program is one of the great unknown successes at Google. It may not be as famous as Gmail, Search, and AI, but many of those better-known products would not have been possible without it.

And Marissa's success points to another key attribute for leaders— the ability to nurture and develop talent from within. Hiring stars is expensive, and sometimes impossible, because there are only so many of them, and the right talent may not be available at any given time. Moreover, constantly bringing in outsiders doesn't build and strengthen the culture the same way that developing in-house talent does. To quote Barry Diller, renowned for developing young talent at his various companies, "If you hire people at senior positions, you are a failure as a leader."

The stars Marissa helped to shape at Google eventually shot out into the larger tech universe, landing at other companies. Marissa herself eventually did likewise, moving to Yahoo in 2012. It was a company that pioneered many of the online services we take for granted today. But it had failed to capitalize on those achievements and, having burned through four CEOs in five years, was in desperate need of a turnaround when Marissa arrived.

In the midst of this dire situation, Marissa couldn't hire an entirely new team at scale. But she could create the team that she needed out of the employees she had.

The problem at Yahoo was not a lack of talent—Marissa could sense early on that there was plenty of that. But the energy and enthusiasm required to activate that talent lay dormant, stifled by layers of bureaucracy and years of mismanagement. During Marissa's first week, she recalls an employee walking up to her and saying: "There's a whole bunch of us that have been here for years, waiting for the leadership and the board to figure itself out. Is it go-time? Can we actually run, do stuff, build stuff?" Marissa assured him that it was, indeed, "go time"—and that part of the reason she was at Yahoo was to clear away the obstacles so people could focus on bringing their ideas to life.

This notion of a leader being someone who "clears the path" was an idea Marissa had picked up from her former boss at Google, Eric Schmidt. Marissa recalls Eric frequently saying: "As a leader, you don't get to do the hands-on work anymore of, say, writing code or designing things. Your job is to point the team in a direction and get everything else out of their way. In order for them to do the best work they can do, you've got to clear the pathway for them."

To think of leadership in this way flips the script: The leader becomes the one doing the unglamorous grunt work that enables others to shine—in football terms, the blocker who fends off opponents and creates an opening for a teammate to score the touchdown. It's a core principle of servant leadership, which inverts business convention by encouraging the leader to try to understand and address the problems and needs of employees, rather than the other way around. Shellye Archambeau, former CEO of the risk-management platform MetricStream, says that as a servant leader, "my job is to be running slightly ahead of everyone else, knocking out the boulders, making sure the trees aren't blocking the road. My job is to make their jobs easier. I have to figure out what problems they've got, and how I can help them solve those issues."

At Yahoo, Marissa immediately started clearing away the boulders and dead trees blocking her team's path forward. One of her first moves was to appoint a "Red-Tape Machete" specialist, whose job was to identify obstacles caused by Yahoo's excessive bureaucracy. "We wanted people to report processes that didn't make sense to them," recalls Marissa. This led to weekly sessions called "PB and J" meetings, which stood for process, bureaucracy, and jams. Anyone in the company could suggest a problem for the Red-Tape Machete to take on, as long as they also proposed a solution for it. Those fixes started to make Yahoo function better—and also had the effect of empowering the people who worked there to be part of the solution.

Marissa also wanted to encourage new ideas to flourish. Yahoo wasn't the fresh slate that Google had been, so Marissa didn't have the opportunity to seed the primordial goop of a new company. But what she could do was surface the ideas that she suspected were already out there, buried in the muck. She decided she would take the employees she had and turn them into the idea-generating machines she needed.

So she issued the CEO Challenge, inviting anyone, anywhere in the company, to propose new ideas to build the business. And there was a big potential payoff: If an idea generated $5 million a year extra, the prize was $50,000 for each individual behind it. "I thought we'd get about two dozen ideas, maybe greenlight six of them," Marissa says.

Instead, she got more than eight hundred. Marissa and her team greenlit almost two hundred of them. The outpouring of new ideas at Yahoo led to big innovations (like streaming ads on the home page) and new revenue on a large scale.

Cultivating the skills you need in the people you already have is easier at a smaller startup. The company culture is still being formed; you have a longer timeline. It's not impossible to do at a larger company—but you have to keep your eye on the clock. At Yahoo, the clock was ticking from the time Marissa got there. Many of its investors had already lost faith; the only real value they saw left in the company was its ownership stake in the Chinese internet giant Alibaba.

At the start of Marissa's tenure, Yahoo's Alibaba investment had kept Yahoo afloat and even helped fund some of Marissa's early efforts to revive the company. But when investors became eager to cash out the Alibaba holdings, Marissa and her team simply ran out of time. It's worth noting, however, that in the last six quarters of Marissa's tenure, Yahoo consistently beat Wall Street projections, as well as the company's own forecasts; and in five years, the company had created almost $2 billion of entirely new invented revenue from inside the company. Marissa thinks if she'd had another year to work with, Yahoo could have turned the corner.

Turnarounds don't always work out, but even when they don't, there are lessons to be learned. Marissa showed that her strategy for developing talent from within could get big results—not only at a high-flying company like Google but even at a down-and-out one like Yahoo.

REID'S THEORIES ON LEADERSHIP

The drum major

A great leader's drumbeat doesn't force people to follow them; it inspires them to move in the same direction of their own volition. Your drumbeat depends on your temperament, your experiences, and your company. Your drumbeat might be focused on efficiency, or innovation, or work-life balance. Or perhaps a mix of all these.

The compassionate leader

A core tenet of compassionate leadership is being willing to see everything through the lens and perspective of the people around you. It also requires some self-examination and reflection—and an effort to resist emotional, gut reactions. By paying attention to the people you lead and being willing to learn from them, you're helping your people find their own rhythm.

The truth-teller (and seeker)

As a truth-teller, be prepared to document the criteria or principles driving your decisions. Doing so creates a clarity in your own mind and helps you communicate your thinking to other people. And while free-flowing feedback is nonnegotiable for radically transparent companies, it's important to develop protocols and guidelines to keep disagreements and criticism moving in a constructive, positive direction.

The connector

Whether your staff is seventy thousand people or a team of seven, a leader needs two things to create a strong unified team: an elevated mission and everyday human contact. Inspire people with a guiding mission, then connect them with each other. And then watch them take ownership of that mission and become leaders themselves.

The ship captain

Many startups have piratical qualities in their early days—scrappiness, inventiveness, a willingness to venture into unknown areas. Rather than trying to tame those qualities by imposing a new culture from the top down, encourage the pirates to help shape and guide the necessary transformation to a culture that looks more like the navy—with rules of engagement, lines of communication, and long-term strategy.

The star-maker

Hiring stars is expensive and sometimes impossible because the right talent may not be available. The best leaders are those who are able to nurture and develop talent from within. Your role then becomes to identify bottlenecks and clear away obstacles so your new stars can shine.

10

The Trojan Horse

Howard Schultz grew up in public housing in the neighborhood of Canarsie, on the eastern shore of Brooklyn. Howard's father was a World War II veteran who didn't experience the American dream he thought he was coming home to after the war.

Howard's father returned home with yellow fever and struggled to make ends meet. The economy was booming in postwar America, but as a high school dropout, he didn't have a lot of options. The worst in his series of dead-end jobs was as a delivery driver picking up and delivering cloth diapers. During one delivery, he slipped on a sheet of ice and fractured his ankle and broke his hip. The injury got him fired. No workman's compensation, no health insurance, no safety net.

"When I was seven years old I came home from school, opened the apartment door, and saw my father laid out on a couch with a cast from his hip to his ankle," Howard says. "At the age of seven, how could I possibly understand the impact that would have on me? But I know it scarred me to witness the hard time my parents went through. It sensitized me to people living on the other side of the tracks."

Years later, at his own company, **Starbucks**, Howard tried to build "the kind of company my father never got a chance to work for. A company that would try to balance profit with conscience." Howard began thinking about how to maintain this delicate balance from the earliest days in his career.

In 1986, Howard was living in Seattle, and working for the original Starbucks—a relatively small, local operation with just a handful of stores. But a fateful business trip to Milan gave him a bigger idea of the role coffee could play in people's lives. "I became enamored with the fact that on every street there were two or three coffee bars. What I witnessed was the romance, the theater and joy of espresso.

"I would go back to these coffee bars every day I was in Italy, and I began to witness something: I would see the same people who were doing this routinely. They didn't know each other, but there was a camaraderie between them because there was a sense of place, a sense of community, and there was human connection over coffee."

Howard returned to Seattle, left Starbucks, and founded his own upstart company, with several Milan-style coffee bars. Meanwhile, the original Starbucks acquired Peet's Coffee, based in Berkeley, California. The overextended owners realized they had bitten off more than they could chew—and decided to sell Starbucks. They gave Howard first dibs.

Howard was able to attract investors with his vision of a new kind of coffee shop and raised the money to acquire Starbucks—then six stores and an old roasting facility—for the modest sum of $3.8 million. By the end of 1987, he had eleven stores, one hundred employees, and a dream of expanding the "theater and romance" of Italian coffee culture nationwide.

But before undertaking this next wave of early expansion, he had another priority in mind: He started planning a benefits package for those one hundred employees. For Howard's private investors, learning of this plan was just the first of many befuddling encounters.

"You can imagine this conversation," says Howard. "We were small, losing money, with a not-yet-proven business model. And I say, 'I want to provide health insurance and equity in the form of stock options for every person who works for the company.'"

They thought this decision was, shall we say, misguided.

But Howard laid out the business case for conscience: "I want to invest in our people," he said, "and I think I will be able to prove that we will lower attrition, raise performance, but most importantly create the kind of company in which people feel part of something larger than themselves."

Thus, Starbucks became the first company in America to provide comprehensive health insurance to everyone—full-time and part-time workers alike (those working twenty hours or more). "And we figured out a way to provide equity in the form of stock options to every single employee, again, even part-timers," Howard recalls.

Notice that when Howard first pitched the concept to his investors, he didn't say, "I want to invest in our people because it's the right thing to do" or "I want to invest in our people because no one invested in my father." Instead, he said, "I want to invest in our people, *because it's good for our business.*" That's the kind of reasoning that investors can get behind.

"When I look back on what we've been able to achieve today, there's no doubt in my mind—none whatsoever—that the twenty-eight thousand stores we have in seventy-six countries would never have been accomplished without the culture, values, and guiding principles. If the core purpose of the company wasn't defined by putting our people first, and ensuring success, we would not be here. I know that for a fact."

This idea of doing well by doing good is far from universal today. And it was much less common when Howard took the reins at Starbucks in the late 1980s. His board members, at the time, didn't quite know what to make of him. But he made the right bet—as demonstrated by Starbucks' remarkable long-term growth in the years that followed.

Many great founders have a secondary purpose, something outside their main business objective they're trying to get done in the world. In fact, you could say that every successful company is like a Trojan horse carrying the founder's second purpose forward.

In this final chapter, we'll consider some of the ways to bring that second purpose to the fore—whether by smuggling it into the world

Trojan horse–style, by making it a foundational feature of your business, or by finding a way to graft purpose onto an existing business.

When your business scales massively, you touch lives on many different levels. Your decisions impact employees, customers, entire communities. You have the opportunity to shape the world, for better or for worse. And that creates an opportunity and even a responsibility to ask: *What do we want to stand for? How can we make people's lives better? And how can we do that in a way that strengthens our business?*

It's not about telling yourself, "I'm a good person, so my company will do good things." It's about asking, "What kind of positive impact can I have that will also support my core business?" And these concerns don't have to be mere side effects of your business; if you're strategic about it, they can, and should, become the beating heart of your business.

Struggling startup founders may think that's a nice idea for later on . . . something they can think about *after* they scale. But the best scale entrepreneurs think about their social impact from day one.

Twin questions: "How do I do good?" and "How do I do good business?"

From the earliest days of Starbucks, Howard Schultz imagined a future where the company's success would be intertwined with that of its employees. "I have many of these old journals that I kept," Howard recalls. "I wrote something early on about how the business plan of this new company was going to be to achieve the fragile balance between profit and conscience."

A balance of profit and conscience sounds simple on paper, but it gets complex when it meets the world. "I started thinking about: What does that really mean?"

"What's important to understand is we had no money to build traditional marketing, or advertising, or PR," Howard says. "We had none of that. And so we defined the brand by the experience in our stores. And we said early on that the equity of the brand would be defined by the managers and leaders of the company exceeding the expectations of our people—so that they could exceed the expectations of the customer.

"And because coffee is so personal and it's frequent, we had an opportunity to create an intimacy with the customer that built the equity of the brand."

Healthcare and stock options turned out to be only the beginning for Howard—he shocked his investors again when he announced he was going to provide a free college education to many Starbucks employees.

"When we started looking at the cost of free tuition, there was great trepidation and concern that we could not afford to do it," he says. "But like anything else, when you get a group of smart people in a room and you leave your ego outside, you can say, *We're not going to leave the room until we solve the problem.* The problem was how do we make this cost-neutral? And we figured out a way."

In 2014, Starbucks introduced a first-of-its-kind partnership with Arizona State University to cover, in full, college tuition for every American Starbucks employee working twenty or more hours a week. Starbucks and ASU split the tuition costs sixty-forty. The degrees were exclusively offered online, allowing employees to stay in their jobs and ASU to keep their costs contained.

Note that once again, Howard and his team approached the issue of free tuition like they would any other piece of their business. He didn't say, "Education is priceless, so any cost is okay." Instead he argued, "Let's figure out how to get the best value."

Starbucks' benefits plans can seem extravagantly generous at first glance. But this generosity pays off, as it did in China—eventually.

These days Starbucks has more than forty-eight hundred stores in China, with a new one opening every fifteen hours.

But it wasn't always so.

"We lost money for nine consecutive years in China," says Howard, "and investors said, 'This isn't working, it's a tea-drinking society, close it up.'"

On top of losing money, Starbucks was having trouble retaining its Chinese workers. Howard's years of focus on employee well-being, though, had helped him spot the pivotal role Chinese parents play in guiding their kids' careers. Most of the people running Starbucks stores in China are college graduates. Howard realized that their parents had the feeling *I sent my son or daughter to college and now they're serving coffee as opposed to working for Apple, or Google, or Alibaba. It's not right*. The influential parents' dissatisfaction with their child's job status was leading to high employee turnover, hampering growth.

Howard's solution: Show the Chinese parents the clear benefits of a Starbucks job, and the people-first philosophy behind it. First, the company extended health insurance not only to every employee but to their parents, too. As hoped, retention rates soared. Then to truly demonstrate the company's understanding of Chinese family-centric values, Howard told his board, "I want to have an annual meeting of the parents of our employees in China."

Remember, Starbucks opens a new store in China every fifteen hours. When Howard says, let's meet "the parents of our employees in China," he's talking about more than a few symbolic handshakes. As you can imagine, this was a huge line item for a market that was still finding its feet and took some convincing of the board about its business value.

The Starbucks' parents event, though, was a big hit with Chinese parents and employees alike, and it has become an annual institution. "The meeting of parents is a celebration of *families* who are working at Starbucks, of us highlighting their children," Howard says. "We fly parents to Shanghai or Beijing who have never been on an airplane. We surprise our partners who don't know their parents are coming, and it's very emotional. It is the thing every year that I refuse to miss."

The appeal of these family meetings in China isn't just that they helped solve a business problem, although staff retention rocketed, and that had a cascading effect on customer retention. Rather, for Howard, the meetings' focus on employee loyalty and happiness captures the essence of the global company—its humanity. "These kinds of moments are so emotionally alive with the spirit and culture and values of Starbucks," he says. "What we've learned through all of this is that we are all longing for human connection."

As companies reach the kind of massive scale that Starbucks achieved, though, they inevitably face a new set of challenges. The twin questions—"How do I do good?" and "How do I do good business?"—become more complicated as your opportunities, and your responsibilities, scale. And it becomes harder to prevent customers from becoming "revenue" and employees from becoming "headcount."

Howard thinks Starbucks has mostly managed to avoid those pitfalls because the company's commitment to doing good was established early—and then, as Starbucks grew over the years, those values became clearly linked to the company's success.

"Starbucks is not profit driven," says Howard. "Starbucks is values driven, and as a result of those values, we have become very profitable. Not every business decision should be an economic one. Our financial performance is directly linked to the enduring values and culture that we are constantly trying to enhance and preserve."

REID'S ANALYSIS | What wall do you want to break down?

We all know the story of the original Trojan horse. An enormous towering wooden horse on wheels appears at the gates of ancient Troy. It was sent by the Greeks as a peace offering during a brutal ten-year war. But inside that horse, lying in wait, was the great warrior Odysseus and an elite team of thirty Greek warriors. The horse is wheeled into the city. The soldiers wait until nightfall, they sneak out of the horse, and they open the gates to the rest of the army. And that was it for Troy.

Okay, so bloodthirsty soldiers carrying out a massacre don't *exactly* speak to the higher purpose of business. Neither do the "Trojan horse" viruses that your IT department fights. But imagine instead that the perimeter you're trying to breach isn't the wall of a sovereign city or the firewall of an unsuspecting internet user. Instead, you're trying to break through a different kind of wall:

A wall of systemic prejudice.

Or intractable disease.

Or entrenched inequity.

Or lazy assumptions.

Imagine the army you want to unleash from the horse's belly isn't there to inflict violence, but to tear down walls that limit the human experience. A Trojan horse is only as good or as bad as its intended purpose. And a business or a career can be a kind of virtuous Trojan horse—a well-built construction that carries the founder's second purpose forward. The company's mission builds a great business, but also an important transformation of society.

Create the change you want to see

Linda Rottenberg has a nickname: *Chica Loca*. It means "crazy woman." And to Linda, that's a compliment.

She got the nickname a couple of decades ago while living in Latin America, where she was trying to raise money for local entrepreneurs. At the time she launched Endeavor, startups were popping up—and raising money quickly—all over the United States, but in Latin America, "no one was starting a business," Linda recalls. In fact, there was so little awareness about the possibilities of entrepreneurship that she recalls there wasn't even a word for "entrepreneur" in Spanish at the time.

Her company aimed to change all that.

But first Linda had to find backers. She managed to get a ten-minute meeting with one of Argentina's top real estate magnates, Eduardo Elsztain, at his office in Buenos Aires. Eduardo's business at one point had been funded by the billionaire George Soros. "So as soon as I go in to meet Eduardo he says, 'I get it, you want a meeting with George Soros. I'll see what I can do.'

"I said, 'No, Eduardo—you're an entrepreneur. I'm an entrepreneur. And Endeavor is an organization of, by, and for entrepreneurs. I want your time, your passion—and $200,000.'"

At that point, Linda recalls, "Eduardo turns to his right-hand guy and says, *'Esta chica es loca.'*" Linda then pointed out to Eduardo that he had once famously walked into Soros's office and then walked out with a $10 million check. "So you're lucky I only asked you for two hundred grand," Linda said.

Eduardo wrote her the check and became chair of Endeavor Argentina. "And today he says it was the best investment he ever made," Linda says.

Meanwhile, Linda decided to embrace that word *crazy* as a badge of honor. "Everyone had been calling my Endeavor idea crazy, and I didn't think it was crazy. And I realized, **entrepreneurs don't think what they're doing is crazy—though other people do, because it's threatening to the status quo.**"

Linda's crazy Endeavor idea—that there was entrepreneurial talent in unexpected places around the world, and that these people could build innovative, scalable businesses that could create jobs—turned out to be not so crazy at all. And it's also a prime example of one of the most important ways any successful entrepreneurial company can contribute to the larger world—by paying it forward.

Paying it forward can take any number of forms, from mentoring programs, to investing in other startups, to focusing on specific areas—geographic regions, or underrepresented groups of people—with the goal of helping to encourage, strengthen, and diversify the next generation of entrepreneurial leaders.

As Linda tried to build an entrepreneurial culture in Central and South America, one of the first people Endeavor backed was **Wences Casares**, a kid who'd grown up on a sheep farm in Patagonia. In his early twenties, he created the area's first internet service provider—then it got taken over and he was thrown out of the company with nothing. No problem: Wences decided he'd simply start the first e-commerce company in Latin America. The only problem being he didn't have any capital.

"So we meet him and he had been turned down by thirty local investors," Linda says. "He had his sister and his best friend working for him—never a good sign. But as soon as we met him we said, 'This guy is on to something.'" Endeavor helped Wences raise capital from Flatiron Partners and Chase Capital. They found him a COO. And a year later, Banco Santander bought Wences's company for three quarters of a billion dollars.

Wences went on to other successes, including starting the bitcoin wallet Xapo, which aims to "democratize money" by promoting a more stable universal currency. But at the time Linda Rottenberg approached Wences, he was skeptical that an outsider would have any interest in his business ideas. Linda says that after she helped him get going, he confessed something to her: "When I first approached him," Linda says, "he thought I was running a cult. So yes, even Wences thought I was crazy."

After Wences's big success, word started to spread in South America. "It became a rallying cry," Linda says. "People were saying, 'If Wences can do it, I can, too.'"

And just like that, an entrepreneurial culture was beginning to develop in the region. That's how it happens, Linda says—local success stories inspire other local people to jump into the fray. And it can all be rapidly accelerated if those local successes then pay it forward in their communities by supporting other local entrepreneurs.

"Many local cultures have two or three successful businesspeople that create companies," Linda says. "But if they don't pay it forward and reinvest in the ecosystem—becoming mentors, becoming angel investors, inspiring their employees to start new companies—then it stops. The network effect is key to scaling an entire business community."

One of the most important things Linda's firm has done to encourage this virtuous cycle is to help convince successful local business leaders that it's in *their own* interest to support the growth of an entrepreneurial ecosystem in the region—that it creates a bigger local talent base, opens up opportunities to collaborate with business partners, and strengthens the local economy.

With more business leaders now paying it forward, entrepreneurialism should continue to flourish in Latin America. And it helps that there is finally a word for it in Spanish. A number of years ago, Linda got a call from the editor of a Brazilian Portuguese dictionary who wanted her to know that, in part because of Endeavor's work, they were adding the words *emprendedor* and *emprendedorismo* to the lexicon. "So today," Linda says, "people can say, 'Hey, I'm an *emprendedor.*'" And as Linda has long believed, "if you can name it, you can be it."

Create what you want to see

It started, as so many big ideas do, with a bit of frustration.

Franklin Leonard was a junior executive for Leonardo DiCaprio's film production company, Appian Way. And if "junior executive for Leonardo DiCaprio" sounds like a fun job, what it entailed was reading a lot—a *lot*—of scripts. Think of the script as the table stakes of making a Hollywood movie—it's the starting point for studios to find the stories and writers they can start making movies with. The only way to find out if a script is useful or not is to sit down and read it. That was Franklin's job, and he read a *lot*.

Let's do some quick calculations: A screenplay is usually between 90 and 120 pages, with a median length of 106. In a single weekend, Franklin might read thirty scripts. That's over 3,000 pages, every single week.

And this is how everyone in the film industry was doing it—Franklin was only one of thousands of movie folks toting home a banker's box full of scripts on the weekend.

"You know, trying to boil the ocean is an approach, but it's not an efficient approach," Franklin says.

The Black List was born in a moment of frustration with that approach. Near the end of 2005, Franklin ran a data-gathering experiment. He made a list of his peers across all the production companies he could think of, emailed them anonymously, and asked: What are the best scripts you read this year that are not currently in production? The scripts you genuinely *liked*, the scripts that would make movies you'd want to see? He compiled the results in a spreadsheet, found some clear winners, and published it anonymously, calling it the Black List.

And it went viral. Franklin started getting the Black List emailed back to him: "Have you seen this?" He even found himself fielding pitches from agents for films "that will be on next year's Black List"—which was funny, because he hadn't compiled it yet. From the reaction, it was clear his peers in Hollywood had been looking for something like the Black List all along, a tool to uncover high-quality writing that could be turned into award-winning movies. His peers were as frustrated as he was with the state of the industry—to the point where this famously closed culture willingly shared their own favorite scripts with him, anonymously.

"Everybody in Hollywood is standing in a field full of haystacks, trying to find a bunch of needles," Franklin says. "And they don't know which needle they're going to use when they find them, but they have to start with a needle. We invented a metal detector."

Something else the metal detector found? A meaningful number of the scripts on the first Black List came from first-time writers, from women, from people outside of Hollywood's systems and networks. Including *Juno*, from first-time scriptwriter Diablo Cody—which became the beloved film starring Elliot Page and Michael Cera. There

was something about the anonymous submission process that surfaced wisdom that departed from the conventional.

"There are lots of different ways in which the industry's conventional wisdom is all convention and no wisdom," Franklin says, "and
some of them are more pernicious than others. The undervaluing of
writers, okay? We're probably making less money because of that. We
could be making better movies, if we didn't think that way."

Just after the next year's annual Black List came out, Franklin's
anonymity was over—and so was his job with Appian Way. But the list
opened other doors for him as it grew in importance each year. He created specialized Black Lists that highlighted LGBTQ authors, authors
of color, and other groups. He started a beloved reading series in L.A.
where well-known actors did table reads of the year's top scripts.

But there was more he could do, he realized. Most of the scripts
on any given year's Black List already had some toehold in the Hollywood system—the writers were represented by agents, or the story
was optioned by a studio even if it was sitting in turnaround. But there
was a wider world of scriptwriters out there, Franklin knew, who
needed help getting past the studio gates. Whose scripts were just as
good, but who couldn't get that first meeting, that first nod of approval
to get into the Hollywood network.

"We should be out there trying to find these people, not hoping
they come to us," he realized.

Franklin's truly big idea, and his scale business: Leverage the
power of the annual Black List to create a platform to help unknown
scriptwriters get their work reviewed and read—and help moviemak-
ers find the best of these scripts.

To return to our metaphor, it's like holding a metal detector up in
the air and asking the haystacks to come to you. On the Black List
platform, anybody can upload a screenplay to the website for a small
fee. Writers can pay a reasonable fee to have their scripts evaluated.
"And then," Franklin says, "we share the information about the good
scripts, the ones that were reviewed positively by our readers. And
because of the credibility that we had built over the previous eight
years at this point, people might take our word for it."

Why is it worth breaking down the Hollywood gates to allow in
more scriptwriters from outside the system? It all comes back to mak-

ing the movies Franklin wants to see, the kind with great, honestly told stories that resonate with fellow humans.

"For me personally, I'll take an attempt at screenwriting from somebody who's been living a 'normal life' over someone who was able to come to Hollywood because their parents worked in the industry, their parents gave them a trust fund, whatever it is. My personal experience would suggest that those people have more insight in telling an emotional, human story than folks who have not."

If the Black List is a Trojan horse, the outside of the horse has a big sign on it that reads: GREAT SCRIPTS! SCRIPTS THAT MAKE GREAT MOVIES! SCRIPTS THAT MAKE MONEY!

What's inside the Trojan horse is a vision of a more inclusive society—both in the movies we see on screen, and in the industry that makes them. As a Black man from Georgia, whose great-great-grandfather was born an enslaved person, Franklin finds that this vision of inclusiveness resonates with him deeply.

"If I sat here and said, 'That was part of a master plan,' I'd be lying to you. I thought this was a selfish pursuit of a list of good scripts so that I could read them, and the transaction I was making was what was necessary for me to get what I wanted."

But by staying true to the mantra of creating what he wanted to see, he's created a larger virtuous cycle. "All of the work of the Black List has been explicitly about unlocking those networks for people who have the talent, for the benefit of both those people and the economics of this closed network that has been undermining themselves, not even realizing how much money they're leaving on the table."

Founders speak a common language

As a kid growing up in Guatemala, **Luis von Ahn** didn't dream of founding a digital, crowd-fueled, language-learning app. He didn't dream of being a "unicorn" startup founder.

"I wanted to become a math professor," Luis says.

The best math programs at the time were in the United States, and so Luis had plans, as a high school senior, to apply to college in the United States. "But to come to college in the United States you have to take an English proficiency test," Luis remembers. He made plans to take the TOEFL (Test of English as a Foreign Language), but there was one small problem. "The country of Guatemala ran out of seats for this test."

"I freaked out. I thought I couldn't apply to college anymore."

Luis looked around for other options, and learned that there were available TOEFL test seats in the neighboring country of El Salvador. "Fortunately, I had enough means to be able to fly to El Salvador to take that test," Luis says. But that was no small thing. "Guatemala is kind of a dangerous country. At the time El Salvador was an even more dangerous country. But I had to go there. I had to take the test.

"And at the time I thought: I'm going to do something to kill the TOEFL."

Luis aced the TOEFL, was admitted to Duke University, and came to the United States for college. And he put aside his desire to kill that language test—for a while.

But years later, when Luis was a computer science professor at Carnegie Mellon, his instinct surfaced. His expertise was in a specific kind of crowdsourcing, and he wanted to create a tool that harnessed the efforts of many people's contributions. And also, "I wanted to do something related to education that could help a country like Guatemala, which is why I thought of language learning," Luis says.

Once he learned that people all over the world spend between $5 and $10 billion a year to learn and prove they've learned English, he thought he could build something that would allow people to learn English from anywhere, for free. And **Duolingo** was born.

Today, Duolingo lets you learn language in bite-sized lessons, motivated by achievements and prompts. It has over three hundred million users who complete over seven billion exercises a month. And much of the course content is created by its passionate users. That's why, alongside the likes of Spanish, Chinese, and Arabic, you can find more esoteric languages like Esperanto, Navajo . . . and even Klingon.

When Luis launched Duolingo, it only offered Spanish and German (because he made the Spanish course himself and his Swiss co-founder made the German course). He had some early success, but to really grow, he knew he needed more languages. "It occurred to me, maybe we can crowdsource this—get people to actually help us add the courses themselves," Luis says.

Luis gave it a shot: When people wrote asking if he offered a particular language translation course, he would reply: "No, we don't have that—can you help us create it?" People started saying yes, so Luis opened up and shared his tools for creating language courses for Duolingo. And in the first week, about fifty thousand people applied to add a language. These contributions have been so valuable that Duolingo is now hailed as one of the best examples of how crowdsourcing can be used to generate business success.

Luis was able to quickly grow Duolingo because people not only responded to the mission he was pursuing—making language learning easily accessible to people around the world—they also wanted to be part of it. You might say that with Duolingo, goodness was baked in as a key ingredient.

At Duolingo, Luis has taken pains to live up to that mission. He created a contract to make sure all of the unpaid contributors who help him to create language courses retain ownership of the content they create. And he has worked to keep the language courses free, to live up to the promise of making language learning available to anyone.

"We didn't want to charge for content," he says, "even though the standard way to make money in education is to charge for courses." Instead, Luis simply ran an automated ad at the end of the lesson. He thought it might bring in a few bucks. "Now it's tens of millions of dollars from those little programmatic ads." Then he added a subscription feature that allowed you to turn off the ads. "Quickly, the subscription made more money than the ads," he says. Today, Duolingo makes more money than any other education app, and Luis never went back on his promise of not charging for content.

A product offering perhaps most satisfying to Luis is Duolingo's own version of the TOEFL—that anachronistic English test that he and millions of others had to take if they wanted to study in the United States. It's cheap ($49) and you don't have to travel anywhere (like into a war zone) to take it.

• • •

Generosity can be found in the DNA of companies featured in every chapter of this book. **Sallie Krawcheck's** startup Ellevest is focused on closing the "gender investment gap" by helping women to become more active and smarter investors. **Payal Kadakia** of ClassPass built her business around the vision of helping people become more active and find their fitness passion. **Anne Wojcicki** of 23andMe started her genetic testing business with the goal of empowering people to gain more control of their healthcare information. And **Charles Best** launched DonorsChoose with the express purpose of helping to fund worthwhile school projects by matching them up with donors.

As these organizations that are "born good" gradually begin to scale, the acts of goodness often start to expand and multiply. An example of this is Bumble, the online dating startup from **Whitney Wolfe Herd.** As we saw in Chapter 3, Whitney started Bumble in part because she wanted to improve the online dating experience for women by giving them more control in that situation (including the ability to make the first move).

But Whitney and Bumble also went a step further in empowering women, by introducing the Bumble Fund—which provides early-stage investments for U.S. businesses founded and led by women of color and those from underrepresented groups.

Meanwhile, Bumble continues to expand around the world, introducing its app—and in turn, its message of female empowerment—to women across different cultures.

"The highlight of my career," says Whitney, "is going into different cultures and understanding the way women think there. The most interesting, so far, for our team has been India. Going into a culture that has traditionally repressed women in dating and in love and assigned them a life—not just a love life, but very much assigned them a life from the time they're very young."

Whitney acknowledges that Bumble is a tiny step in bringing cultural change in India, but nevertheless, "it's just giving people something that has already been within them. And so going into India, a place where women now are more empowered than they've ever been, their voices are finally being heard."

A hundred million users later, while Bumble continues to focus on

REID'S ANALYSIS | **Harness the power of the crowd to help you do good**

I believe crowdsourcing can scale your business in unexpected ways—as long as you align your mission with your crowd's motivation.

Luis von Ahn uncovered a hugely valuable resource in crowdsourcing. In fact, it was *the* resource that would shoot Duolingo to massive scale. And he found it by reaching out to his passionate crowd of users who loved the company's mission of offering a free way to learn language enough to help him fulfill it.

A similar effect happened with Charles Best when he created the first crowdsourcing platform, DonorsChoose.org, back in 2001. Charles knew that there was a passionate crowd waiting to support teachers like himself if they could feel a connection to the classroom projects they were funding. Charles's particular do-good mission aligned perfectly with his crowd's motivation: so much so, in fact, that he also was able to recruit a volunteer crowd of experienced DonorsChoose teachers to authenticate all the other teachers' project requests, saving time and money.

And this is the kind of alignment you need to get crowdsourcing right. Crowdsourcing is a way to tap skills—and scale—that you don't have in-house. When it works, it opens extraordinary opportunities. It lets you scale faster and further than you ever could on your own. But if you get the alignment wrong, you can end up with anything from a weak fizzle to a fiery disaster.

Rallying people who share your mission to gather beneath your banner is the Holy Grail—or maybe the Rosetta Stone in Luis's case—of crowdsourcing. To keep them there, you have to make sure you're directing their efforts toward something that engages them and feels like a worthwhile use of their passion.

Now, keep this in mind when you reach out to users and offer to be partners with them in a shared mission: You've just raised the stakes. If you let them down, they'll lose faith in your commitment—and your product. And that powerful crowd you've worked so hard to assemble will disperse—as will their willingness to work with you.

creating a dating ecosystem that feels comfortable and safe to women, Whitney's second purpose has shifted beyond the one-on-one world of dating and networking.

"I think that a lot of people are craving community," says Whitney. "Loneliness is an epidemic these days. That's something that you are never going to be able to cure by just introducing one person to one person."

Whitney's new focus is on *How can we not just make a safer ecosystem for dating but one that focuses more broadly on community?* Looking forward, she says, "I think that's going to happen both inside Bumble and outside of Bumble in terms of our physical presence in the world."

Good as an add-on feature

Yes, this chapter begins with the suggestion that you should launch your business's social mission on day one. But there are also plenty of examples of social good as an add-on feature.

Tasks for Good, from TaskRabbit, is an example of add-on goodness done right. After improving the company's relationship with taskers, **Stacy Brown-Philpot** wanted to bring more of an element of community service into TaskRabbit.

When Stacy joined TaskRabbit as CEO, its mission around revolutionizing everyday work really spoke to her. But Stacy gradually saw the possibility for a second purpose: *How do we use technology to enable many more middle-class jobs?* She began looking closer at how TaskRabbit could be made more accessible to people who don't have high school degrees or access to expensive technology.

In 2016, Stacy became a fellow in the Aspen Institute's Henry Crown Fellowship program. All fellows were asked to launch a venture designed to increase their impact on society. Stacy's idea, TaskRabbit for Good, opened up the TaskRabbit platform for people and nonprofits that might not otherwise be able to access it.

Along with partnering with community-based organizations to help people in need earn a meaningful income as taskers, TaskRabbit for Good invited their current taskers to volunteer to be matched with regional nonprofits focused on homelessness, job creation, and disaster relief operations who need some extra hours on the weekend or upcoming weeks. This not only offered the taskers an easy way to get involved in causes they cared about, it also allowed these organizations to access volunteers without having to pay for coordination and administration—the TaskRabbit platform does all of that for them.

"We send people to these disaster-relief situations," says Stacy, "because the extension of what TaskRabbit is about is, yes, we're helping people to make a meaningful income, but we also aim to impact the community, and that might mean helping people in the community who can't afford the service at all."

TaskRabbit for Good was a natural progression for TaskRabbit—it took advantage of the company's existing resources and expertise and then applied that to a related area of need. And it shows that even for companies offering a product that's not directly associated with improving the world, it can be worthwhile to take a close look at their offering—because there may be some hidden purpose waiting to be discovered and unlocked.

That was certainly the case for Instagram's **Kevin Systrom**, who says that as an entrepreneur, his life goal has always been to do something bigger, beyond just leaving the world with more beautiful photos.

After the sale of Instagram to Facebook, Kevin and his co-founder, Mike Krieger, got to thinking about their legacy. They were grateful that the company was successful and growing larger every day. But they also recognized the unique opportunity in front of them: to leverage their giant platform to bring about social change. So they sat down together and asked, *What kind of effect can we have on the world that goes beyond our product?*

Kevin and Mike were very aware that young people were spending a ton of time on Instagram. Those kids were learning about their world through Instagram, expressing themselves artistically through Instagram, and interacting with friends, family, and classmates also on that platform. The two co-founders were bothered, however, by how nasty those interactions could be.

This was a personal concern for Kevin and Mike, both of whom planned to have children; and in fact it was during this period that Kevin's daughter Freya was born. Kevin asked himself, *What legacy do we want to leave so that when Freya grows up and uses social media, she doesn't have to face the stuff that I see kids face today online?*

The co-founders vowed to find a way to bring more kindness to the internet. Kevin challenged his team: "What tools can you guys build using machine learning to make the internet more kind via Instagram?" At first everyone just looked at each other and shrugged. But Kevin stuck with this idea, telling his team, "The hard problems are the ones we need to attack."

It turned out that the same machine learning and artificial intelligence technology they used to filter out spam could also be used to detect bullying or harassment. Just as it can detect a spam comment, their technology could also detect people being nasty to each other.

The way it works is relatively simple. First, Instagram gets a lot of data in from users saying, *Hey, I think this post or comment is bullying.* Then a trained team of employees goes through all of those flags to decide which reports seem legit and feeds them into a neural network.

Finally, their algorithms use criteria such as how well the people involved know each other, their previous interactions, and how many followers they have. The combination of those signals—and others—helps to determine whether any given comment or post in fact constitutes bullying. If this turns out to be the case, Instagram will hide the bully's posts. "We've seen this effect where you as a bully don't want to be the *only* bully," says Kevin. "It's broken windows theory—if there are a bunch of broken windows or graffiti around you, you feel, 'Oh, it's okay for me to do that.' If people are not seeing bullying by others, they don't feel it's okay to be the only one doing it. By cleaning it up, we've seen it has this interesting scaled effect."

Instagram's bullying filter allows them to monitor kindness on the platform via technology and metrics. "Bit by bit, I think it is making the internet slightly more kind," says Kevin. "The hardest thing still is, how do you measure kindness?" He says he's not sure he has it figured out exactly, but his hope is that if Instagram can crack that problem, they could share the kindness tools and algorithms with other companies.

Kevin never expected that his social media company would take on this kind of challenge. But he now views his anti-bullying crusade as one of his key achievements.

Pivoting to good

A lot of entrepreneurs have the idea of doing something good for the world in mind from the outset. **Scott Harrison** was not one of those people.

On the contrary, early in his career, Scott was pretty much focused on one thing: having a good time. And by some people's measure (including his own at the time), he was living the dream.

After leaving home at eighteen determined to rebel against his conservative upbringing, Scott went in search of money, glamour, and fun. And he found it in his work as a club promoter, working at forty different nightclubs. "I was always with the most beautiful girl in the room," he says. "And I couldn't believe that you could get paid to drink alcohol in New York City, but I did."

The wild ride was enjoyable for a while—but after a decade, Scott realized that all those good times he'd been having weren't doing him much good. He began to wonder about other roads he might have taken.

Then Scott asked himself a fascinating question: *What would the opposite of my life look like?*

"I thought, well, if I'm this selfish, hedonistic, drug-addled night-club promoter who's done nothing much for anyone else," Scott says, "then what would it look like to actually help people in need? What if I quit and did one year of humanitarian service?"

Scott didn't just wonder; he acted. He sold most of his belongings, gave up his apartment in New York, and began applying to every charity he could think of. After months of rejection, Mercy Ships—which dispatches ships staffed with medical personnel throughout the developing world—offered to take him on. *If* he was willing to pay Mercy Ships $500 a month and go live in postwar Liberia, that is.

Scott's reaction? "Perfect—it's the opposite of my life. Here's my credit card, when does it start?"

Three weeks later, Scott found himself living on a five-hundred-foot hospital ship with a group of maxillofacial surgeons. He was given the role of photojournalist, so his job was to document every patient, pre-op and post-op. It was harrowing work, but also exhilarating. Scott's storytelling instinct emerged, and he felt compelled to share his experiences with people back home.

He sent photos of massive facial tumors to the thousands of people on his club email lists. Not everyone wanted to see these startling images in their inboxes. But a surprising number of Scott's old friends were moved by what they saw and interested in helping in some way. "A lot of them were saying, 'I had no idea that this world of sickness and lack of access to healthcare existed.'"

Scott knew he was on to something. "I had this aha moment early on that the photos seemed to move people in a way that the words couldn't." Then, during his time with Mercy Ships, Scott encountered a gut-wrenching problem with a relatively simple solution.

"I saw the water crisis for the first time in Liberia," he remembers. Mercy Ships was donating small amounts of money to help people build wells, and Scott was sent to take pictures. "I saw the water people were drinking—and I'd never seen anything like that." He remembers it looked to him like "thick chocolate milk." He learned that 50 percent of the country was drinking bad water, and it was the source of much of the illness that plagued Liberia.

Scott had found his cause. As he hatched a plan to launch a nonprofit, however, he heard the same jaded view over and over again from his New York friends. "They said, 'Oh, I don't give to charities, charities are ineffective, they're bureaucratic, the CEO is probably just trying to make millions of dollars for himself and driving a Mercedes-Benz around.'"

In that cynicism, Scott saw an opportunity. He would launch a nonprofit designed to bring clean water to the world *and* inspire generosity by tackling cynicism head-on.

The nonprofit he created, Charity: Water, was based on a three-pronged plan. The organization would commit to total, radical transparency about where every penny of donated money was being spent; he would guarantee that 100 percent of public donations went directly to the water projects; and he would create a brand that inspired—one that used photos and videos to tell the kind of true stories that people would yearn to be part of, stories they would share with others.

Scott would make positivity the very fabric of Charity: Water. "We would have these sayings at the organization, *Hope, not guilt. Invitation, inspiration.* The images that we would take would be people getting clean water—not the child drinking dirty water. We would say,

'Here is what we're about, we're providing this life-giving party and there's *before the water* and there's *after the water*. Do you want to be a part of that solution?'"

As chief evangelist for his company, Scott knew he had to spark a global virtuous cycle with Charity: Water. He took stock of the resources at his disposal. He had his photographs. He had a commitment to transparency. He had an email list of movers and shakers.

And he had an idea for how to make good use of something we all get once a year, whether we want it or not. *Our birthdays.* The idea was that instead of getting birthday gifts, people could ask friends and loved ones to donate that gift in their name to Charity: Water.

The idea to let people give their birthday to Charity: Water was simple. It was invitational. And it tapped into the fact that people build their strongest emotional relationships with other people, not brands or charities.

"The idea just exploded as people of all ages started giving up their birthdays," says Scott. The birthday initiative went on to become one of Charity: Water's signature methods of fundraising. In 2014, they raised $45 million and helped a million people get clean water that year—twenty-five hundred every day of the year.

Charity: Water's donations soared for years . . . until they didn't. "The problem for our organization," says Scott, "was that people did one birthday for Charity: Water, then said, 'I did it, I built my well, I raised my $1,000.' We didn't have any sort of repeatability in that."

It was a big setback, but Scott looked around and drew new inspiration from what was going on in the culture. Individuals were subscribing to an increasing number of online entertainment services. Scott wondered, *What if I build a subscription program for pure good, where a lot of people show up for a little bit every month knowing where 100 percent of their money is going?*

Scott dubbed his monthly subscription idea "The Spring." With the ten-year anniversary of Charity: Water coming up, Scott devised a grand plan to introduce The Spring in a twenty-minute online video telling the entire decade-long journey of Charity: Water.

To say this was a video that got passed around is an understatement: It got ten million views, and counting. And the subscription program just kept expanding geographically, to one hundred countries.

This pivot of Charity: Water's business model from once a year (if they were lucky) donations to monthly subscription led to growth of 35 percent a year. With subscribers from one hundred countries giving an average of $30 a month, it meant more than $70 million coming in each year. A decade and a half after pivoting from party boy to nonprofit visionary, Scott Harrison's personal passion has funded fifty-six thousand water projects across twenty-nine countries, bringing clean water to more than ten million people.

Scott's story is proof that if you are going to try to scale good intentions, one of your greatest tools is the ability to tell a compelling, inspirational story (and so much the better if there are pictures). "The real power of inspirational storytelling," Scott says, "is that it creates a loop that feeds into people's desires to share. And then they open up their networks to the cause, and the inspirational story spreads."

The other lesson from Scott? You don't necessarily have to start out "good"—but you can still get there, eventually.

Liberating the human spirit

When it comes to paying it forward, nobody pays better than **Robert F. Smith**. At least that's what the students at Morehouse College must have thought. As the founder and CEO of Vista Equity Partners—and one of the most successful investors in the United States—Robert was invited to give the 2019 commencement speech at Morehouse, a historically Black college. During the speech, he unexpectedly announced that he would personally pay the student debt of every graduating senior.

And that wasn't the only instance of his extreme generosity: Robert also had made a public ripple in 2016 when he donated $20 million to help build the Smithsonian's National Museum of African American History and Culture.

The seeds of Robert's passion were planted when he was very young, growing up in a tight-knit Black neighborhood in Colorado during the school-busing integration era. On his first day of first grade,

Robert was put on a bus that took him forty-five minutes away to a community of students who looked nothing like the kids he was accustomed to. But he soon found that, like him, they all loved to run fast and have fun and tell jokes.

"We didn't see each other through the lens of color or economic position," he says. "We figured out that we had more that was alike than was different. As we grew up, I went to birthday parties, bar mitzvahs, all those sorts of things. It created a wonderful connectivity as a human being."

Only one bus came to Robert's neighborhood. He later learned that there had been a number of buses drafted to force the desegregation process in local schools, but someone burned a third of those buses before the process even got started. So just a single bus made it to Robert's neighborhood, and only a few blocks of kids got the opportunity to be on that bus. Looking back, Robert deems this a "lucky" bus.

"When you look at all the kids who were on that bus and their lives now on a relative basis versus the kids in my neighborhood who didn't get on the bus," he says, "you see a vast difference in socioeconomic progress, in educational opportunities, in what they bring to the communities that they live in now."

Perhaps the most formative experience of Robert's youth was when his mother brought her seven-year-old son to the March on Washington to see Rev. Martin Luther King, Jr., give his "I have a dream" speech.

"The impact of her bringing me there," he says, "was for me to understand that our community stood for something, our community was striving for something, and it was important that we were a part of it. I think that's part of my soul today. Which is, I have to give back and help my community move forward in this wonderful country called America."

When Robert was in high school, he found out there was a Bell Labs nearby in Denver and called them up asking for a summer internship, even though it was only January. And they replied, "If you're between your junior and senior year in college, why don't you come and apply?" Robert admitted he was only in high school, and for most kids, that would've been the end of that. Except Robert kept calling Bell Labs weekly, for five months. They finally relented and gave him the internship.

It was pretty clear by this point that there was no stopping Robert F. Smith.

After getting his MBA at Columbia University, Robert went into investment banking at Goldman Sachs, advising on billion-dollar mergers and acquisitions for tech companies such as Microsoft, Apple, and Texas Instruments. He left Goldman in 2000 to become founder of Vista Equity Partners.

What the outside world saw over the next twenty years was Vista's incredible financial performance. What insiders knew was that Robert was just as focused on creating a *diverse* company as a *successful* company, and those two missions were not in conflict; rather, they seemed to reinforce each other. When it came to hiring, Robert's company developed a methodical approach to identifying and nurturing innate skills and talent so that they could spot potential in people who might not have come from privileged backgrounds or gone to the top schools. That resulted in a diverse workforce that brought a wide range of skills and perspectives to the company—now a market-leading investment firm that manages $57 billion in assets.

Robert describes this as a "holistic approach to business," and says it tends to spark more creative thinking and greater work output at Vista. He believes companies and communities will benefit if businesses, particularly in the tech and financial sectors, can actively construct on-ramps via education and training for people of all ethnicities, races, and genders to participate in these businesses. It's what Robert calls the "Fourth Industrial Revolution dynamic."

At the same time, Robert serves as a model of a founder who looks beyond the business to serve the community in other ways—many of them inspired by a lunch meeting with the widow of anti-apartheid activist Stephen Biko in South Africa, where they discussed the concept of Ubuntu—the Bantu term for the love of humanity. It's a powerful word and concept that was on Robert's mind on the day he made his pledge to the Morehouse College graduating students. "I thought about the Morehouse community of these young African American men," says Robert. "They have an unfair burden in this country on so many different levels. I wondered, *How can I help them with those burdens?* One way would be to alleviate the debt, not only for them, on them, but the debt that most of them are also responsible around their families."

On that graduation day in 2018, Robert told the 396 newly minted graduates, "On behalf of the eight generations of my family who have been in this country, we're going to put a little fuel in your bus," as he shared the news about the grant to pay off their loans. Later, Robert added: "Now, my young brothers, you figure out how you're going to practice Ubuntu. How are you going to deliver back to your community?"

He confesses that he hopes "a quarter of them decide that they're going to be teachers and teach programming and engineering in their communities. I hope a quarter of them become brilliant chemical engineers—because I like them, generally. I hope another quarter of them become doctors and deal with the healthcare disparities that our community faces in this country. And I hope a quarter of them become politicians and use their strength and capacity to change policies—so that we don't have to have only one bus in the neighborhood."

Robert believes that when you invest in people, you "liberate the human spirit. And when you're able to liberate the human spirit and see that spirit really become its best self," he says, "that is the greatest thrill on the planet."

REID'S THEORIES ON DOING GOOD, WELL

Think of your company as a Trojan horse

Social transformation shouldn't just be side effects of your business—if you're strategic about it, social good can, and should, become the beating heart of your business. It's not about saying, "I'm a good person, so my company will do good things." It's about asking, "What kind of positive impact can I have that will also support my core business?"

Bake in goodness from day one

If a company has a mission that is rooted in goodness—*and* if you can effectively communicate that mission to the world and then live up to it—it can become one of the driving forces that helps you scale.

You can always pivot to good

You don't necessarily have to start out "good"—but you can still get there. There may be bumps as you have to shift to get your business model right, but if you are going to try to scale good intentions, one of your most powerful tools is the ability to tell a compelling, inspirational story that describes your target future.

When good is an add-on feature

Even for companies offering a product that's not associated with improving the world, it can be worthwhile to take a close look at that offering—because there may be some hidden purpose waiting within to be discovered and unlocked. One good place to look is always your employees and engagement with your local communities.

Paying it forward

One of the most important ways any successful company can contribute to the larger world is by paying it forward. This can take the form of mentoring programs, investing in other startups, or focusing on specific areas—geographic areas or underrepresented groups of people—with the goal of helping to encourage, strengthen, and diversify the next generation of entrepreneurial leaders. Marc Benioff's 1-1-1 program at Salesforce is a model of commitment.

First, do no harm

Entrepreneurs bear a responsibility to society. Without the infrastructure of society, we wouldn't be able to create our businesses and reap the rewards of success. We should follow the principle of the Hippocratic Oath: First, do no harm. As entrepreneurs, we should strive to leave society better off than we found it.

ACKNOWLEDGMENTS

First, a thank-you to every guest of *Masters of Scale* and *Masters of Scale: Rapid Response*—and especially to their hard-working assistants and communications teams, the good people who made space for ninety-minute interview slots in ridiculous schedules, who coordinated sanitized microphone delivery and pickup during a pandemic . . . and who joyfully shared every episode with the world.

Masters of Scale team past and present

Executive producers: June Cohen and Deron Triff
Supervising producer: Jai Punjabi
Editor at large: Bob Safian
Producers past and present: Jordan McLeod, Cristina Gonzalez, Marie McCoy Thompson, Chris McLeod, Dan Kedmey, Jennie Cataldo, Ben Manilla, Steph Kent, and Halley Bondy
Writers: Adam Skuse and Katharine Clark Gray
Managing editor: Emily McManus
Music director: Ryan Holladay
Music: Daniel Nissenbaum, Daniel Clive McCallum and the Holladay Brothers

Audio editing: Keith J. Nelson, Stephen Davies, and Andrew Nault

Mixing and mastering: Bryan Pugh and Aaron Bastinelli

Production: Adam Hiner and Chaurley Meneses

Production support: Colin Howarth, Eric Gruber, Chineme Ezekwenna

Designers: Sarah Sandman, Kelsie Saison, and Tim Cronin

Audience growth: Anna Pizzino and Ben Richardson

Special thanks: Mina Kurasawa

And to all our WaitWhat team and alumni!

Thank you to the team at Greylock Partners and Reid Hoffman's office: Elisa Schreiber, David Sanford, Greg Beato, Chris Yeh, and Saida Sapieva.

Thanks to Christy Fletcher and her team at Fletcher & Co. for their brilliance at pitching, advising, and getting this book into many hands.

Thanks to Warren Berger and Laura Kelly, whose work and insight helped this book gel into what it has become. And to Cary Goldstein for thoughtful edits and guidance along the way.

INDEX

PHOTO: © DAVID YELLEN

As an entrepreneur and executive, REID HOFFMAN played an integral role in building many of today's leading consumer technology businesses; as an investor, he has been instrumental in the success of iconic companies such as Facebook and Airbnb and has helped fast-growing newcomers like Aurora and Convoy get to scale.

His unique understanding of consumer behavior and a clear-eyed ability to guide startups from inception through ramped-up "blitzscaling" has made him a sought-after advisor, partner, and investor. Reid was a board observer for Airbnb and currently serves as a board director for Apollo Fusion, Aurora, Blockstream, Coda, Convoy, Entrepreneur First, Microsoft, Nauto, Neeva, Xapo, and a few early-stage companies still in stealth. Reid's core focus is on businesses with network effects.

In 2003, he co-founded LinkedIn, the world's largest professional network that today has more than 650 million members and a diversified revenue model that includes subscriptions, advertising, and software licensing. Before LinkedIn, Reid served as executive vice president at PayPal, where he was a founding board member and responsible for all of the company's external relationships. Reid joined Greylock in 2009, where he focuses on early-stage investing in products that can reach hundreds of millions of participants. He serves on several not-for-profit boards, including Kiva, Endeavor, CZI Biohub, Do Something, New America, the Stanford Institute for Human-Centered AI, and the MacArthur Foundation's 100&Change. Reid has received various awards for his philanthropic work, including the CBE from the Queen of England and the Salute to Greatness Award from the Martin Luther King Center.

Reid is a frequent public speaker, known for his approachability and skill at explaining complex topics with lucidity. He is the co-author of *Blitzscaling* and two bestselling books: *The Start-up of You* and *The Alliance*. He is the longtime host of the podcast *Masters of Scale*.

PHOTO: © LORI PEDRICK

June Cohen is the co-founder and CEO of WaitWhat, a media invention company that makes podcasts, live events, professional courses, and more, with a unique business model that develops horizontal integration around strong brands, such as the award-winning business podcast *Masters of Scale,* the tech+ethics show *Should This Exist?,* the creativity podcast *Spark & Fire,* and the nothing-else-like-it hit *Meditative Story.* Prior to co-founding WaitWhat in January 2017, June headed up media for TED, building its digital media operations from the ground up. In 2006, she launched TED Talks on the internet. And in 2009, she introduced the TED Open Translation Project, the largest subtitling effort in the world, with 120 languages, 20,000 translators, and 100,000 translations. She co-hosted the annual TED Conference with Chris Anderson and co-founded the annual TEDWomen with Pat Mitchell. Under her leadership, TED's media efforts earned seventeen Webbies, eight iTunes Best Podcast of the Year awards, a National Design Award, and a Peabody. Prior to TED, June was VP of Content at HotWired.com, the pioneering website from *Wired* magazine, which introduced many of the conventions now commonplace on the web (yes, she helped introduce the world to the banner ad!) and authored *The Unusually Useful Web Book*. As a student, she led the Stanford team that developed the world's first networked multimedia magazine in 1991. June holds a BA from Stanford, where she was editor in chief of *The Stanford Daily*.

PHOTO: © LORI PEDRICK

DERON TRIFF is the co-founder of WaitWhat, a media invention company that makes podcasts, live events, professional courses, and more, with a unique business model that develops horizontal integration around strong brands, such as the award-winning business podcast *Masters of Scale,* the tech+ethics show *Should This Exist?,* and the nothing-else-like-it hit *Meditative Story.* Prior to co-founding WaitWhat in January 2017, Deron Triff served alongside June Cohen on the executive team at TED, where he built nearly 100 partnerships that grew TED's audience to more than 100 million per month. His love and unique skill set for creative partnerships resulted in hits including the *TED Radio Hour* on NPR, *TED Weekends* on *The Huffington Post, TED in Cinemas* with Fandango, TED shows on Netflix, TED English with National Geographic Learning, and international collaborations throughout Asia, Latin America, the Middle East, and Europe—as well as a joint venture with Simon & Schuster to relaunch TED Books. Prior to TED, Deron served as vice president of digital ventures for PBS, where he launched the kids cable network Sprout. He holds an MBA from McGill University in Montreal.

mastersofscale.com
@mastersofscale
Instagram: @mastersofscale

Available from #1 *New York Times* bestselling author

REID HOFFMAN

MASTERS of SCALE Courses App

Cultivate the **entrepreneurial mindset** through 10-minute Daily Practices

What factor does every successful entrepreneur have in common?

It's not luck, or skill, or credentials — it's a mindset.
In fact, it's a suite of entrepreneurial mindsets:
a bias to action, a comfort with chaos, a capacity for quick decisions, grit, optimism, and more.

Do they all come naturally? No — but they can be cultivated.

Inside the Masters of Scale Courses App, you'll find curated lessons, each centered on a 10-minute Daily Practice, that will help you cultivate the entrepreneurial mindset.

Learn more at **join.mastersofscale.com**

Other great podcasts from the creators of **MASTERS of SCALE**

Meditative Story combines human stories with meditation prompts embedded into the storylines — all surrounded by breathtaking music. Think of it as an alternative way into a mindfulness practice through story.

www.meditativestory.com

Spark & Fire celebrates the hero's journey behind every creative practice — including yours.

www.sparkandfire.com